Complete Japanese

Helen Gilhooly
with
Mikiko Kurose

For UK order enquiries: please contact
Bookpoint Ltd, 130 Milton Park,
Abingdon, Oxon OX14 4SB.
Telephone: +44 (0) 1235 827720. *Fax:* +44 (0) 1235 400454.
Lines are open 09.00–17.00, Monday to Saturday, with a 24-hour
message answering service. Details about our titles and how to order
are available at www.teachyourself.com

For USA order enquiries: please contact
McGraw-Hill Customer Services, PO Box 545,
Blacklick, OH 43004-0545, USA.
Telephone: 1-800-722-4726. *Fax:* 1-614-755-5645.

For Canada order enquiries: please contact
McGraw-Hill Ryerson Ltd, 300 Water St,
Whitby, Ontario L1N 9B6, Canada.
Telephone: 905 430 5000. *Fax:* 905 430 5020.

Long renowned as the authoritative source for self-guided learning –
with more than 50 million copies sold worldwide – the *Teach Yourself*
series includes over 500 titles in the fields of languages, crafts, hobbies,
business, computing and education.

British Library Cataloguing in Publication Data: a catalogue record
for this title is available from the British Library.

Library of Congress Catalog Card Number: on file.

First published in UK 2008 as Teach Yourself Japanese by
Hodder Education, part of Hachette UK, 338 Euston Road, London NW1 3BH.

First published in US 2008 as Teach Yourself Japanese by
The McGraw-Hill Companies, Inc.

This edition published 2010.

The *Teach Yourself* name is a registered trade mark of Hodder Headline.

Copyright © 2008, 2010 Helen Gilhooly

Typeset by MPS Limited, A Macmillan Company.

Printed in Great Britain for Hodder Education, an Hachette UK Company,
338 Euston Road, London NW1 3BH, by CPI Cox & Wyman, Reading,
Berkshire RG1 8EX.

The publisher has used its best endeavours to ensure that the URLs for external
websites referred to in this book are correct and active at the time of going to
press. However, the publisher and the author have no responsibility for the
websites and can make no guarantee that a site will remain live or that the
content will remain relevant, decent or appropriate.

Hachette UK's policy is to use papers that are natural, renewable and
recyclable products and made from wood grown in sustainable forests.
The logging and manufacturing processes are expected to conform to the
environmental regulations of the country of origin.

Impression number 10 9 8 7 6 5 4 3 2 1

Year 2014 2013 2012 2011 2010

Acknowledgements

Thank you to all these people for their invaluable comments and feedback in writing this book:

Niamh Kelly of Dublin City University, Ginny Catmur and Alexandra Jaton at Hodder Headline, Marianne Forgan for producing the roughs for the Japanese script and cultural artwork and an especially big thanks to John, Rosie and Bonnie for just being there!

I've dedicated this book to a much-missed friend, Richard Gibson.

Credits

Front cover: © Star Pix / Alamy

Back cover and pack: © Jakub Semeniuk/iStockphoto.com, © Royalty-Free/Corbis, © agencyby/iStockphoto.com, © Andy Cook/iStockphoto.com, © Christopher Ewing/iStockphoto.com, © zebicho – Fotolia.com, © Geoffrey Holman/iStockphoto.com, © Photodisc/Getty Images, © James C. Pruitt/iStockphoto.com, © Mohamed Saber – Fotolia.com

Pack: © Stockbyte/Getty Images

Contents

Only got a minute?

Everyone says Japanese is a difficult language to learn, so it must be, musn't it? Let me reassure you. There are aspects of the Japanese language that are surprisingly straightforward:

- There is no masculine and feminine in Japanese and most words don't have a plural.

- Verb endings remains the same regardless of who does the action: *kaimasu* can mean *I buy, he buys* or *we buy*.

- There are only two main tenses – the past and the present/future: *kaimasu* covers *buy* and *will buy*, *kaimashita* means *bought*.

- Pronunciation is relatively easy and very regular.

So you aren't going to be grappling with a lot of complex grammar rules when you start learning Japanese. Of course, much of the vocabulary is new, but even in this aspect there is a pleasant surprise – the Japanese language has always been a great 'word borrower' and it is rich with loanwords from English, for example, *aisukuriimu* (ice cream), *kompyūtā* (computer).

Even if you have never studied Japanese before, because of the huge economic and cultural influence that Japan has had worldwide you will almost certainly already be familiar with many Japanese words and terms such as: *karaoke*, *origami*, *sumō*, *sushi* and *manga*.

There are more challenging aspects to learning Japanese, but this is the case when you learn any language, and it is often these challenges that give the greatest satisfaction. And you certainly won't be alone in your quest to master Japanese – about 3 million people worldwide are currently learning Japanese.

Complete Japanese aims to help you to interact with Japanese people through a range of everyday situations. It is an in-depth self-study course that will take you from beginner's to intermediate-level Japanese via a logical step-by-step approach. By the end of the course you will feel confident enough to speak, read and understand Japanese in a wide range of practical situations.

5 Only got five minutes?

Japanese is spoken by 126 million people both in Japan and around the world, especially in North and South America, and it is the second language of older Chinese and Korean people who either live in Japan or had to learn Japanese during the occupation of their countries. And with Japan's rapid worldwide industrial growth from the 1970s onwards, people around the world are keen to learn Japanese. It is the fifth most popular foreign language in the USA, the first modern foreign language on the curriculum in many Australian and New Zealand secondary schools and a popular non-European language in secondary schools in the UK. Currently about 3 million people around the world, including 2 million Chinese, are learning Japanese.

Is it a difficult language? A popular perception is that Japanese is very difficult and people will always be impressed when you tell them you are learning the language. Of course, it would be misleading to say it does not have any difficult elements and it is generally held that it takes about five years to reach a similar level in Japanese as you would in three years in a European language. However (and you may wish to keep this secret so you can keep on impressing your friends and colleagues!), there are some features of the Japanese language that make it very simple and logical, especially when you compare it with the irregularities of the English language. Here are three of those features:

1 Regular grammar rules:

- There is no masculine and feminine in Japanese and most words don't have a plural.
- There is no conjugation of verbs, so the verb ending remains the same regardless of who does the action. For example *I go*, *he goes* and so forth are all covered by **ikimasu** in Japanese.

- There are only two main tenses, the past and the present/future, with a 'probably' used for future events which are not certain (e.g. the weather).
- There is no definite/indefinite article (the, a).

2 Regular pronunciation rules:

- Japanese has relatively easy pronunciation rules. Sounds are created by combining the five standard vowel sounds, a, i, u, e and o, with one of the 19 consonant sounds (e.g. ka, ki, ku, ke, ko). These sounds are always pronounced in the same way and so, once learned, are easy to remember and use.
- Unlike English, there is no stress accent. In other words, every syllable has equal stress. For example, the city name Hiroshima should be pronounced Hi-ro-shi-ma and not Hi-RO-shi-ma or Hi-ro-SHI-ma.
- Some Japanese words using identical sounds are distinguished in pronunciation through use of high and low pitch. The word hashi can mean either bridge or chopsticks. Háshi means chopsticks and hashí means bridge (the accent above the syllable is my way of showing you where the high pitch is). However, pitch is neither as strong as stress accent nor as complex as in tonal languages such as Chinese.

3 Loan words:

The Japanese language is rich with words borrowed from other languages, particularly English. This means that, although Japanese is not related structurally to English, you will find many recognizable clues. Can you work out the meaning of these words?

Food and drink:	**1** kēkī	**2** kōra	**3** sandoitchi	**4** hottodoggu
Technology:	**5** terebi	**6** kompyūta	**7** mausu	**8** shii dii
Sports:	**9** sakkā	**10** barēbōru	**11** gorufu	**12** tenisu

Answers: 1 cake, 2 cola, 3 sandwich, 4 hotdog, 5 TV, 6 computer, 7 mouse, 8 CD, 9 soccer/football, 10 volleyball, 11 golf, 12 tennis

There are also many Japanese or Japanese-invented words and brands which have become part of everyday English language. For example:

walkman, pokemon, karaoke, kimono, samurai, discman, Nintendo, Mitsubishi, Toyota, Sony, Kawasaki . . .

I said that it would be wrong to give the impression that there are no difficult features in Japanese, but I believe it is because of these challenges that people become truly fascinated with Japanese, the wonderfully logical way in which the language works and the way in which the language reflects Japanese culture and vice versa. Here are some of those features:

- Apart from loanwords, there are no links between English and Japanese. The Japanese language originated in Central Asia and it is structurally closest to Korean. It is not structurally linked to Chinese but it is from China that it received and developed its complex writing system.

- There is a respectful language system which has many layers of polite and humble words and structures. However, as a foreign speaker of Japanese, you can safely use the neutral polite form known as the **masu/desu** form, which is relatively straightforward.

- The sentence order is different to English. Japanese sentence order has the basic pattern of SOV (subject object verb), with the verb spoken at the end of the sentence. English, on the other hand, has the pattern of SVO (subject verb object). For example, in English we would say *I* (subject) *eat* (verb) *meat* (object), which in Japanese translates as **watashi wa niku o tabemasu** meaning literally *I meat eat*. This means that, essentially, Japanese sentence order is 'backwards' to English and the main point to remember is that the verb comes at the end of the sentence.

- Japanese has a system of grammar markers, known as particles, which have no intrinsic meaning but mark the function of most nouns in a sentence. In the sentence **watashi wa niku o tabemasu** (*I eat meat*) the subject (**watashi**) is marked with particle **wa** and the object (**niku**) is followed by particle **o**.

- There is a very wide vocabulary, with the influences of China, Korea and the west adding to the rich tapestry of words which make up the Japanese language.

The aim of *Complete Japanese* is to help you to interact with Japanese people through a range of everyday and useful situations such as meeting and greeting, speaking on the phone, business interactions, sightseeing, eating out, shopping and visiting a Japanese home. It is an in-depth self-study course that will take you from beginner's to intermediate-level Japanese via a logical step-by-step approach and by the end you will feel confident enough to speak and understand Japanese in a wide range of practical situations.

Here are some key Japanese words and phrases to give you a flavour of this wonderful language and to help you begin to build or review your vocabulary knowledge.

Greetings: **konnichiwa** *good afternoon/hello*, **ohayō gozaimasu** *good morning*, **konbanwa** *good evening*, **oyasumi nasai** *good night*

Titles: **san** (said after a first or family name): **Tanaka-san** *Mr/Ms/ Mrs Tanaka*, **Robert-san** *Robert*. You should always attach **san** to names except when you refer to yourself or your family/in-group

Your name: **Tanaka desu** *I am Tanaka*, **Robert desu** *I am Robert*. Attach the word **desu** (*I am*, *s/he is*, *you are* etc.) after your name

Please and thank you: **onegaishimasu** *please*, **dōmo arigatō** (**gozaimasu**) *thank you (very much)*

Goodbye: **sayōnara** *goodbye* (if you are not going to see someone for a while), **jā mata ne** *see you later* (casual)

Introduction

Welcome to *Complete Japanese*!

This is an in-depth self-study course that will take you from beginner's to intermediate-level Japanese via a step-by-step approach. This approach will help you to gain confidence and essential skills in understanding and communicating in Japanese and the practical content will enable you to transfer your learning easily to business and social situations both in Japan and in your own country. You will also gain many insights into Japanese culture and the ways in which language and culture influence each other and are closely bonded.

A particular feature of this course is the opportunity to learn to read Japanese, a skill often considered to be the most difficult to acquire when learning Japanese. This book offers a practical and logical approach to reading which breaks down traditional barriers and turns the skill of reading into an enjoyable and achievable challenge. However, if you wish only to focus on the speaking and listening aspects of the language you can work through the main course without the need to read Japanese script.

I have found after many years of teaching that students are often tempted to skip the dialogues in language books because they don't understand them, so in this book I give you a number of pre-dialogue activities to help you understand from the very start of every unit.

You will find *Complete Japanese* useful whether you are planning a trip to Japan, want to communicate better with Japanese colleagues or friends or simply want the personal satisfaction of mastering Japanese.

How does the course work?

Complete Japanese is divided into two main parts. Part 1 (Units 1–7) teaches the basics of Japanese and employs a primarily topic-based approach with a thorough foundation in structures (the 'nuts and bolts' of the language). A range of language is introduced to help the learner communicate in everyday situations such as greetings and introductions, counting, shopping, daily routine, going out, travelling, directions, descriptions, likes, dislikes, hobbies and illness.

Part 2 (Units 8–13) begins to explore the language in more depth and to guide the learner into manipulating the language to express more complex and rich concepts such as opinions, advice, requests and commands. The learner will begin to feel much more confident about saying longer sentences and taking part in conversations on a variety of topics. You will also explore the layers of politeness that are so important and fundamental to Japanese language and society. Although Part 2 includes a lot of important structures, it will still retain a topic-based and practical focus, in other words, you will be learning language that you can *use*.

A different approach to learning

Traditional language courses begin with a dialogue from which explanations and activities are developed. This can be quite daunting because it often leaves you unsure of the meaning of the dialogue until the end of the unit. In *Complete Japanese*, each unit begins with an **opening** and **build-up activity**, which explore a relatively simple aspect of Japanese to help you build your confidence and skills straightaway. In addition, Units 1–5 have a short opening dialogue so that you can see and hear the language you have already learned in a practical situation. You then work through **key sentences** and **explanations**, which include lots of practice before you meet the **main dialogue**. The intention is that you will find it much easier to understand the dialogue by this stage and so be able to take a much more active part in it. This is followed by a **learn to say** section to really get you talking and then **activities** and **end-of-unit challenges** to help you consolidate your learning.

An opportunity to read Japanese

A new feature of the *Complete Japanese* course is the inclusion of Japanese script. The main body of the book is written in **rōmaji** (Romanized script – a, b, c . . .), however, the final part of each unit is devoted to reading. You do not have to work through these reading sections if you do not choose to – they are stand-alone sections designed to offer an opportunity to those who wish to learn to read without being 'a step too far' for those who wish to focus on speaking and listening. It is also perfectly possible to work through the main units first and then return to the reading sections once you feel more confident of your other skills. The choice is yours but the opportunity is there to be taken and the teaching approach is very much based on the way the author has learned to read – through visual and pictorial links that help you to break down the script into recognizable parts and make it fun to learn.

How to be successful at learning Japanese

- A little, often, is far more effective than a long session every now and then. So try and put in about 20–30 minutes of regular study (where possible twice or three times per week or more). Try to make it at a regular time so that you can get into the habit of studying 'a little, often'.

- Find a balance between moving through the book and revising what you have already learned so that you can build gradually and *effectively* on your learning. Set aside one session every now and again (maybe once every five sessions) to look back at previous units and recap on your learning. A good place to start is with the activities and challenges – if you have difficulties with a certain structure, look back to the explanation and examples.

- Find time to study in a quiet room where you can *speak out loud*. This will help you to focus on building up your speaking and listening skills in an environment where you can concentrate and, literally, hear yourself speak.

- Don't be too harsh on yourself! Learning a language is a gradual and cumulative process and everyone makes mistakes. You mustn't expect to be perfect straightaway and you can't be expected to remember every item of vocabulary and every new structure. Let your learning grow slowly and surely and don't be impatient with yourself.

- Seek out opportunities to use your Japanese. You don't have to go to Japan to do this: find out about Japanese societies, join a Japanese class, go to a Japanese restaurant and practise ordering in Japanese (but be careful – people working in Japanese restaurants are not always Japanese), ask a Japanese friend to speak with you in Japanese or visit Japanese shops and areas where you can hear Japanese being spoken around you.

- But, most importantly, remember that learning and using a foreign language should be FUN!

Listening to Japanese

To benefit fully from the course, it is best to use the accompanying recordings but you can work through the course without these. However, the recordings will help you to pronounce Japanese correctly and to acquire an authentic accent. The recorded dialogues and activities will also give you plenty of practice in understanding and responding to spoken Japanese. The pronunciation guide and the new words in the first few units are also recorded to help you speak Japanese correctly in the important early stages of your study. If you don't have the recording then there are some activities that are 'listen only' but you will find that the material will also be covered by other activities.

Getting the best from the recording

You will find plenty of advice for making the most from listening as you work through this course. Here are some general tips:

- The recording contains a variety of listening passages to develop different skills such as listening for gist, learning vocabulary, improving pronunciation and listening for specific information. You will find you can listen to and learn parts of the recording such as vocabulary lists and 'learn to say' passages while doing something else such as travelling to work; for other passages such as activities you will need to be more focused. In either case, don't listen for too long otherwise you will probably find you have switched off – *stay focused*.

- Use the pause button (or on/off button on car systems) when you are practising chunks of dialogue. This will help you to focus on accurate pronunciation and thus to develop your Japanese accent. Use it too when memorizing new words or dialogue – you will have better results if you memorize small chunks at a time.

- In the listening activities, try to develop the speed of your listening and understanding by listening to the whole activity without using the pause button initially. You won't get all the information the first time, but it will help you to develop the skill of picking out the essential points and processing them in your brain more quickly.

- Once you have listened to the whole activity once or twice, break it down into manageable chunks using the pause button, so that you can complete the information required.

Introducing the main characters

There is a storyline running throughout the book involving characters from various backgrounds who eventually all meet or have dealings with one another. The characters are:

- *Robert Franks* (British) – married to Rie, living in Tokyo and working as a journalist for *Japan Now* (an English-language newspaper)

- *Rie Franks* – married to Robert and working as an English-speaking receptionist in a Japanese hotel

- *Tatsuya and Naoe Hondo* with their two daughters, *Eri*, aged 10 and *Yuki*, aged 16. Tatsuya-san works for a Japanese electronics company and Naoe is a full-time mother and carer for her elderly father

- *Ian Ferguson* (New Zealander) and *Katie Mears* (American). Katie teaches English in a private language school and Ian works for a Japanese company

- *Roger Wilson* (Australian) is studying Japanese at university in Australia and currently in Japan for one year at Tokyo University

- *Miki Sugihara* has spent 5 years teaching Japanese in the United States and is a Japanese and English teacher in a private language school in Tokyo

- *Takeshi Ishibashi* is studying engineering at Tokyo University and plays in a boy band at weekends

Meaning of symbol

◀) recording

Pronunciation guide

◀) **CD1, TR 2**

The Japanese 'alphabet' (it is actually a phonetic system) is made up of a number of sounds created by combining the five Japanese vowels (a, i, u, e, o) with consonants (letters that are not vowels). Each sound is a single 'beat' or syllable and these are combined to form words. Unlike English with its various pronunciation and spelling rules, in Japanese each sound is *always* pronounced in the same way. For example, the vowel sound **a** in English can be pronounced:

m*a*n m*a*te m*a*yor m*a*rsh . . .

However, the Japanese vowel sound **a** is always pronounced as the **a** in 'm*a*n'. The five Japanese vowels in order are:

a as in m*a*n
i as in h*i*t
u as in bl*u*e
e as in *e*xtra
o as in sh*o*t

Here's a bizarre 'headline' to help you remember these sounds:

Man hits two extra shots
a   i   u   e   o

How to pronounce syllables

◀) **CD1, TR 3**

You are now going to practise pronouncing Japanese using the sound chart of Japanese syllables that follows. Use the recording if you have it, listen to a line at a time, then pause the recording and say those sounds out loud. There are also notes written alongside the chart so if you don't have the recording, remember the correct pronunciation of the five vowel sounds and work through the chart line by line, speaking out loud and reading the additional notes as you go along.

Sound chart

a	i	u	e	o	
ka	ki	ku	ke	ko	
sa	shi	su	se	so	
ta	chi	tsu	te	to	**tsu** is an unfamiliar sound for English speakers; it is only one syllable (or beat); squash the **t** and **s** together as you say them

na	ni	nu	ne	no	
ha	hi	fu	he	ho	**fu** is a soft sound, between f and h. Your front teeth don't touch your lips as you say it; air is let out between your teeth and lips

ma	mi	mu	me	mo	
ya		yu		yo	
ra	ri	ru	re	ro	**r** is a soft sound, somewhere between r and l, and not like the French 'r' sound
wa				n	**n** has a full beat. There are examples in the next section
ga	gi	gu	ge	go	**g** as in *get* not *gin*
za	ji	zu	ze	zo	
ba	bi	bu	be	bo	**there** is no **v** sound in Japanese and **b** is substituted for foreign words. For example *Valerie* becomes *Ba-ra-ri-i*

pa	pi	pu	pe	po	
da			de	do	

The final set of sounds in the sound chart is made up of a consonant plus **ya, yu** or **yo**. These also have a single beat (i.e. they are one syllable) although English-speaking people sometimes mistakenly pronounce these sounds with two beats. For example, you may sometimes hear the first sound of the city name **Kyoto** being wrongly pronounced **ki-yo** instead of **kyo**.

Practise saying these sounds carefully:

kya	kyu	kyo	
sha	shu	sho	
cha	chu	cho	**ch** as in *chance*
nya	nyu	nyo	
hya	hyu	hyo	
mya	myu	myo	
rya	ryu	ryo	
gya	gyu	gyo	
ja	ju	jo	**ja** as in *jam*
bya	byu	byo	
pya	pyu	pyo	

How to pronounce words

◀) **CD1, TR 4**

Equal stress

Every syllable in Japanese is given equal stress, whereas in English we give more stress to some parts of the word than others. Look at this example:

(English)	A-ME-ri-ca	(the stress is on *me*)
(Japanese)	A-me-ri-ka	(each syllable has equal stress)

English-speaking people often add stress to Japanese words. For example:

Hi-ro-SHI-ma	(the stress is on **shi** whereas there should be
Hi-ro-shi-ma	equal stress)

So, to make your accent sound more authentic, try not to stress parts of words in the English style; instead, give equal stress to each syllable. Now listen to the recording for examples.

Long syllables

In this book, a macron is used over vowels to indicate long sounds. Here is an example:

Tōkyō	(you hold the sounds with macrons for about twice the normal length)
To-u-kyo-u	(say the word smoothly)

Macrons are not used when the place name appears as part of an English text or translation, only as part of a Japanese dialogue.

The n sound

n is a syllable by itself. For example, the greeting *hello* is:

ko-n-ni-chi-wa

When n is followed by **p**, **b** or **m** its sound softens to **m**:

ga*m*batte	*good luck*
sa*m*paku	*three nights*

Double consonants

◀ **CD1, TR 4, 01:08**

A double consonant indicates that you should pause slightly before saying it, as you would in these English examples (say them out loud):

headdress	(you pause slightly after *hea* – you don't say *head dress*)
bookcase	(you pause after *boo*)

You will come across these double consonants in Japanese – **kk, ss, tt, pp**. Listen to the recording and speak out loud:

gambatte	good luck
Hokkaidō	north island of Japan
Sapporo	capital of Hokkaidō
massugu	straight on

You *always* build in this slight pause when there is a double consonant.

Silent vowels

🔊 **CD1, TR 4, 01:40**

Sometimes **i** and **u** become almost unvoiced. This is indicated here by bracketing the vowel. Listen to the recording and say these examples out loud:

des(u)	it is
s(u)ki	I like
ikimas(u)	I go
hajimemash(i)te	how do you do?

Non-Japanese words

🔊 **CD1, TR 4, 02:02**

Foreign words are adapted to the Japanese sound system. Look at these examples and listen to the recording: for example, there is no **th** sound in Japanese, so **s** is used instead.

Ajia	Asia
Sumisu	Smith
Robāto	Robert
marason	marathon
kōhī	coffee
hoteru	hotel
terebi	television

Practice

To practise and consolidate your learning so far, turn to Explanation 1.7, listen to (or read) the greetings in the chart and practise saying the words out loud. These words cover most of the pronunciation rules you have just learned. Now you are ready to begin the course!

Meet the author

Helen Gilhooly is the language college director of Aldercar
Community Language College, a specialist language secondary
school in Derbyshire. She is also a teacher-trainer and special
lecturer at Nottingham University. She teaches Japanese to
people of all ages, has lived and worked in Japan, is a graduate
of Churchill College, Cambridge, and has an MA in Japanese.
She is author of the following Teach Yourself titles: *Get Started in
Japanese*, *Read and write Japanese scripts* and *Speak Japanese with
confidence*. She was also the language consultant and translator
for *Fast-track Japanese* (Elisabeth Smith).

Mikiko Kurose has given native-speaker support during the
writing of this book. She was born in Kyoto, Japan, has an MA
in Linguistics and is a qualified Japanese teacher currently working
at Aldercar Community Language College. She has also worked as
a translator and interpreter. She has proofread and advised Helen
on previous Teach Yourself titles and has also produced English–
Japanese dictionary support for Sharp software.

Part one

Building the foundations

1

Hajimemashite, Robert Franks to mōshimasu

How do you do? I'm called Robert Franks

In this unit you will learn
- *basic Japanese sentence structure*
- *introductions, greetings and farewells*
- *words for countries, nationalities and family members*
- *how to say 'it is' and 'it is not'*
- *how to count from 1 to 10 (with actions!)*

Welcome to the first unit of *Complete Japanese*. If you haven't read the introductory section and pronunciation guide yet, please do so now! It isn't too long and will help you to understand how this book works. This, in turn, will help you to progress through it successfully. If you have the recording, listen to and repeat the activities in the pronunciation guide. Otherwise, read the hints in the pronunciation guide and say the sounds out loud. You could even record yourself and give yourself a mark from 0 to 10!

Insight

You will be asked at different stages throughout the book to listen to words, dialogues and sentences. If you don't have the recording, take the instruction listen to mean read. You don't have to have the recording but it really will help your progress and, in particular, your pronunciation of Japanese. In the early units, certain letters are bracketed to show that they are not pronounced or at most very slightly (see pronunciation guide).

Getting started

In Units 1–5, before you begin the main section of the unit, there is a list of 10 new words and phrases for you to listen to/read and repeat out loud (always out loud if you can; if you simply 'say' words in your head you can't really improve your pronunciation and confidence). You will then listen to a short opening dialogue and see if you can pick out those 10 words. The aim of this opening section is to ease you into the new unit.

◄» CD1, TR 5

<table>
<tr><td rowspan="10" style="writing-mode: vertical-rl">QUICK VOCAB</td></tr>
<tr><td>hajimemash(i)te</td><td>pleased to meet you</td></tr>
<tr><td>(name) to mōshimas(u)</td><td>I'm called (name) (formal language)</td></tr>
<tr><td>dōzo yorosh(i)ku</td><td>pleased to meet you</td></tr>
<tr><td>yorosh(i)ku onegaishimas(u)</td><td>pleased to meet you (also used when you feel indebted to someone)</td></tr>
<tr><td>watashi</td><td>I</td></tr>
<tr><td>watashi no</td><td>my</td></tr>
<tr><td>meishi</td><td>business card</td></tr>
</table>

des(u)	am, is, are
arigatō gozaimas(u)	thank you
kaisha no eigyō buchō	company sales manager

Insight

Try saying these phrases out loud. Say the sounds smoothly:
do-u-zo yo-ro-sh(i)-ku; yo-ro-sh(i)-ku o-ne-ga-i-shi-mas(u);
a-ri-ga-to-u go-za-i-mas(u).

Opening dialogue

◀) CD1, TR 6

Robert Franks, a British journalist working for a Japanese newspaper company in Tokyo, is about to interview Tatsuya Hondo who works for an electronics company.

Robert	Hajimemashite, Robāto Franks to mōshimasu. Dōzo yoroshiku.
Hondō-san*	Hajimemashite, Hondō Tatsuya to mōshimasu. Yoroshiku onegaishimasu.
Robert	[*Handing over his business card*] Watashi no meishi desu. Dōzo.
Hondō-san	Arigatō gozaimasu. [*Hands over his business card*] Watashi no desu. Dōzo.
Robert	Ā, Hondō-san wa kaisha no eigyō buchō desu ne. Oisogashii deshō ne.
Hondō-san	Sō desu ne . . .

[* Use of the *san* ending after a name is examined in Explanation 1.4.]

Robert	*How do you do? I am called Robert Franks. Pleased to meet you.*

Mr Hondo	*How do you do? I am (called) Tatsuya Hondo.*
	Pleased to meet you.
Robert	*(Here) is my business card. There you are.*
Mr Hondo	*Thank you. (Here) is mine. There you are.*
Robert	*Aah, Mr Hondo, you are the company*
	sales manager, aren't you? You must be busy.
Mr Hondo	*Indeed . . .*

Did you manage to pick out those 10 words and phrases? Listen again and this time pause the recording after each sentence and repeat out loud. This will help you to build confidence in pronunciation and in remembering the new vocabulary.

Key sentences

◀》 **CD1, TR 7**

This section in each unit gives example sentences of the key grammar points you will learn. Read them, listen to the recording, repeat them and check the English meanings and new vocabulary list that follow. Before you read the grammar explanations, see if you can work out how the sentence fits together:

1 Watashi wa jānaris(u)to des(u).
2 Kanai no namae wa Rie desu.
3 Kazoku wa go-nin desu.
4 Musuko wa roku sai desu.
5 Musume wa jussai desu.
6 Robāto-san wa Amerikajin desu ka.
7 Robāto-san wa Amerikajin dewa arimasen.
8 Kochira wa shachō no Takahashi-san desu.
9 Kore wa Furansu no wain desu.
10 Are wa Tōkyō Ginkō desu ka.

....

Insight
Listening is an activity you can often carry out while driving, cleaning the house, relaxing in the garden and so

on. However, it will depend on the purpose of the activity whether you can simply listen while doing other things or whether you need to sit with the book and focus. So whereas you can drive along in your car and repeat sentences out loud (you might get some funny looks from other drivers but you're not going to worry about that!), it is both dangerous and illegal to try to refer to the book while driving and will certainly require some good multitasking skills to do so while manoeuvring the vacuum cleaner!

In other words, adapt the listening task to the situation – it's a great use of time to listen to the recording on the way to work but do some preparation beforehand so that you are familiar with the vocabulary already before you set off on your journey. Or simply listen to the recording and check the book later.

◀) **CD1, TR 8**

jānaris(u)to	*journalist*
kanai	*(my) wife*
no	*'s* (possessive, to show belonging)
namae	*name*
kazoku	*family*
go	*five*
nin	*people* (counter)
musuko	*(my) son*
roku	*six*
sai	*years old*
musume	*(my) daughter*
jussai	*10 years old*
Amerika	*America*
jin	*person* (nationality)
Amerikajin	*American* (person)
ka	*spoken question mark*
dewa arimasen	*is not, am not, are not*
kochira	*this* (person)
shachō	*company director*
kore	*this (one)*

QUICK VOCAB

Furansu	France
Furansu no	French (items)
wain	wine
are	that (one) over there
ginkō	bank

English translation of the key sentences

1 *I am a journalist.*
2 *My wife's name is Rie.*
3 *My family is five people (there are five in my family).*
4 *My son is 6 years old.*
5 *My daughter is 10 years old.*
6 *Is Robert an American? (or: Are you, Robert, an American?)*
7 *No, he is not an American. (or: No, I am not an American.)*
8 *This is the company president, Mr Takahashi.*
9 *This is French wine.*
10 *Is that (over there) the Tokyo Bank?*

Language explanations

The language and grammar explanations in this book will be given through a step-by-step approach using language that is accessible and straightforward. There may well be times when you don't entirely understand but you will often find that it all becomes clearer as you work through the examples and activities. Also, there will be plenty of reinforcement throughout this book with language points being revisited and further developed so that you gradually, but in a logical way, develop your knowledge and understanding.

Insight

Remember, grammar is basically the skeleton of language – it forms its frame and structure – and once you have a grasp of this you can 'flesh it out' with the words and sentences you want to say.

Here is a list of the grammar and language points you will learn in this unit:

1 basic Japanese sentence structure
2 different uses of the word 'no', showing possession
3 countries and nationalities
4 how to address people
5 words for family members
6 formal and informal introductions
7 greeting and farewells
8 'this', 'that' and 'that over there'
9 saying 'it is' and 'it is not' (affirmative and negative)
10 counting from 1 to 10 (with actions!)

Explanation 1.1 Basic Japanese sentence structure

Each of the 10 key sentences used the basic structure 'noun **wa** noun **desu**'.

What are nouns? Here is a quick recap of the meaning of the word 'noun' – it is the word for a person, place, item, idea or emotion. Proper nouns are names and are spelt (in English) with a capital letter (Peter, Tokyo, Mitsubishi). If you can put *the* or *a* in front of the word, then it is a noun.

Grammar markers (also called grammar particles) will be discussed in more detail in later units. They are placed after words and serve to tell you the function of a word in the sentence. So **wa** tells you that the word it is placed after is the main topic of the sentence.

Here are two examples:

Watashi wa eigyō buchō desu   *I am a sales manager*
Musuko wa roku sai desu   *My son is 6 years old*

This is one of the most basic Japanese structures. The person (or item or place or idea) that is being talked about is followed by the grammar marker **wa** (this has no meaning in itself). More information is then given about this noun ('sales manager', '6 years old') and the sentence ends with **desu** ('is', 'am', 'are'). It ends with **dewa arimasen** if you want to say 'is not/am not/are not'. Did you notice that the sentence order is different from that of English? The word for 'is' is spoken at the end of the sentence.

Now see if you can say (and write down) these simple sentences in Japanese (look back at the key sentences if you need help). The answers are given in the key at the end of the book.

1 I am a journalist.
2 This is the Tokyo Bank.
3 My family is six people.
4 I am American.
5 I am not 10 years old.

Explanation 1.2

The particle **no** is inserted between two nouns to show some type of ownership or belonging – the first noun 'owns' the second noun, the second noun belongs to the first. Look at these examples:

Watashi no pen	*my pen* (I own the pen)
Rie-san no wain	*Rie's wine* (Rie 'owns' the wine, it belongs to her)

No can also connect a noun with its place of origin or place of work:

Furansu no wain	*French wine*
Amerika no kaisha	*American company*
Tōkyō Ginkō no Takahashi-san	*Mr Takahashi of the Tokyo Bank*

You can leave out the second noun, as in these examples:

Watashi no desu	*it's mine*
Rie-san no desu	*it's Rie's*
Furansu no desu	*it's French*

No is also used when connecting a person's role with their name. For example:

shachō no Takahashi-san   *Mr Takahashi, the company director*
musume no Yuki-chan   *my daughter, Yuki*
kanai no Rie   *my wife, Rie*

Explanation 1.3

◀ฺ **CD1, TR 9**

This leads us on to nationalities, countries and languages. Many countries in Japanese sound very close to their native tongue pronunciation. Here is a short list for you to read through and say out loud. Can you work out which countries they are? Use the map which follows to help.

1 Ingurando	2 Itaria	3 Nyū Jīrando	4 Supein
5 Porutogaru	6 Mekishiko	7 Burajiru	8 Doitsu
9 Aruzenchin	10 Ōsutoraria		

Insight

Not all country names in Japanese are derived from their native language; some have a Japanese name. These include: **Kankoku** (Korea), **Chūgoku** (China) and, of course, **Nihon** (Japan). Some countries have an additional Japanese name as well as their native-tongue-derived name. These include: **Beikoku** (America), **Eikoku** (England). England is most commonly referred to as **Igirisu**.

When you add the word **jin** to the end of a country word, it indicates a person from that country. Say these nationalities in Japanese, then check your pronunciation with the recording:

American (person)   *German*   *Australian*
English (person)   *Italian*

You should have said:

◀ CD1, TR 9, 00:46

| Amerikajin | Doitsujin | Ōsutorariajin |
| Igirisujin | Itariajin | |

When you add the word **go** to the end, it means language. Say these languages in Japanese, then check your pronunciation with the recording:

| *French (language)* | *Chinese* | *Portuguese* |
| *Korean (language)* | *Spanish* | |

You should have said:

◀ CD1, TR 9, 01:01

| Furansugo | Chūgokugo | Porutogarugo |
| Kankokugo | Supeingo | |

By the way, the word for English (language) is: **Eigo.**

And finally, if you want to talk about the country of origin of an item, you attach **no** (see Explanation 1.2).

The main point here is that what is covered by one word in English has three possibilities in Japanese. So 'Spanish' could be said in the following ways:

| Supeinjin | Supeingo | Supein no |

It all depends on whether you are talking about a *person*, a *language* or an item's *origin*.

By the way, if you wanted to say 'Spanish teacher' you have a choice:

Supeinjin no sensei	*a Spanish [nationality] teacher*
Supeingo no sensei	*a Spanish language teacher*

It depends on which you want to say but don't forget **no** connects the two nouns.

Explanation 1.4

You will learn a lot about formal and informal Japanese language throughout this book. In Japanese society a distinction is made between the 'in-group' (myself, my family, my work colleagues, my friends) and the 'out-group' (my seniors, people from other families and workplaces). Politeness is an important traditional aspect of Japanese life and this is reflected strongly in the language used when speaking to those in the out-group. More informal language is generally used within the in-group.

First of all there is the use of **san**. This is attached to the end of a name (either first or surname) and is best translated in English as Mr, Mrs, Miss or Ms. It shows respect for the person you are addressing but you never use it to refer to yourself or your family.

More casual titles are:

- **kun,** used to address boys and between male friends (again never for yourself)
- **chan,** used for children and between friends, particularly girls
  Other titles are:
- **sensei,** used for teachers and professors
- **sama,** used in more formal situations and when addressing letters

Insight
All titles are attached after the name and it is important to use these titles when talking to other people whether you address someone by their first or their surname. If in doubt, it is safest to use the surname and **san**.

Explanation 1.5

Continuing the theme of in-group and out-group language, there are two sets of words for family – my family and other families. Here are some family terms for you to read out loud and learn. You will notice that often you simply attach the word **san** to make the 'other family' term and also attach the respectful **go** at the beginning of some words.

English	my family	other family
father	chi chi	otōsan
mother	haha	okāsan
son	musuko	musukosan
daughter	musume	musumesan
husband	shujin	go-shujin
wife	tsuma/kanai	okusan
brothers and sisters	kyōdai	go-kyōdai
family	kazoku	go-kazoku

Refer back to this box when you need to look up family terms.

Explanation 1.6

You learned a very formal way of introducing yourself in the opening dialogue. Look back at this now to remind yourself.

The phrase '*(name)* to mōshimasu' is a very formal way of saying 'I am called'. A more neutrally polite way to say your name is to say '*(name)* desu'

Dōzo yoroshiku and **yoroshiku onegaishimasu** are both ways of saying 'pleased to meet you'. The phrases more importantly encompass the idea of working together and being indebted/tied in to each other. You can combine the two phrases to make the more formal **dōzo yoroshiku onegaishimasu**.

If you want to introduce someone else you use **kochira** (this person): This (person) is Ms Takahashi.

Kochira wa
Takahashi-san desu
*This person is
Ms Takahashi*

For own family it would be over-polite and inappropriate to use **kochira.** You can use the more informal **kocchi** instead:

kocchi wa kanai desu   *this is my wife*
kanai desu   *my wife (simpler version)*

For children you can say: **kono ko** (*this child*).

Insight

You may have noticed that Japanese people say their surname before their first name (or you may not have if you are not yet familiar with Japanese names!). When you say your own name it is best to keep to the western order: first name then surname because most Japanese people are familiar with this, but be aware that Japanese people always give their surname before their first name.

Explanation 1.7

◀ CD1, TR 10

In Japanese, there are specific greeting words for different parts of the day and not one general word to cover the meaning 'hello'. Here they are – listen to the recording and say these new words out loud to really master them.

English	Japanese (formal)	Japanese (informal)
good morning	ohayō gozaimas(u)	ohayō
good afternoon (from 11ish)	konnichiwa	
good evening	konbanwa	
good night	oyasumi nasai	oyasumi
goodbye	sayōnara	bai bai/ja mata ne
when leaving the office	osaki ni	
excuse me, sorry	sumimasen	

Explanation 1.8

◀ CD1, TR 11

Read out loud the following table.

this (one)	*that (one)*	*that one over there*	*which one?*
kore	sore	are	dore
this	*that*	*that over there*	*which?*
kono	sono	ano	dono

Did you notice that as well as *this* and *that*, Japanese also has a word meaning *that over there*? You use this word when the object is near neither the speaker nor the person being spoken to. There are two sets of 'this and that' words (one set ends in **no** and the other in **re**) and here are examples of their different uses. Can you work out the rule?

kore wa Furansu no wain desu	*this is French wine*
kono wain wa Furansu no desu	*this wine is French*
sore wa Nihon no ginkō desu	*that is a Japanese bank*
ano ginkō wa Furansu no desu	*that bank over there is a French* (one)

Have you worked out how the **no** and **re** set are used differently?

- You use **re** when you want to say this or that one and there is no other word before **wa** (technically speaking **kore, sore** and **are** are nouns in their own right). Think of them as meaning 'this one, that one . . .' and you won't go far wrong
- The **no** set describe nouns and must be followed immediately by the item (noun) which is being described

Try saying these short sentences in Japanese to help you understand the difference:

1 This business card is mine.
2 That one is Robert's.
3 That wine is Italian.
4 That one over there is Spanish.

Explanation 1.9

Look at the following table.

am, is, are	am not, is not, are not (formal)	informal (more informal)
desu	dewa arimasen	ja arimasen (ja nai desu)

Notice that **desu** covers all the different words we use in English (*am, is, are*). This means you have fewer words and changes to remember! And often you don't need to say *I, you, it, she, he* or *they* either (there is more about this in Unit 2). Here are some examples:

Robāto-san wa jānarisuto desu	*Robert is a journalist*
Igirisujin desu	*(He) is English*
Amerikajin dewa arimasen	*(He) is not American*

Explanation 1.10

🔊 **CD1, TR 12**

Finally in this section you are going to learn to count from 1–10. It's easy! Do the actions to help you remember:

1 = ichi	(scratch your shoulder – you have an *itch*!)
2 = ni	(now scratch your *knee* – *itchy knee*!)
3 = san	(make a circle with your arms – the *sun* (pronounce it **san** though!))
4 = shi	(point to a girl – *she*)
5 = go	(do a jogging motion – off you *go*!)
6 = roku	(play your air guitar – you're in a *rock* band)
7 = nana	(pretend to knit like your grandma or *nana*)
8 = hachi	(lift up the *hatch*back of your car)
9 = kyū	(stand up straight in a *queue*)
10 = jū	(wave your fingers like *dew* falling on the grass!)

Go through the actions with numbers backwards and forwards and out of order until you feel confident. Then listen to the recording (or read the numbers with the pronunciation guide in mind) and concentrate on the correct pronunciation. You will find that sometimes the endings of 1 and 6 are cut short.

Insight

This matching of Japanese numbers to English words is only approximate and may lead to mispronunciation so, if you have the recording, listen carefully to the correct pronunciation or ask a Japanese friend to say the numbers and record them yourself.

These numbers can be used with counters – you have learned two in this unit:

counter	example	English
nin (person)	**gonin**	*five people*
sai (years old)	**gosai**	*5 years old*

Sometimes the number changes or 'squashes' depending on the counter that follows it. For example:

| jussai | *10 years old* |
| yonin* | *four people* |

You'll learn more about this in later units.
*Yo (yon) is another way of saying 'four'.

Main dialogue

◀ CD1, TR 13

Now you are going to see how well you have taken in these 10 explanations plus all the new vocabulary. Listen to (or read) the main dialogue three times. Each listening will have a different purpose as follows:

1 Listen and simply see how much you understand and how many words and phrases you recognize. You could even keep a tally on a piece of paper – make a mark every time you recognize a word
2 Listen and pause after each 'chunk' of conversation then repeat out loud
3 Answer the following questions (in English – answers in the key)

Robert's interview with Mr Hondo is part of his research on the work/home balance for Japanese fathers. As part of this research he meets Mr Hondo's family at home.

Hondō-san	Ā, Robāto-san, konnichiwa! **Yōkoso!**
Robert	Konnichiwa.
Hondō-san	[*Gestures to Naoe*] Kanai no Naoe desu.
Naoe-san	Hajimemashite, Hondō Naoe desu. Dōzo yoroshiku.
Robert	Hajimemashite. **Kochira koso**. Dōzo yoroshiku.

Hondō-san	Kono ko wa musume no Yuki desu. Kono ko wa Eri desu.
Yuki and Eri	Dōzo yoroshiku.
Eri-chan	Watashi wa jussai desu. **Ano**, Robāto-san wa Amerikajin desu ka.
Robert	Iie, Igirisujin desu. *Japan Now* **shinbun** no jānarisuto desu.

Insight

Additional words will sometimes appear in the main dialogues of each unit but they are not key to understanding the overall meaning. When you listen to or read a language you *do not* have to understand every word – the true skill is to pick out the key information.

yōkoso	*welcome*
shitsurei shimasu	*excuse me for interrupting*
kochira koso	*the pleasure is all mine*
ano	*hey, erm* (used to get attention)
shinbun	*newspaper*

QUICK VOCAB

Learn to say: My family

◄⁾ **CD1, TR 14**

Committing chunks of language to memory is a great way to improve confidence and pronunciation. Learning a language requires a fair amount of memorization of words and sentences and this can seem both difficult and tedious at times. And people say that they find it harder to memorize as they get older. But did you know that scientists have proved that, just as muscles need physical exercise to keep them in shape, the memory needs mental exercise to keep it sharp, whatever your age? In other words, 'use it or lose it'! And what better way to use it than to learn Japanese!

This section in the first five units will focus on one practical use of the language you have used so far. Listen to it or read it as many times as you need to; keep pausing and repeating the recording until you can say it all off by heart. It is worth persevering with because you will really begin to feel that you can speak Japanese.

Naoe Hondo is describing her family:

Kazoku wa yonin desu. Shujin no Hondō Tatsuya to musume no Yuki to Eri desu. Yuki wa jū roku sai desu. Soshite Eri wa jussai desu. Shujin wa eigyō buchō desu. Watashi wa shufu desu. Yoroshiku onegaishimasu.

Now have a go at introducing your own family. You may not have all the information you need but do as much as you can or make up a family if that is easier at this stage. Remember to speak out loud; you may also find it useful to write your speech down.

....

Insight
Meishi Business cards

Meishi are very important in Japan and all working adults carry them. Their purpose is not simply to provide name, workplace and other contact details – more importantly, they indicate a person's status and therefore with what level of respect they should be addressed. Always treat a **meishi** with respect – look at it with interest and then put it carefully away in your wallet or purse. Don't write on it, bend it or treat it casually – this may cause offence.

....

```
TOKYO
COMPUTERS

社長
田中　健一

東京コンピューター会社
〒１０３－２０４４東京六本木区２－１９
Phone (03) 1234-5678
Fax  (03) 9876-5432
```

Activities

In this section, you will have the opportunity to practise what
you have learned so far through a variety of activities and
exercises. The answers are all at the back of the book. Keep a
tally of your score – if you are scoring less than half marks, it
might help to go back over the unit and then try the activities
again. You can look back at vocabulary at any time (or use the
lists at the back).

Activity 1.1

You meet a Mrs Suzuki Naomi at a business conference. Can
you say your side of the conversation out loud? Use the English
prompts to help you. You might find it useful to listen once
more to the opening dialogue before you try this to refresh your
memory:

Suzuki-san	Hajimemashite, Suzuki Naomi desu.
	Yoroshiku onegaishimasu.
You	**1 Introduce yourself.**
Suzuki-san	Watashi no meishi desu. Dōzo.

You	2 Say thank you and hand over your business card.
Suzuki-san	Arigatō gozaimasu.
You	3 Comment that Mrs Suzuki is a sales manager for the Tokyo Bank.
Optional extra	4 Comment that she must be busy.

Activity 1.2

How well do you remember the greetings? Look at each picture and say the greeting out loud then refer back to Explanation 1.7 to refresh your memory.

Good morning   Hello (Good   Excuse me
afternoon)

See you!   Goodbye   Good evening

Good night

Activity 1.3

Think back to countries, nationalities and languages
(Explanation 1.3) and to the use of **no** (Explanation 1.2).
You are now going to play the part of an English-to-Japanese
translator (at a very simple level, of course!). You have a list
of English labels with incomplete Japanese translations. Can
you provide the correct missing information in Japanese? Keep
asking yourself – do I need nationality, language or country of
origin?

1 American whisky   _____ uisukī
2 a book in French   _____ hon
3 a Japanese bank   _____ ginkō
4 a newspaper in English   _____ shinbun
5 my Chinese wife   _____ kanai
6 a Korean teacher   _____ sensei

Activity 1.4

Look back to the 'learn to say' section. This time *you* are going
to introduce Naoe Hondo's family. Remember you are not
part of her in-group so you need to use the other family terms
(Explanation 1.5). And don't forget **san** and **chan** for other people
too (Explanation 1.4). Speak out loud then write it down.

Activity 1.5

This activity will practise the different uses of *this* and *that* (look
back to Explanation 1.8 to refresh your memory). Simply choose
the correct Japanese word from the box to complete each of the
following sentences. You can only use each word once so tick it off
once you have used it.

1 _____ hon wa watashi no desu. (this book is mine)
2 _____ sensei wa Takahashi-sensei desu. (that teacher over there
is Miss Takahashi)

3 _____ uisukī wa Amerika no dewa arimasen. (that whisky is not American)

4 _____ wa musuko no Tadashi desu. (this is my son, Tadashi)

5 _____ wa Suzuki-sensei desu. (this is Professor Suzuki)

6 _____ wa chichi no kaisha desu. (that over there is my father's company)

> sono   kocchi   kono   ano   are   kochira

Activity 1.6

Finally, here are some statements taken from this unit. You have to decide if they are true or false and in the gap at the end of each sentence write either **desu** (it is, he is . . .) or **dewa arimasen** (it is not/he is not). How well have you been paying attention? **Gambatte!** (Good luck!)

1 Robāto-san wa Igirisujin _____.

2 Hondō-san wa jānarisuto _____.

3 Yuki-chan wa jussai _____.

4 Naoe-san wa Hondō-san no okusan _____.

5 Hondō-san no go-kazoku wa gonin _____.

6 Naoe-san wa shufu _____.

7 Hondō-san wa Nihonjin _____.

You will find the End-of-unit challenge after the reading section.

Introduction to reading Japanese

The final section of each unit in this book will be devoted to learning how to read Japanese. You may decide that you want to focus on spoken Japanese only in the initial stages. If so, simply leave out this section and move on to the next unit – all the reading sections are independent of the rest of the book. However, the Japanese system of reading is both fascinating and challenging as well as offering an important insight into Japanese culture and the Japanese psyche. So whether you decide to work through the reading sections now or later, give them a try because they will open up a whole new aspect of Japanese language to you.

Described as 'the Devil's tongue' by 16th-century European missionaries, the Japanese reading system has been berated by some as being 'overcomplicated' and 'cumbersome' to learn. Three scripts and the need to learn 2000 Chinese characters to read a newspaper may seem daunting but here are some interesting considerations:

- At almost 100%, Japan has the second highest literacy rate in the world (Iceland takes number one place)
- Japan has the highest readership of newspapers in the world
- Kanji (Chinese characters) are very visual – good news for visual learners!
- The sound system and written symbols are phonetic, meaning that in Japan there is none of the dyslexia associated with spelling rules
- Japanese people are avid readers – you see people reading everywhere in Japan, on trains, buses and in bookshops
- Reading 'high-brow' newspapers in English requires an extensive vocabulary – in other words, it still requires a lot of work in English to be able to read a newspaper
- If you visit Japan without being able to read Japanese, it is that much more difficult to be able to get around (there *are* signs in English, but not always)

Insight

I'd also like to add to the list that learning to read Japanese can be fun and can give you a real sense of satisfaction and progress as well as challenging and stretching that grey matter! I hope I have convinced you to have a try. You can now choose either to move on to learning how to read Japanese or put this off (for now) and move on to Unit 2 – the choice is yours but don't forget to do the End-of-unit challenge.

A brief history

Before the 6th century AD Japanese was a spoken language only and **kataribe** (messengers) travelled around to convey important information to people orally. The ancient Chinese had developed a writing system in the 14th century BC that spread to the Korean Peninsula and from there to Japan in the 4th and 5th centuries AD (there are also many Korean and Chinese influences on Japanese culture and religion). Both Korea and Japan adapted these **kanji** (Chinese characters) to fit their own language and, even in China, the **kanji** developed over 3000 years ago have been revised, changed and abbreviated over many years.

Insight

People often assume that Chinese and Japanese are similar. In fact, the Chinese language is very different from Japanese in structure and is not in the same family of languages. Therefore, the writing system which came from China had to be adapted to fit the structure and rules of the Japanese language.

An introduction to the different scripts

There are three scripts in Japanese (four, if you include **rōmaji** or romanized script; in other words, the western alphabet). These three scripts are **kanji** (Chinese characters), **hiragana** and **katakana**. Each has its own specific function and the three are used in combination in written texts. You will also find **rōmaji** used for some foreign words and acronyms, e.g. NATO. Let's look at each individually, beginning with **kanji**.

Kanji (Chinese characters) 漢字

Kanji are ideographs that convey a specific meaning, word or idea. The simplest and earliest of these were pictographs. These were pictures drawn by the Chinese of the world around them, such as the sun, moon and trees, which were gradually standardized into the kanji used today. Here are three examples of this process.

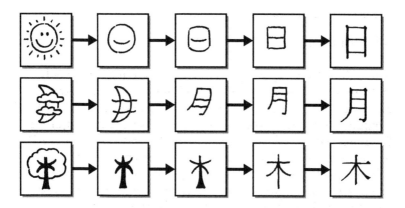

These are very simple examples but there are kanji to represent all aspects of language including concepts, feelings and ideas and extensive kanji dictionaries can have as many as 40–50,000 kanji. However, in 1981 the Japanese Ministry for Education, **Monbukagakushō**, produced an approved list of 1945 kanji for daily use known as the **jōyō kanji**. These are the kanji needed to read texts such as newspapers thoroughly. The learning of these 1945 kanji is spread throughout the nine years of compulsory education.

Insight

Although 1945 kanji sound like a lot to learn, it is worth making a comparison with English because, although we learn the alphabet relatively quickly, it takes much longer to learn our complex spelling and pronunciation rules and we spend many years learning and acquiring vocabulary and understanding different types of text. If you compare English vocabulary to French, for example, you will discover that in a standard dictionary there are over 171,000 English words compared to only about 43,000 French words. Whoever said English was easy?!

In addition to the 1945 jōyō kanji, there are a further 284 more unusual kanji that are used in names and Japanese parents may look even beyond these additions to find auspicious kanji when naming their children (as parents in the west might consult a naming book to find more unusual names). The rules for writing kanji are very precise and the correct order for writing each kanji is learned and practised repeatedly at school (as in the west the rules for correctly writing the alphabet are taught at school).

Insight
Shodō (Way of writing or calligraphy)

Shodō was introduced to Japan with kanji and many styles have developed since. As in China, it is considered to be one of the fine arts in Japan and the mark of a cultured person. **Shodō** is written using kanji and/or kana and the main implements are the **futofude** (thick brush) used for the main part of the text and **hosofude** (thin brush) for the signature or fine writing. **Sumi** (Chinese ink) is made from wood or oil soot mixed with fishbone or hide glue.

Styles of calligraphy

In some styles of calligraphy, such as **kaisho,** the characters are easily recognizable but in others, such as **sōsho** ('grass writing'), the characters are often abbreviated or linked to each other in a rounded and flowing style. A post-war avant garde development has produced styles that are totally abstract and bring calligraphy close to the principles of modern art.

Kana かな

Hiragana and katakana are collectively known as **kana.** They are both phonetic alphabets or syllabaries. This means that each symbol represents a sound (phoneme). This is different from the western (Roman) alphabet system, in which each symbol is a letter and letters are grouped into sounds. Here is an example of this difference:

In English, the word *goodbye* is made up of seven letters:
G-O-O-D-B-Y-E

In Japanese, *goodbye* is **sayōnara** and is made up of five syllables:
SA-YO-U-NA-RA

These are represented by five hiragana symbols: さようなら

Kana was originally developed in the 9th century in order to be able to write the Japanese language phonetically. The first set of phonetic characters were called **man'yōgana** and these were kanji that were chosen, regardless of their meaning, because their pronunciation was the same as the sounds of the Japanese language. For example, the sound **ka** is represented by these kana symbols:

か (hiragana)　　　カ (katakana)

Both symbols were created originally from this kanji: 加 (pronounced **ka**).

All **man'yōgana** were gradually simplified into the hiragana and katakana systems used today. If you look carefully at the **ka** example, you can see that the hiragana symbol is a simplification of the *whole* kanji whereas the katakana symbol has been developed from *part* of the kanji.

Insight

The Buddhist priest, Kukai (774–835) is credited with the invention of the kana syllabary. Both hiragana and katakana represent the same set of 46 basic sounds (plus other combination and modified sounds) but the symbols are written differently. This is not an alien idea to English speakers for there are essentially two alphabets, capital and lower case, which both represent the same letters but in Japanese, the two kana scripts exist for different purposes.

Hiragana ひらがな

The word **hiragana** means *rounded/easy to use* and indicates both the shape and relative simplicity of the script. The hiragana symbols were developed by simplifying the man'yōgana kanji that represented the sounds of the Japanese language. An example of this process was shown in an earlier section. Hiragana was necessary in order to adapt the Chinese writing system to the Japanese language.

It was during the Heian period (794–1185) that hiragana developed to allow for a more pure expression of the Japanese language. Before this, written expression had been very limited in Japan, with the use of many Chinese words and phrases and restricted mainly to official documents written by men. The Chinese system continued to be used for official matters but the kana system allowed for more creative writing and became essentially the writing system of the Imperial Court and, more importantly, of aristocratic court ladies and their female attendants.

Insight

The Heian Court women used the kana writing system to express themselves through poetry, prose and diaries and so it is that the heights of creativity in Heian literature were achieved mainly through women writers using hiragana, which was given the name **onnade** meaning 'women's hands'. Two famous female authors from this time are Murasaki Shikibu who wrote the world's first novel, *Tale of the Genji,* and Sei Shonagon (*The Pillow Book*)

Today, hiragana symbols are used to write the grammatical parts of words and sentences and Japanese words that have no kanji. You will learn more about this in units to follow.

Katakana カタカナ

This word means *partial* because katakana symbols were developed from part of kanji characters. You saw an example of this in the previous **kana** section.

Katakana was thought to have been invented by the Buddhist priest Kukai in order to write out Chinese and Sanskrit Buddhist texts phonetically. Today, its main use is for writing non-Japanese words that have been introduced into the language. These fall into two categories:

1 *Loan words* **gairaigo**, for example, コンピューター (**kompyūtā**) *computer*
2 Foreign names such as countries, cities and personal names, for example, アメリカ (**Amerika**) *America*

There are also three ways in which katakana is used for writing *Japanese* words:

1 to make words stand out, for example, in advertising: トヨタ (Toyota)
2 to classify species of plants and animals, for example in botanical gardens
3 to write onomatopoeic words

In overall appearance, katakana symbols are more angular in shape and hiragana are more rounded. Here are the first five sounds of each script (a, i, u, e, o). Compare these two sets of symbols and see if you can identify these features:

Hiragana あ い う え お
Katakana ア イ ウ エ オ

Insight

Japanese is traditionally written downwards (**tategaki**) and you begin reading from the top right of a page. This means that books are opened from what we would consider to be the back. Nowadays, however, books, newspapers and magazines are often written western style, in horizontal lines (**yokogaki**) from left to right and, in these cases, the book is opened from our (western) understanding of the front.

Reading activity 1.1

Here is a short piece of Japanese text. Some parts have been underlined and numbered 1, 2 or 3. Each of these numbers relates to kanji, hiragana or katakana. Can you work out which number relates to which script? Remember: hiragana is more rounded, katakana is more angular and kanji characters are more complex.

サラダのアレンジが広がる シンプルサラダと相性のいい ソース三種

In Units 2–6, you will be gradually learning how to read hiragana. In Units 7–12, you will learn a total of 82 kanji and 52 compound words and finally, in Unit 13, you will be introduced to katakana.

End-of-unit challenge

◂) CD1, TR 15

Every unit ends with a challenge or fun test so you can assess your progress. Keep an eye on your score in each test – if you score over 80% then you are definitely ready to move on to the next unit; if you score between 50 and 80% you may find it helpful to read over the explanations for that unit again; if you find you are scoring below 50% then read through the explanations in that unit again and try some of the practice activities once more before you move on to the next unit.

For the Unit 1 challenge you are going to test yourself on numbers. How well do you remember them? Follow the instructions below then listen to the recording (or refer back to Explanation 1.10) to see how well you did.

1 Say the numbers 1–10 out loud and as quickly as you can.
2 Now say them backwards from 10 – as quickly as you can!
3 Now say all the even numbers in order – 2, 4, 6 . . .
4 And now the odd numbers – 1, 3, 5 . . .
5 And, finally, teach someone else the numbers with the actions – it'll help you to remember them even better!

2

···

Mainichi terebi o mimasu
I watch TV every day

In this unit you will learn
- *how to use verbs and particles in sentence structures*
- *how to say* **shall we** *and* **let's**
- *how to say* I don't
- *time expressions and telling the time (1)*
- *how to count from 11–99*
- *months of the year*

Getting started

There will be opening and build-up activities in each unit from now on; they are designed to get you speaking Japanese straightaway.

The main objective of Unit 2 is to learn about Japanese verbs. You can think of verbs as action or 'doing' words, or as words in front of which you can put *I*, *you*, *she*, *he*, *it* or *they*: *I eat, you slept, they watched*.

Opening activity

◀) **CD1, TR 16**

You'll be pleased to learn that Japanese verbs have an easy-to-recognize pattern. Switch on the recording and repeat the following then pause the audio.

34

tabemas(u)	*eat* (I, you, s/he, they, we, it)		
nomimas(u)	*drink*		
mimas(u)	*watch, look, see*		
shimas(u)	*do, make, play* (a sport or instrument)		
hanashimas(u)	*speak, talk*		

By the way, the 'u' is bracketed to show it is barely/softly spoken.

Good news! – it doesn't matter who does the action – the ending *masu* is always the same.

Build-up activity

◀ **CD1, TR 17**

Here are five items. Listen to the recording and repeat out loud then press the pause button:

gohan	*rice*	sōji	*cleaning*
kōhī	*coffee*	Nihongo	*Japanese*
terebi	*TV*		

Now you are going to say: *I eat rice, I drink coffee, I watch TV . . .* Listen and repeat:

Gohan o tabemasu.	Sōji o shimasu.
Kōhī o nomimasu.	Nihongo o hanashimasu.
Terebi o mimasu.	

Insight
Have you noticed that the order is different from English – in Japanese, the verb always comes at the end of the sentence – *rice eat.*

You will have noticed **o** between the item and the verb. This is called a particle or grammar marker and it is said after the item you eat, drink, watch etc. You will learn more about this later in this unit.

Opening dialogue

Listen to Naoe Hondo as she explains her morning routine. First listen to (read) and then *repeat out loud* the 10 new words to improve your pronunciation and confidence. Then listen to the opening dialogue and see if you can pick out these 10 words and also the verbs and items you learned in the opening activity.

◀》 **CD1, TR 18**

asa	*morning*
asagohan	*breakfast* (**asa** + **gohan** = 'morning rice')
hayaku	*early*
okimasu	*get up*
to	*with, and*
itsumo	*always*
nyūsu	*news*
tokidoki	*sometimes*
sorekara	*and then*
kinjo no hito (to)	*neighbour* (*with*)

◀》 **CD1, TR 19**

Now over to Naoe-san:

Asa hayaku okimasu. Kazoku to asagohan o tabemasu. Itsumo terebi nyūsu o mimasu. Soshite kōhī o nomimasu. Tokidoki kinjo no hito to hanashimasu. Sorekara sōji o shimasu.

I get up early in the morning. I eat breakfast with my family. I always watch the TV news. And I drink coffee. Sometimes I talk with the neighbour. Then I do the cleaning.

How did you get on? Did you manage to pick out those 10 words? Listen again and this time pause the recording after each sentence and repeat out loud. This will help you to build confidence in pronunciation and in remembering the new vocabulary.

Key sentences

This time we'll start with you doing some of the work. Here are some short sentences in English. Can you say them in Japanese? Remember to refer back to previous vocabulary lists in this unit to help you (or use the vocabulary index at the back). Check your answers with the recording and at the back:

◀) **CD1, TR 20**

1 I eat my breakfast with my family.
2 Sometimes I watch the TV.
3 I always drink coffee.
4 I speak Japanese with my neighbour.
5 I do the cleaning in the morning.

Now here are some example sentences of the key grammar points you will learn in Unit 2. Read them, listen to the recording, repeat them and check the English meanings and new vocabulary list that follow. Before you read the grammar explanations, see if *you* can work out how the sentence fits together:

◀) **CD1, TR 21**

1 Rokuji ni okimasu.
2 Asagohan ni tōsuto to tamago o tabemasu.
3 Gohan o tabemasen.
4 Kaisha de hirugohan o tabemasu.
5 Ano resutoran de bangohan o tabemashō!
6 Ashita Furansu ni ikimasu.
7 Issho ni resutoran ni ikimashō ka

ji	*o'clock*
ni (1)	*at/for/on/in*
tōsuto	*toast*
tamago	*egg*
tabemasen	*don't eat*

QUICK VOCAB

de	*at/in* (after place)
hirugohan	*lunch*
resutoran	*restaurant*
bangohan	*evening meal*
tabemashō	*let's eat*
ashita	*tomorrow*
ni (2)	*to* (a place)
ikimasu	*go*
issho ni	*together*
ikimashō ka	*shall we go?*

Insight

You may have noticed that there is a word common to the three meal words – **asagohan, hirugohan, bangohan** – this word is **gohan**. **Gohan** means *rice* and rice is the fundamental component of all traditional Japanese meals, including breakfast.

English translation of the key sentences

1 *I get up at 6 o'clock.*
2 *For breakfast, I have toast and eggs.*
3 *I don't eat rice.*
4 *I eat lunch at work (the company).*
5 *Let's eat dinner at that restaurant over there!*
6 *Tomorrow I will go to France.*
7 *Shall we go to a restaurant together?*

Language explanations

Here is a list of the grammar and language points you will learn in this unit:

1 a number of useful **masu** verbs
2 more about particles (grammar markers): **wa, o, ni** and sentence structure

3 **to** meaning *and* or *with*
4 more about **shimasu** (*do, make, play*)
5 three useful verbs to say *go*, *come* and *return*
6 the particle **ni** plus some useful time expressions; telling the time (1)
7 saying *where* an action takes place and the particle **de**
8 how to say *shall we* and *let's* (**mashō ka, mashō**)
9 how to say *I don't* (**masen**)
10 the numbers 11–99 plus the months of the year

Explanation 2.1 More verbs

So far in this unit, you have been introduced to seven Japanese verbs. Now you are going to double that amount! Look at the following table and familiarize yourself with the 14 verbs listed by doing the following: look, cover, say out loud then check until you feel familiar with them.

tabemasu	*eat*	**nomimasu**	*drink*
shimasu	*do, make, play*	**hanashimasu**	*talk, speak*
ikimasu	*go*	**mimasu**	*watch, see, look*
okimasu	*get up*	**kikimasu**	*listen*
yomimasu	*read*	**kaimasu**	*buy*
kakimasu	*write, draw*	**hatarakimasu**	*work*
nemasu	*go to bed*	*****tsukurimasu**	*make, build*

Insight

Pronunciation tip: The sound **tsu** is a single syllable (beat) and the **u** is very soft. Your tongue should touch the top of your mouth and the sound almost 'whistles' through. It is very similar to the last sound in the word 'ca*ts*'.

Now practise what you have learned by saying these simple sentences in Japanese. Say them out loud and check your answers in the back:

1 I eat lunch.
2 I sometimes read a newspaper.
3 I always listen to the news.
4 I work with my father (**chichi**).
5 Tomorrow I will go to Japan.
6 I draw a picture (**e**).
7 I make lunch.
8 I go to bed early.
9 I will buy a TV.
10 My mother does the cleaning in the morning.

Explanation 2.2 The topic of the sentence

haha wa asa sōji o shimasu   *my mother does the cleaning in the morning*

This was your final sentence in Explanation 2.1. You probably missed out the **wa** after you said **haha** because you hadn't had any practice or explanation of this yet in Unit 2. But you did meet **wa** in Explanation 1.1. Its function is to mark the topic or subject of the sentence. Let's think about this further.

In English, the order of the sentence tells us which is the subject and which the object. The subject, by the way, is the thing or person that carries out an action, whereas the object is the thing or person that has the action done to it. Some examples will show this:

my mother drinks coffee (mother = subject; coffee = object)
I do the cleaning (I = subject; cleaning = object)

The sentence order tells us which is subject and object with the standard pattern being: subject, verb, object (SVO).

Here are two examples of Japanese sentence structure. What is the order?

Haha *wa* kōhī *o* nomimasu   Watashi *wa* sōji *o* shimasu

You should have worked out the order as subject object verb (SOV).

In addition, Japanese uses grammar markers (known commonly as particles) to indicate subject and object – **wa** for subject, **o** for (direct) object.

You will have noticed by now that the word for *I* (**watashi**) isn't always spoken in the Japanese sentences you have been listening to and saying. This is the same for *they, she, he, it* and *we* – if it is obvious who the subject is or once the subject has been established it is not necessary to say or keep repeating these words. But the words do exist and are used when you need to clarify, introduce or emphasize who did what. The following table contains the words for he, she . . . for you to learn.

I	**watashi** (**boku** is often used by men)
we	**watashitachi**
you	**anata** (**anatatachi** – plural)
he	**kare**
she	**kanojo**
they	**karera**

Now use them in these sentences. Don't forget **wa** and don't worry too much about exact sentence order as long as the verb comes at the end – the order is actually quite flexible in Japanese:

1 She will go to Korea tomorrow.
2 You guys get up early!
3 We always eat dinner together.
4 He works with his father.
5 You will go to the restaurant with your family?

We need to mention the particle **ni** briefly in this explanation. It has some different uses but we will focus on two now. The first is to convey the meaning *to* with verbs of movement (e.g. go, arrive, return). 'I go *to* France' is:

(Watashi wa) Furansu *ni* ikimasu

You say **ni** (to) after the place or location you are going to (arriving at, returning to).

The second use of **ni** is to say 'for' as in 'for breakfast':

Asagohan <u>ni</u> tōsuto o tabemasu   *I eat toast <u>for</u> breakfast*

Insight

You will find these facts about Japanese grammar markers (particles) useful as you get to grips with Japanese grammar:

- Particles are always placed <u>after</u> the word they mark
- Most nouns in a sentence will need a particle, except nouns followed immediately by **desu**

Explanation 2.3 Kazoku to *With my family*

To has two meanings – *and*, *with*. Here are two examples you have already come across:

Kazoku <u>to</u> asagohan o tabemasu   *I eat breakfast <u>with</u> my family*

Asagohan ni tōsuto <u>to</u> tamago o tabemasu   *For breakfast I eat toast <u>and</u> egg*

Try saying these sentences out loud then check your success in the back. Remember to put **to** meaning *with* after the noun that the action is done with. **To** meaning *and* works the same as in English:

1 In the mornings I always buy a newspaper and a coffee.
2 I sometimes watch TV with my brothers and sisters.
3 I always make dinner with my mother and my husband.

Explanation 2.4 Shimasu *I do*

Shimasu is a useful general verb covering the meanings of *do, make, play* depending of context. Look at these examples and new words:

sakkā o shimasu	*play football*
sōji o shimasu	*do the cleaning*
denwa o shimasu	*make a phone call*

Now here is a table of 10 verbs using **shimasu** for you to learn and refer back to.

sōji (o) shimasu	*do the cleaning*
denwa (o) shimasu	*make a phone call*
gorogoro shimasu	*chill out, slob around*
benkyō (o) shimasu	*study*
shigoto (o) shimasu	*work (do a job)*
sakkā o shimasu	*play football*
gorufu o shimasu	*play golf*
shokuji (o) shimasu	*have a meal*
ryokō shimasu	*travel, take a trip*
kaimono (o) shimasu	*do the shopping, go shopping*

You will have noticed that for many of these new words, **o** is in brackets to show that often it isn't spoken or needed – in the case of *to travel*, it isn't used at all but look at the following:

| Furansu o ryokō shimasu | *I travel (in) France* |
| Nihongo o benkyō shimasu | *I study Japanese* |

In these two examples, **o** is still used to mark the object, in these cases *France* and *Japanese*.

Explanation 2.5 Ashita Nihon ni ikimasu *Tomorrow I will go to Japan*

The verb **ikimasu** is one of a group of verbs that describe movement. These verbs don't have a 'direct object' – instead you talk about the places you go <u>to</u>, return <u>from</u> or come <u>to</u>. In English, the word 'to' or 'from' is usually required to convey the movement; in Japanese, we use **ni** or **e** (see Explanation 2.2) for *to* and **kara** for *from*.

Here is a short table of places you are going to use to practise using verbs of movement.

uchi	*home*
jimusho	*office*
depāto	*department store*
sūpā	*supermarket*
koreji	*college*

Insight

Pronunciation tip: Make sure you say syllables with a macron (line) over them as a double 'beat', but say the sound smoothly not as two separate sounds: su-u-pa-a, de-pa-a-to.

The three verbs you will use are: **ikimasu** (*go*); **kaerimasu** (*return*) and **kimasu** (*come*). When you go to your home or home town or the country you come from, you should use **kaerimasu** (*return*) and *not* **ikimasu** (this has the meaning more of *go out/go away from home*). Now try these sentences (say them out loud if you can):

1 I will go to the office tomorrow.
2 I will go to the supermarket with my son.
3 I sometimes go (return) home early.
4 My father will come to college in the morning.
5 I will return to Japan tomorrow.

Explanation 2.6 Time expressions and telling the time

These are the time expressions you have learned so far:

tokidoki	*sometimes*
itsumo	*always*
asa	*(in) the morning*
ashita	*tomorrow*
ji	*o'clock*

The first four of these are general times and you do not need to use a particle after them – they stand alone. However with ji (o'clock), just as we would say *at 6 o'clock* you also need an equivalent particle in Japanese. This particle is ni. Look at these examples:

rokuji <u>ni</u>	<u>*at*</u> *6 o'clock*
nichiyōbi <u>ni</u>	<u>*on*</u> *Sunday*
nigatsu <u>ni</u>	<u>*in*</u> *February*

You haven't learned days of the week or months yet but they are here to show you how ni works – don't worry about learning them as vocabulary yet.

So you have seen in this unit alone that there are different uses of the particle ni – ni meaning *for* (*for breakfast*), ni meaning *to* (with movement verbs) and ni meaning *at*, *on* or *in* with precise time expressions.

I hope you realize, by the way, that saying the time on the hour is easy – say the relevant number followed by ji (*o'clock*). Say *1 o'clock*, *5 o'clock* and *10 o'clock* out loud now.

This is what you should have said: ichiji, goji, jūji.

There are some changes to the numbers – remember that four people was yonin? Well, 4 o'clock is yo ji. Two other changes are:

7 o'clock	shichiji (shichi is the alternative to nana for *seven*)
9 o'clock	kuji

◄) CD1, TR 22

Now listen to the times from 1 o'clock to 12 o'clock being spoken on the recording and use the pause button to repeat each one out loud.

Finally, here are a few more general time expressions (they stand alone – no particle needed) to add to your growing collection. You should see a pattern, which will make them easier to remember.

	mai ~ (every ~)	kon ~ (this ~)	rai ~ (next ~)
nichi (day)	mainichi (*every day*)	kyō (*today*)	ashita (*tomorrow*)
shū (week)	maishū (*every week*)	konshū (*this week*)	raishū (*next week*)
getsu/tsuki (month)	maitsuki (*every month*)	kongetsu (*this month*)	raigetsu (*next month*)
nen/toshi (year)	mainen/maitoshi (*every year*)	kotoshi (*this year*)	rainen (*next year*)

And three more frequency time expressions:

taitei	*usually*
tabitabi	*many times, over and over again, frequently*
tama ni	*occasionally*

Explanation 2.7 Uchi <u>de</u> bangohan o tabemasu
I eat dinner <u>at</u> home

Here's another particle with a precise meaning. When you talk about the place in which an action takes place, you use the particle **de** after the place word. (Remember that particles are placed *after* the word they mark.) It means *on* or *at* in English. And a quick word about sentence order – if there is a time expression, it usually but not always comes first followed by the place then the object then the verb. If you are going to say the subject, you can say this at the very beginning. Look at this example:

Watashi wa	mainichi	kaisha de	hirugohan o	tabemasu
I	every day	at the company	lunch	eat
Subject	**time**	**place**	**object**	**verb**

I eat lunch every day at the company

Now try these sentences – look back to Explanation 2.5 for a table of place words:

1 I drink coffee at the office every day.
2 I occasionally buy a newspaper at the supermarket.
3 My son will play football at college next week.
4 Tomorrow I will eat with my family at the restaurant.

Insight

At this stage I think you will find it useful to have a short
summary of the particles you have met so far:

wa marks the subject of the sentence – the doer of the action:
<u>haha</u> **wa** bangohan o tabemasu – *Mum eats dinner*

o marks the object of the sentence –the action is done to
this: haha wa <u>bangohan</u> **o** tabemasu – *Mum eats <u>dinner</u>*

ni means *to* with movement verbs: Nihon **ni** ikimasu – *I go
<u>to</u> Japan*

ni also means *for*: asagohan **ni** – <u>*for*</u> *breakfast*

ni also means *on, in, at* when used with time expressions:
goji **ni** – <u>*at*</u> *5 o'clock*

to means *and, with*: haha **to** bangohan o tabemasu – *I eat
dinner <u>with</u> my Mum*; haha **to** chichi – *Mum <u>and</u> Dad*

de marks the place where an action happens: uchi **de** haha to
bangohan o tabemasu – *I eat dinner with Mum <u>at</u> home*

Explanation 2.8 Resutoran de tabemashō ka *Shall we eat at a restaurant?*

If you want to make a suggestion (*shall we?* or *let's*), you change
the **masu** part of the verb to **mashō (ka)**:

Resutoran de tabe**mashō ka**	*Shall we eat at a restaurant?*
Resutoran de tabe**mashō!**	*Let's eat at a restaurant!*

Try making these suggestions in Japanese:

1 Let's go to that department store over there. (Remember *that?*
ano, Explanation 1.8)
2 Let's buy sushi in this supermarket.
3 Shall we go (return) to my house?

Explanation 2.9 Saying *I don't*

Saying *I don't* is easy too – change **masu** to **masen**:

Gohan o tabemasen   *I don't eat rice*

Often in negative sentences particle **o** is changed to **wa** to emphasize the thing that is *not* done, especially if there is no other **wa** in the sentence:

Kōhī wa nomimasen   I don't drink *coffee* (but there *are* lots of things I do drink)

Try these sentences:

1 I don't drink coffee.   **3** My wife doesn't clean the house.
2 He doesn't work.

Explanation 2.10 More on numbers

Now you are going to learn how to count from 11 to 99. First of all try to count from 1 to 10 from memory then look back at Explanation 1.10) to double-check that you have remembered them correctly.

If I tell you that you only need to know the numbers 1–10 to be able to count up to 99 then can you work out what 11 will be (don't look yet!).

◀) **CD1, TR 23**

If you guessed that the pattern is 10 + 1, you were right! Here are the numbers 11–19. Listen to them on the recording then use the pause button and repeat out loud. Think what 20 is going to be as you go through them:

11 jū ichi   **16** jū roku
12 jū ni   **17** jū nana (jū shichi)
13 jū san   **18** jū hachi
14 jū shi   **19** jū kyū
15 jū go

And 20? If you have a mathematical mind then this pattern may have occurred to you:

$2 \times 10 = nij\bar{u}$

Before we go further you need to know that there are alternative numbers 4 and 7 (you know this already from learning the time):

4 = shi, yon (yo)   7 = shichi, nana

···

Insight

By the way, the word **shi** also means 'death' in Japanese, which is why you will never find a room or floor numbered 4 in a hospital or hotel!

◀ **CD1, TR 23, 00:30**

Now try counting in tens from 20 to 90 (40 is **yonjū** and 70 is **nanajū**) then listen to the recording and try pausing and repeating. To count 21, 22, 23 . . . , you add the single number like this: nijū ichi, nijū ni, nijū san, etc.

◀ **CD1, TR 23, 01:27**

And finally, before you begin the main dialogue and activities, a word about the months of the year. In Japanese, they say one month, two month, three month . . . for January, February, March and so on, using the word **gatsu** for month:

ichigatsu	*January*	shichigatsu	*July*
nigatsu	*February*	hachigatsu	*August*
sangatsu	*March*	kugatsu	*September*
shigatsu	*April*	jūgatsu	*October*
gogatsu	*May*	jūichigatsu	*November*
rokugatsu	*June*	jūnigatsu	*December*

Listen to the names for all 12 months on the recording.

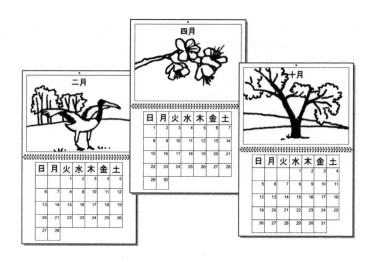

Main dialogue

◄》 CD1, TR 24

Now you are going to see how well you have taken in the
10 explanations in this unit plus all the new vocabulary. As with
Unit 1, listen to (or read) the main dialogue three times. Each
listening will have a different purpose, as explained in Unit 1.
To summarize:

1 Listen for words and phrases you recognize. Keep a tally
2 Listen in 'chunks', pause, repeat out loud
3 Answer the questions

*Robert is interviewing Mr Hondo about his daily routine as part of
his article on work/home balance.*

Mr Hondo	Mainichi rokuji ni okimasu. Asagohan ni **taitei** tō suto o tabemasu. Soshite kōhī o nomimasu.

	Densha de jimusho ni ikimasu. Itsumo hachiji ni **tsukimasu. Osoku made** hatarakimasu. Soshite tabitabi jimusho no hito to resutoran de bangohan o tabemasu.
Robert	Nan ji ni kaerimasu ka.
Mr Hondo	Jūji, jūichiji **goro** desu. Tsuma to terebi o mimasu. Soshite nemasu.
Robert	Nichiyôbi ni **nani** o shimasu ka.
Mr Hondo	Tokidoki jimusho no hito to gorufu o shimasu ga **taitei** kazoku to uchi de gorogoro shimasu.

Questions

1 What time does Mr Hondo get up?
2 What does he have for breakfast? (two items)
3 What time does he arrive at work?
4 What does he frequently do after work?
5 What sort of time does he get home?
6 What does he do then?
7 Describe his Sundays.

taitei	*generally, usually*
densha	*train*
densha de	*by train*
tsukimasu	*arrive*
osoku	*late*
osoku made	*until late*
goro	*about* (used with times)
nani (nan)	*what*

QUICK VOCAB

Learn to say: My routine

◀) **CD1, TR 25**

Remember that the aim of this section is to get you memorizing chunks of language and getting that grey matter working to improve confidence and pronunciation.

....

Insight

In this unit, you are going to commit a daily routine to memory. Remember you can listen to it, pause it or read it as many times as you need to and remember to keep persevering because you will really begin to feel that you can speak Japanese. You may find it easier to learn one or two sentences – that's fine, you can always revisit this later and learn some more.

Katie Mears, an American English teacher in Tokyo, is describing her daily routine.

Shichiji ni okimasu. Asagohan wa tabemasen **ga** itsumo kōhī o nomimasu. Asa tabitabi kinjo no hito to depāto de kaimono o shimasu. Soshite resutoran de shokuji o shimasu. **Gogo** tokidoki sūpā ni ikimasu. Soshite uchi ni kaerimasu. Tama ni uchi o sōji shimasu. Itsumo terebi o mimasu. **Sorekara** bangohan o tsukurimasu. **Yoru** shichiji **kara** shigoto o shimasu.

QUICK VOCAB	**ga**	*but*	
	gogo	*afternoon, pm*	
	sorekara	*and then*	
	yoru	*(in the) evening*	
	kara	*from*	

Insight

Japanese breakfast

There is such a range of food and dishes in Japan that it would be impossible to list them all within this book but breakfast is a good place to start! Traditional Japanese breakfast consists of three staple items: **miso** (bean paste) soup, pickles and grilled fish.

Other components of a Japanese breakfast may be a raw egg to whisk into the hot rice, **nori** (wafers of dry seaweed) to eat with rice, **natto** (fermented bean curd – an acquired taste!) to mix with rice and greens such as spinach or mountain roots. Green tea is normally served with a Japanese breakfast. This meal involves a fair amount of preparation and the busy lifestyles of Japanese people nowadays may mean they choose to eat a simpler western-style breakfast instead. This is often something like toast, coffee, some kind of simple salad and maybe a fried egg.

Activities

Activity 2.1

You have learned about sentence order and particles in this unit. Can you reorder the following Japanese words to make Japanese sentences that match the English meanings? You will need to supply the particles and think about the sentence order.

Example: For breakfast I eat rice and miso soup: miso shiru, asagohan, gohan, tabemasu = Asagohan ni gohan to miso shiru o tabemasu.

1 For lunch I eat egg and toast. And I drink coffee.

tōsuto, kōhī, tamago, hirugohan, nomimasu, tabemasu, soshite

2 I get up every day at 6 o'clock. Then I make breakfast.

asagohan, mainichi, rokuji, okimasu, tsukurimasu, sorekara

3 Tomorrow I will play golf with my neighbour.

gorufu, kinjo no hito, ashita, shimasu

4 In the afternoons I usually read the newspaper. Sometimes I watch the news.

shinbun, gogo, taitei, tokidoki, nyūsu, yomimasu, mimasu

5 I always return home late. Occasionally I eat dinner with my family.

itsumo, tama ni, uchi, kazoku, osoku, bangohan, kaerimasu, tabemasu

Activity 2.2

Use the English prompts to say things that you DON'T do. Where appropriate use particle **o** rather than **wa** but remember that **wa** can be used instead for emphasis (Explanation 2.9).

Example: You don't watch TV in the evenings. (evenings = yoru)
Yoru terebi o mimasen.

1 You don't have meals with your family.
2 You don't talk to your neighbour.
3 You don't drink coffee for breakfast.
4 You don't clean the house.
5 You don't go to work early.

Activity 2.3

Here are some questions in Japanese about Mr Hondo's daily routine using **nanji** (what *time?*) and **nani** (*what?*). Can you match them with their correct English meaning?

Japanese questions
1 *Nan ji* ni uchi ni kaerimasu ka
2 *Nan ji* ni okimasu ka

3 *Nan ji* made hatarakimasu ka
4 Nichiyōbi ni *nani* o shimasu ka
5 Asagohan ni *nani* o tabemasu ka

English meanings
a What time does he get up?
b What does he have for breakfast?
c What time does he work until?
d What time does he go home?
e What does he do on Sundays?

Check your answers and then see if you can answer the questions in Japanese. Refer back to main dialogue for any information you need.

Activity 2.4

Can you write in the correct particles to complete the sentences? To quickly find words you can't remember, use the vocabulary lists at the back of the book.

1 Sūpā___ tamago ___ kōhī ___ kaimasu.
2 Uchi ___ shujin ___ nyūsu ___ kikimasu.
3 Rokuji ___ kinjo no hito ___ depāto __ ikimasu.
4 Ashita issho ___ resutoran ___ ikimashō ___.
5 Mainichi kaisha ___ jimusho no hito ___ hirugohan ___ tsukurimasu.

Activity 2.5

This activity is designed to help you review all the verbs you have learned in this unit. See how many you can remember without looking back. Write them in the table (or just say them) both in the **masu** and **masen** forms then search for the ones you didn't remember. Keep coming back to this activity at later stages to see how many more you can remember.

English meaning	I do/will do (masu)	I don't/won't (masen)
drink	_____	_____
eat	_____	_____
see, watch, look	_____	_____
listen	_____	_____
speak, talk	_____	_____
write	_____	_____
read	_____	_____
work	_____	_____
make	_____	_____
buy	_____	_____
go	_____	_____
return	_____	_____
come	_____	_____
do	_____	_____
get up	_____	_____
go to bed	_____	_____
play golf	_____	_____
chill out	_____	_____
do work	_____	_____
study	_____	_____
play football	_____	_____
do the shopping	_____	_____
travel	_____	_____
have a meal	_____	_____
make a phone call	_____	_____

How to read hiragana (1)

In this section you will learn:

- the first 15 hiragana symbols
- ideas to help you remember the symbols
- how to read some simple words

Introduction

In Unit 1, you learned about the three different scripts and had a brief introduction to each of them. In the next six units you will gradually learn how to read hiragana. In this unit, you will learn the first 15 hiragana.

Insight

Hiragana is the phonetic script that Japanese children learn first. They then gradually learn kanji and, as they do so, replace hiragana words or parts of words with these kanji. In a similar way, you will first develop your skills in reading hiragana before adding some useful everyday kanji.

Start reading

You learned about the phonetic sounds of Japanese in the pronunciation guide in the Introduction this book. Look back to this section now, focus on the first 15 sounds (a–so), listen to the recording if you have it and say each sound out loud.

Here are those 15 hiragana symbols with their pronunciation underneath. Look at them and say each sound out loud.

あ	い	う	え	お
a	i	u	e	o
か	き	く	け	こ
ka	ki	ku	ke	ko
さ	し	す	せ	そ
sa	shi	su	se	so

How to remember hiragana symbols

It really helps most people if you can create mnemonics to remember each symbol. Mnemonics are sound and picture associations that help you to link the visual symbol with its sound. Here are a few ideas to get you started. Focus on the sounds (for example, aim = e sound) rather than the letters or spellings:

あ (**a**) is for *a*pple

い (**i**) is for *i*gloo

う (**u**) *ooh!* my back hurts

え (**e**) is for *e*scalator

お (**o**) is for *o*strich

き (**ki**) looks like a <u>key</u>

Insight

Try to invent your own mnemonics by looking at the symbols and thinking of pictures to link them with their sounds. Note your ideas down in a notebook and try to fix them into your head – it will make the learning-to-read process go much more smoothly. Here are a few more ideas (although you may prefer to find your own):

〈 (**ku**) for <u>cu</u>ckoo's beak こ (**ko**) for <u>co</u>in し (**shi**) <u>she</u> has long hair す (**su**) for <u>su</u>perman そ (**so**) a string of <u>sa</u>usages

Other ideas to help you remember

- Make flashcards of each hiragana symbol on paper or card. Write the pronunciation on the back then keep testing yourself in random order to see how well you can remember them. Make two piles – those you can remember easily and those you are still unsure of. Keep working on the 'unsure' pile until you have reduced it to zero! Look at the cards every day or on a regular basis to build up your reading skills and recognition of each symbol

- On a large sheet of white paper draw a grid of squares with five squares across and 10 squares down. Begin to fill in the chart with the first 15 hiragana, starting at the top left square and working across from left to right. It should look like the grid overleaf.

Fill in the chart each time you learn a new set of symbols until you have the complete set. Put the poster up on a wall where you can look at it and practise or test yourself.

Similar looking hiragana

The following hiragana symbols look quite similar and you may find this confusing at times. Here are some clues to help you tell them apart:

あ	い	う	え	お
か	き	く	け	こ
さ	し	す	せ	そ

あ, お   the loop in あ (**a**) curls around the vertical line whereas the smaller loop in お (**o**) is a continuation of the vertical line
お (**o**) has an extra 'dash' line above the loop

い, こ   い (**i**) is more or less vertical, こ (**ko**) is horizontal

き, さ   き (**ki**) has two horizontal lines whereas さ (**sa**) only has one

Also note that you may come across this alternative way of writing **ki, sa** and **so** especially when hand written: き, さ, そ.

Reading activity 2.1

Look at the following two columns of hiragana words. The same words are in both columns but in a different order. Can you correctly pair up these words?

1	すし	a	えき
2	あい	b	あき
3	あかい	c	けさ
4	あき	d	こえ
5	けさ	e	うえ
6	えき	f	すし
7	こえ	g	すき
8	あおい	h	あい
9	すき	i	あかい
10	うえ	j	あおい

Reading activity 2.2

🔊 **CD1, TR**

Now you are going to try reading some hiragana words. These are also on the recording so you can either listen and repeat as you look at the words or try reading them yourself first and then check your answers with the recording:

1	え	*picture*	11	けさ	*this morning*
2	あい	*love*	12	こえ	*voice*
3	あう	*meet*	13	すし	*sushi*
4	うえ	*above*	14	せき	*seat*
5	かお	*face*	15	そこ	*over there*
6	あおい	*blue*	16	すき	*like*
7	あかい	*red*	17	せかい	*world*
8	あき	*autumn*	18	せいき	*century*
9	えき	*station*	19	おおきい	*big*
10	くさ	*grass*	20	おいしい	*tasty*

Reading activity 2.3

The words from Reading activity 2.2 are all contained in the following search. Can you find them and highlight them?

あ	い	け	く	こ	う	う	え
え	う	あ	さ	お	か	え	き
く	す	き	け	せ	か	い	こ
さ	し	し	す	い	せ	そ	こ
お	そ	あ	い	き	う	え	え
お	お	せ	か	き	あ	い	く
け	え	き	こ	さ	か	お	し
お	い	し	い	す	い	せ	い

Reading challenge

Here, in random order, are the 15 hiragana symbols that you have learned in this unit. Can you read them all? Speak out loud:

か し う く さ

き そ あ お け

え す い こ せ

Learning to write hiragana

This book focuses on the important skill of reading Japanese script. If you would like to learn how to write it correctly (and this is also a good way to help you remember the symbols), this is covered in *Read and write Japanese scripts* (Helen Gilhooly, Hodder & Stoughton, 2010).

End-of-unit challenge

The challenge for this unit is to count from 11 to 99! You can
either do it now with the book in front of you or find some 'empty'
time to try this challenge – in your car, before going to sleep, while
cleaning the house, walking to the shops . . . find a convenient time
but don't skip this challenge! And if you really want a challenge,
see if you can count backwards from 99! **Gambatte!** (Good luck!)

3

....

Kaimono o shimashō!
Let's do some shopping!

In this unit you will learn
- *essential phrases for shopping*
- *how to count numbers of items*
- *how to say where things and people are*
- *more question words*
- *money amounts and counting above 100*

_____

Getting started

The main objective of this unit is to learn useful words and phrases around the topic of shopping. You will also learn how to say 'there is' and 'there isn't' and to count different types of object and money.

You are going to revisit some of the words and structures you have already learned to get you speaking in Japanese straightaway!

Opening activity

You have learned the numbers 1–10 (ichi, ni, san . . .), but in Japanese you rarely use these numbers by themselves. For example, when listing numbers of any item, you add a counter word. We do have a similar system in English, for example:

*two **loaves** of bread* *six **portions** of rice*
*three **slices** of toast* *one **bottle** of wine*

In English, these counter words are sometimes essential (one bread or two toasts sound rather odd) but we don't use counter words for everything, so it is all right to say, for example, seven cars, six dolls, four computers. By contrast, Japanese *does* use a counter word for everything and so there are lots of them! You will learn just a few in this unit but enough to make you sound authentic!

First of all, say out loud the numbers 1–10 (check in Explanation 1.10 if you need a memory jog). Now you are ready to learn the counters **mai** and **dai**. **Mai** is for counting square-ish, flat-ish objects such as toast, shirts, cards and paper. **Dai** is for counting machines such as cars, computers and televisions. So, off you go – count one slice (of toast), two slices and so on by attaching **mai** after the number, then count cars using **dai**:

> 1 slice, 2 slices, 3 slices, 4 slices, 5 slices, 6 slices, 7 slices, 8 slices, 9 slices, 10 slices
> 1 (car), 2 (cars), 3 (cars) . . . 10 (cars).

Here's what you should have said:

> **ichi-mai, ni-mai, san-mai, yon-mai, go-mai, roku-mai, nana-mai, hachi-mai, kyū-mai, jū-mai** (for cars add **dai**)

Build-up activity

Now you are going to count specific objects. You say the object first then the number – look at the examples:

two cards kādo ni-mai
three televisions terebi san-dai

Now you try. You will need these words:

> **terebi** (*TV*) **kādo** (*card*) **kami** (*paper*) **kompyūtā** (*computer*)
> **tōsuto** (*toast*) **kuruma** (*car*)

1 four cards	**4** nine sheets of paper
2 seven televisions	**5** two computers
3 five cars	**6** one slice of toast

Opening dialogue

Rie Franks, Robert Franks' wife is shopping at her local **baiten** (*kiosk*). Switch on the recording and listen to and repeat the 10 new words. Then listen out for them in the opening dialogue.

◀) **CD1, TR 26**

◀) **CD1, TR 26**

QUICK VOCAB

irasshaimase	*welcome, may I help you?* (used to greet customers)
iie	*no*
ikura	*how much?*
hyaku-en	*100 yen* (en = yen)
jā	*right, ok, in that case*
(o) kudasai	*may I have, I'll have*
Kurisumasu	*Christmas*
kashikomarimashita	*certainly* (used by shop assistants, tradespeople)
zembu de	*altogether, in total*
sen	*1000*

◀) **CD1, TR 27**

Rie Franks, Robert Franks' wife, is shopping at her local **baiten** (kiosk).

Shop assistant	Irasshaimase!
Rie	Sore wa Igirisu no shinbun desu ka.
Shop assistant	Iie, kore wa Amerika no desu. Kore wa Igirisu no desu.
Rie	**Ikura** desu ka.
Shop assistant	Yon-**hyaku en** desu.

Rie	Jā, kore o kudasai. Soshite kono **kurisumasu** kādo o ni-mai kudasai.
Shop assistant	**Kashikomarimashita. Zembu de sen** en desu.

Shop assistant	*Welcome, may I help you?*
Rie	*Is that an English newspaper?*
Shop assistant	*No, this is American. This is an English one.*
Rie	*How much is it?*
Shop assistant	*400 yen.*
Rie	*Ok, I'll have this please. And two of these Christmas cards.*
Shop assistant	*Certainly. Altogether that's 1000 yen.*

Now listen once more, pause after a 'chunk' and repeat out loud to improve your pronunciation.

◀) **CD1, TR 28**

sumimasen	*excuse me* (to get attention), *sorry*	
arimasu (1)	*have, possess*	
zenzen	*nothing, not at all* (+ negative)	
kai	*floor*	
ni-kai	*second floor*	
ya	*and* (when giving examples *not* a complete list)	
arimasu (2)	*there is, there are* (non-living things, inanimate)	
imasu	*there is, there are* (living things, animate – animals and people)	
dare	*who*	
dare mo	*no one* (+ negative)	

QUICK VOCAB

Key sentences

◀) **CD1, TR 29**

Here are some example sentences of the key grammar points you will learn in Unit 3. Read them, listen to the recording, repeat them and check the English meanings and new vocabulary list that follows. Before you read the grammar explanations, see if you can work out how the sentence fits together.

Insight

Here are some tips to help you de-code the key sentences:

- **Ka** at the end shows you it is a question
- Remember the verb is always at the end of the sentence
- **Wa** marks the subject of the sentence and can sometimes be translated as 'as for' (**shinbun wa** – as for the newspaper)
- **Masen** is the negative ending – is not

1 Kono shinbun wa ikura desu ka.
2 Kono kurisumasu kādo o ni-mai kudasai.
3 **Sumimasen**, Furansu no shinbun ga **arimasu** ka.
4 **Ni-kai** ni terebi **ya** kompyūtā ga **arimasu**.
5 **Ni-kai** ni nani mo arimasen.
6 Ano jimusho ni otōsan ga **imasu** ka.
7 Uchi ni **dare mo** imasen.

English translation of the key sentences

1 *How much is this newspaper?*
2 *May I have two of these Christmas cards?*
3 *Excuse me, do you have any French newspapers?*
4 *On the second floor there are TVs, computers etc.*
5 *On the second floor there is nothing.*
6 *Is your father in that office over there?*
7 *There is no one at home.*

Language explanations

Here is a list of the grammar and language points you will learn in this unit:

1 review of this, that and that over there
2 essential phrases for shopping and asking for things

3 counter words – how to say numbers of items
4 asking for numbers of items
5 **arimasu** and **imasu** – saying there is, there are
6 saying where things and people are using particle **ni**
7 question words – **dare, nani** (who, what)
8 asking if there is anyone or anything – **dare ka, nani ka** and saying there isn't anything or anyone – **nani mo, dare mo**
9 money amounts and counting above 100
10 saying *and* – **to, ya, nado, mo . . . mo**

Explanation 3.1

Do you remember this, that and that over there? (**kono, sono, ano**). And also this one, that one, that one over there (**kore, sore, are**). You also learned **dore** (which one) and **dono** (which). Look back to Explanation 1.8 if you need to review this grammar point.

Explanation 3.2

You have learned three essential shopping phrases in this unit:

do you have any . . .	. . . ga arimasu ka
how much is it?	ikura desu ka (. . . wa ikura desu ka)
may I have . . .	. . . o kudasai

Let's add two other useful phrases to this set:

do you sell . . .	. . . o utteimasu ka (pronounce: **u-**_pause_**-te-i-mas(u) ka**)
may I see/please show me . . .	. . . o misete kudasai (**mi-se-te**)

Here is a list of items for you to start shopping for.

tokei	*watch (clock)*
kitte	*stamps*
yukata	*cotton kimono*
sensu	*folding fan*
denchi	*batteries*
bīru	*beer*
kaban	*bag*
hagaki	*postcard*
ningyō	*doll*
o-hashi	*chopsticks*
kamera	*camera*
keitai (denwa)	*mobile phone*
o-sake	*rice wine*
kēki	*cake*
ringo	*apple*
kutsu	*shoes*

Insight

The pictures show some of the typical Japanese souvenirs that you can buy relatively inexpensively in Japan or in Japanese shops around the world. Wooden kokeshi dolls (bottom left picture) are made in many styles and shapes and are often decorated with symbols, pictures and stories from the regions where they are made. The more expensive ones are usually handmade, with the artist's signature on them, and you can visit individual artists' studios to see the very best that money can buy!

Now, using these words and phrases, see if you can say the following:

1 Excuse me (sumimasen), do you have any cotton kimono?
2 Do you have any postcards?
3 Excuse me, do you sell stamps?
4 Do you sell camera batteries?
5 How much is this folding fan?
6 May I see those chopsticks?
7 May I see that doll over there?
8 May I have this rice wine?
9 May I have this watch and this bag?

Explanation 3.3

You've already been introduced to the concept of counters in the **Getting started** section. Let's look at this in more detail now.

System A

This system of counting involves using the numbers **ichi, ni, san** . . . and adding a specific counter depending on the type of item. There are many, many of these in Japanese. Here is a list of some of them.

counter word	type of item	examples
mai	square-ish, flat-ish	 *shirts, folded clothes, stamps, paper, tickets, pizza, CDs*
dai	large machinery	 *cars, lorries, televisions, computers*

counter word	type of item	examples
hon (pon, bon)	long, cylindrical items	bottles, videotapes, films, pens, trees
kai kai*	floors Number of times	
hiki (piki, biki)*	small animals	dogs, cats, fish, mice
tō*	large animals	cows, horses, elephants
nin	people	
ko	round objects	apples, sweets, round fruit, eggs, soap
satsu	books	magazines, comic books, notebooks
soku*	pairs (footwear)	shoes, socks, boots

Insight

The counters marked * are not really used in this book, but they are useful to know. Don't worry about remembering all the counters – I will remind you of the word or refer you back to this chart each time you need to use them.

With some counters, the pronunciation of number or counter changes slightly. The most common change is the 'squashing' or shortening of the numbers 1, 6, 8 and 10. For example, counters beginning with **k** have these changes to 1, 6 and 10:

ikkai	*first floor*	ikko	*one round item*
rokkai	*sixth floor*	rokko	*six round items*
jukkai	*10th floor*	jukko	*10 round items*

And counters beginning with **s** have these changes to 1, 8, and 10:

issatsu	*one book*	issoku	*one pair*
hassatsu	*eight books*	hassoku	*eight pairs*
jussatsu	*10 books*	jussoku	*10 pairs*

For three pairs you may hear **sanzoku**, but it is ok to use **sansoku**.

Finally, counters beginning with **h** have these changes to 1, 3, 6, 8 and 10:

ippon	*one cylindrical item*	**ippiki**	*one animal*
sanbon	*three cylindrical items*	**sanbiki**	*three animals*
roppon	*six cylindrical items*	**roppiki**	*six animals*
happon	*eight cylindrical items*	**happiki**	*eight animals*
juppon	*10 cylindrical items*	**juppiki**	*10 animals*

When you say four or seven, by the way, with all these counters use **yon** and **nana**.

Insight

The best way to get the hang of these number counters is to practise them but there is a lot to remember so, of course, you will make mistakes but you will still be able to be understood in most cases. To help you in the initial stages, the words that change will be <u>underlined</u> to warn you.

To get your mind really working on this one, here are some items and numbers to say out loud as in the example. You can also listen to them on the reccording:

Example: bottles of beer (**bīru**), <u>three</u> (**hon**) = **bīru sanbon**

1 pairs of shoes (**kutsu**), <u>eight</u> (**soku**)
2 apples (**ringo**), <u>six</u> (**ko**)
3 bottles of rice wine (**sake**), five (**hon**)
4 bottles of beer (**bīru**), four (**hon**)
5 cotton kimono (**yukata**), three (**mai**)
6 televisions (**terebi**), one (**dai**)
7 books (**hon**), <u>ten</u> (**satsu**)

System B

This system uses an alternative way of counting from 1–10.
It is used for the many items that don't have a special counter (especially items that don't have a particular shape) and you can, in fact, use it even for items that do have a special counter although you will then sound less authentic.

◀) **CD1, TR 31**

The list may look a little daunting at first but read it as you listen to the recording and speak out loud:

1	=	hitotsu	**6**	= muttsu
2	=	futatsu	**7**	= nanatsu
3	=	mittsu	**8**	= yattsu
4	=	yottsu	**9**	= kokonotsu
5	=	itsutsu	**10**	= tō

Insight

The reason that there are two systems for counting in Japanese is because there is both the imported Chinese system (**ichi, ni, san, shi** . . .) and the native Japanese system (**hito, futa, mi, yo** . . .). These have become intermingled and completely adapted into the Japanese language.

Here are some hints for remembering system B:

- The words for four and seven items are familiar because they use **yo** and **nana**
- 1–9 all end in the item counter **tsu**
- Ten (**tō**) sounds rather like the English word *toe* – and you have 10 of these!
- Two (**futatsu**) has a sound not unlike *foot* (**futa**) and you have two of these!

Now practise using this system with the following items: mobile phones (**keitai denwa**); cakes (**kēki**); cups of coffee (**kōhī**); bag (**kaban**); watch (**tokei**):

8 three cups of coffee
9 two mobile phones
10 one cake

11 10 bags
12 four watches

Explanation 3.4

You know that to say *may I have* or *I'd like*, you say '. . . o kudasai' (Explanation 3.2). To ask for a number of items you say the counter after the item and between the particle **o** and **kudasai**. For example:

May I have <u>three</u> bags   Kaban o <u>mittsu</u> kudasai
May I have <u>a</u> bottle of beer   Bīru o <u>ippon</u> kudasai

Now you try. Ask for the following using system B (**tsu**):

1 two bags
2 five watches
3 four cups of coffee

Ask for the following using system A (counter in brackets – underlined if changes):

4 two (hon) bottles of rice wine (**sake**)
5 six (<u>hon</u>) bottles of beer (**bīru**)
6 three (ko) apples (**ringo**)
7 five (mai) stamps (**kitte**)
8 three (satsu) notebooks (**nōto**)

Explanation 3.5

You have learned how to say *it is, I am, they are* . . . by using the word **desu**:

Nihonjin desu	*She is Japanese*
Robāto-san wa jānarisuto desu	*Robert is a journalist*

And you have learned the negative (*isn't, am not*) using **dewa arimasen** (**ja arimasen, ja nai** – see Explanation 1.9):

Amerikajin dewa arimasen	*(He) is not American*

Now you are going to learn how to see *there is, there are* using **arimasu** and **imasu**. Look at these examples:

Jānarisuto desu	*He is a journalist (they, she, I . . .)*
Jānarisuto ga imasu	*There is (are) a journalist(s)*
Kaban desu	*It is a bag (they)*
Kaban ga arimasu	*There is/are a bag(s)*

Insight

Here are some points to remember when using **arimasu** and **imasu**:

- In general, as with all Japanese sentences, context will tell you whether something is singular or plural
- Note the difference in meaning of **desu** and **arimasu/imasu** (see preceding examples)

- Remember that **arimasu** is for non-living things (inanimate) and **imasu** is for living things (people and animals). Trees and plants are considered to be inanimate objects

You try. Should these sentences end in **imasu** or **arimasu**?

1 haha ga _____
2 tokei ga _____
3 bīru ga _____
4 inu (dog) ga _____
5 ki (tree) ga _____

There is a new particle – **ga**. You can think of it as meaning *a* or *some* in this type of sentence. As you have probably come to expect, you say it after the item. Now try saying these sentences out loud:

6 There is a book. (**hon**)
7 There are some apples. (**ringo**)
8 The neighbour is there.
9 There are some Americans.
10 There are some Americans and some Japanese people.

Finally, to say *there isn't*, *there aren't*, change **masu** into **masen**:

| *There aren't any English people* | Igirisujin ga imasen |
| *There aren't any English books* | Eigo no hon ga arimasen |

The particle **ga** often changes to **wa** with negative sentences to add emphasis: Igirisujin wa imasen – there are no *English people* (but there *are* Americans).

Explanation 3.6

You learned (in Explanation 2.7) that when you want to say where an action took place you use particle **de** after the place:

Uchi *de* bangohan o tabemasu   I eat dinner *at* home

When you use **arimasu** and **imasu** there is no action – these are known as verbs of existence, in other words, you are saying what there is rather than what is happening. If you want to mention the place where something or someone is you use particle **ni** (this is another use of **ni** – you learned others in Unit 2):

Uchi *ni* haha ga imasu — *In* the house there is my mother (my mother is in the house)

Ni-kai *ni* terebi ga arimasu — *On* the second floor there are TVs (there are TVs on the second floor)

So *in*, *on* and *at* are represented by **ni**, which is said after the place. You say the place at the beginning of the sentence. Now try these:

1 My father is at the office.
2 My family are at home.
3 There are bags and (**ya**) watches (etc.) on the first floor. (**ikkai**)
4 On the third floor is a supermarket.
5 There are French and English journalists in that office (over there).

Explanation 3.7

In Activity 2.3, you learned to recognize questions using **nanji** (*what time?*) and **nani** (*what?*). For example:

Nanji desu ka — *What time is it?*
Nanji ni okimasu ka — *What time do you get up?*
Nichiyōbi ni *nani* o shimasu ka — *What do you do on Sundays?*

To answer these questions, you simply replace **nan** or **nani** with the information and repeat the sentence, leaving off **ka** at the end:

Ichiji desu — *It is 1 o'clock*
Shichiji ni okimasu — *I get up at 7*
(Nichiyōbi ni) gorufu o shimasu — *I play golf (on Sundays)*

Let's use this question word with **arimasu**. You want to find out what is on the second floor of the department store so you say the place/floor first then the question:

Nikai ni nani ga arimasu ka

To reply, replace nani with the information:

Terebi ya tokei ga arimasu

Now you try:

1 What is there on the fourth floor?
2 What is there on the sixth floor?
3 What is there in this office?

The question word *who* is **dare** (**da-re**). Now ask the following:

4 Who is in the office?
5 Who is at home?
6 Who is on the third floor?

Explanation 3.8

Building on the question words **nani** and **dare** (Explanation 3.7) you can now learn how to ask: *Is there anyone? Is there anything?*

To do this you add **ka** after the question word (you don't need the particle **ga**):

Nikai ni nani *ka* arimasu ka   *Is there anything on the second floor?*
Uchi ni dare *ka* imasu ka   *Is there anyone at home?*

Now you try:

1 Is there anybody in this office?
2 Is there anything on the first floor?
3 Is there anyone at home?

If you want to reply, yes there is, you simply say **hai** (*yes*) then repeat the sentence without the question word **ka**:

Hai, dare ka imasu	*Yes, there is somebody*
Hai, nani ka arimasu	*Yes, there is something*

To say there isn't anything or there isn't anyone you repeat the question word and add **mo** after it. You change **masu** into the negative – **masen**:

Nikai ni nani mo arimasen	There is nothing on the second floor
Uchi ni dare mo imasen	There is nobody at home

Now you try:

4 There is nobody in this office.
5 There is nothing on the first floor.
6 There is no one at home.

Insight

The Japanese currency is the yen. To give you an idea of value at 2010 prices, a cup of coffee costs between 200 and 400 yen, a meal out at a moderately priced restaurant would cost between 1000 and 2000 yen a head, a night's accommodation in a 'no-frills' hotel would be about 5000–8000 yen per room and a medium glass of beer in a bar would be between 500 and 800 yen. Check on the internet for up-to-date exchange rates.

Explanation 3.9

The money amounts you will be using a lot in Japan are 100s (**hyaku**) and 1000s (**sen**). Like the counters you learned in Explanation 3.3, you use the number system **ichi, ni, san** . . . and attach **hyaku** and **sen** to it. The numbers 'squash' and change by the same rules too. Listen and repeat these numbers out loud:

100	hyaku	1000	sen (issen)
200	nihyaku	2000	nisen
300	sambyaku	3000	sanzen
400	yonhyaku	4000	yonsen
500	gohyaku	5000	gosen
600	roppyaku	6000	rokusen
700	nanahyaku	7000	nanasen
800	happyaku	8000	hassen
900	kyūhyaku	9000	kyūsen

To say amounts such as 150, 220, 2220 you simply say the number amounts in order as you would in English:

150 – hyaku gojū
220 – nihyaku nijū
2220 – nisen nihyaku nijū

To build up your confidence in reading and saying larger numbers try giving these prices as in the example:

Example: The coffee is 250 yen = kōhī wa nihyaku-en desu

1 The chopsticks are 500 yen.
2 The newspaper is 350 yen.
3 The cotton kimono is 4400 yen.
4 The doll is 6800 yen.
5 This camera is 9999 yen.

◀ **CD1, TR 32**

Now listen to the recording to check your answers and practise these amounts again.

You will also need to deal with another higher amount when in Japan. The Japanese count in units of 10,000 called **man**:

| 10,000 | ichiman | 20,000 | niman |
| 30,000 | sanman | 40,000 | yonman (and so on) |

You say these amounts by isolating the units of 10,000 first then saying the rest of the amount. Here is an example:

45,163 yen = 4 × 10,000, 5 × 1000, 163 yonman, gosen,
hyaku rokujū san-en

Insight

Here is a tip for converting large money amounts into: If you count four decimal points from the right end of the number, then everything to the left of that is counted in **man**:

| 4 ǀ 5163 | to left of line remains 4 so **yonman** (40,000) |
| 65 ǀ 7800 | to left of line remains 65 so **rokujū goman** (650,000) |

Now practise converting and saying these Japanese prices:

6 35,600 yen   **7** 356,600 yen   **8** 356,666 yen

Explanation 3.10

There are a number of ways to say *and* in Japanese. Let's focus on the use of *and* between two nouns (books *and* pens, boys *and* girls, peace *and* quiet). You learned **to** in Unit 2:

| Asagohan ni tōsuto *to* tamago o tabemasu | I eat toast *and* eggs for breakfast |

You have been introduced to **ya** in this unit:

Nikai ni terebi *ya* kompyūtā ga arimasu   *On the second floor are TVs, computers (etc.)*

You use **to** when the list is exhaustive (you list everything there is) and **ya** to give a few examples from an implied longer list. You can add **nado** to say *etc./and so on*:

Nikai ni terebi ya kompyūtā
nado ga arimasu
*There are TVs, computers and so
on on the second floor*

If you are only listing two items and want to say *both . . . and* you
use the particle **mo** like this:

Bīru *mo* o-sake *mo* arimasu
Asagohan ni gohan *mo*
tōsuto *mo* tabemasu
*There is both beer and rice wine
I eat both rice and toast for
breakfast*

Can you add the missing *and* word to these sentences:

1 Ikkai ni sensu ___ yukata ___ ga arimasu.
(*there are fans, cotton kimono and so on on the first floor*)
2 Uchi ni haha ___ chichi ga imasu.
(*my Mum and Dad are at home*)
3 Haha ___ chichi ___ kono kaisha de hatarakimasu.
(*both my Mum and Dad work in this company*)

Main dialogue

◀) **CD1, TR 33–36**

Now you are going to see how well you have taken in the 10
explanations from this unit plus all the new vocabulary. In this
unit the focus is on developing your listening skills (but the script
is printed at the back of the book if you don't have the audio). You
are going to listen to four short shopping dialogues. For each one,
listen out for the following information:

- What item(s) does the shopper buy?
- How many of each item do they buy?
- How much is each item?
- What is the total cost?

Insight

To build up your understanding of the recording, please follow these steps:

1 Listen to the whole recording (all four dialogues) through once without writing anything down. Aim: to get an overall sense of the dialogues
2 Listen to the whole recording again and this time listen out for any words or phrases you recognize. Only jot them down if you have time and/or keep a tally
3 Listen to the whole recording again and focus on specific information related to the questions. For example you could decide to just listen out for items, or numbers or prices (or a combination)
4 Now listen to one dialogue at a time and try to answer the questions. You will probably need to do this several times

<table>
<tr><td rowspan="5">QUICK VOCAB</td><td>de gozaimasu</td><td>= humble/polite form of desu</td></tr>
<tr><td>koko</td><td>here (soko = there, asoko = over there)</td></tr>
<tr><td>doko made</td><td>where to?</td></tr>
<tr><td>kiro</td><td>kilo</td></tr>
<tr><td>banana</td><td>banana</td></tr>
</table>

Learn to say: At the post office

◆ **CD1, TR 37**

Remember that the aim of this section is to get you memorizing chunks of language and getting that grey matter working to improve confidence and pronunciation. Focus on the customer's part. Listen to the recording, pause after the assistant's part and say your part out loud then listen to the recording to check:

Post office assistant	Irasshaimase!
You	Hagaki o utteimasu ka.

Assistant	Hai, koko de gozaimasu.
You	Kono hagaki o misete kudasai.
Assistant	Hai, dōzo. Ichimai hyaku-en de gozaimasu.
You	Jā, kore o yonmai kudasai.
Assistant	Kashikomarimashita.
You	Soshite kitte o yonmai kudasai.
Assistant	Doko made desu ka.
You	Amerika made desu.
Assistant	Ichimai hachijū en desu. Zembu de nanahyaku nijū-en de gozaimasu.

Activities

Activity 3.1

🔊 **CD1, TR 38**

You are going to start this section with a listening activity based around numbers. You will listen to short dialogues and then choose the correct time/price/number or month from a choice of three per question. The aim of this activity is to develop your skills of listening for specific information – you do *not* have to understand everything!

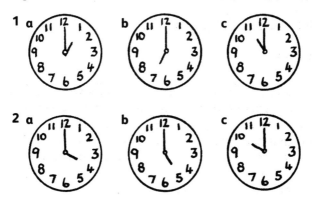

3

a 200 yen
b 2000 yen
c 1000 yen

4

a 31,000 yen
b 32,000 yen
c 72,000 yen

5

a September
b May
c June

Activity 3.2

How confident do you feel with the months of the year? You are probably still trying to work out which number relates to which month. To help you with this, try this simple activity – match the Japanese month with its English equivalent:

1 shichigatsu	**a** January	**7** nigatsu	**g** July
2 kugatsu	**b** February	**8** gogatsu	**h** August
3 hachigatsu	**c** March	**9** jūnigatsu	**i** September
4 shigatsu	**d** April	**10** sangatsu	**j** October
5 ichigatsu	**e** May	**11** rokugatsu	**k** November
6 jūichigatsu	**f** June	**12** jūgatsu	**l** December

Activity 3.3

Now you are going to practise asking for amounts of items using the phrase 'May I have . . .' (. . . o **kudasai**). You need to use the correct counter and to put the counter word in the correct place (between o and **kudasai**). Remember you can use system B if you don't know or aren't sure of the correct counter but the answers will give the usual counter used. Use the pictures as prompts for this activity and speak out loud. Look back to the list of shopping items in Explanation 3.2 for the vocabulary:

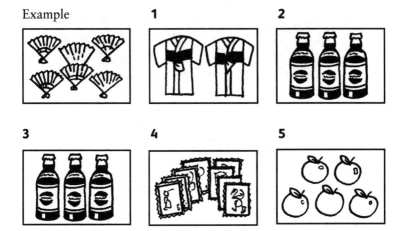

Example | 1 | 2
3 | 4 | 5

Example: sensu o roppon kudasai

Activity 3.4

You have learned about **arimasu** and **imasu** (*there is/are*) in this unit. Now see how well you can use them. The following sentences have gaps requiring either **arimasu** or **imasu**. You also need to add particles **ni** and **ga** in the correct place. Be careful because sometimes the sentence is in the negative:

1 Nikai ___ terebi ya kompyūtā ___ _____. (*there are TVs, computers etc. on the second floor*)
2 Ano depāto ___ haha ___ _____. (*my mother is in that department store over there*)
3 Kuruma ___ kamera ___ _____. (*there isn't a camera in the car*)
4 Resutoran ___ dare mo _____. (*there isn't anyone in the restaurant*)
5 Sono sūpā ___ dare ___ _____ ka. (*who is there is that supermarket?*)

Activity 3.5

You have also learned how to say *someone* or *something* using
dare ka and **nani ka,** and no one or nothing using **dare mo** and
nani mo + the negative. Put in the correct words to complete these
sentences:

1 Uchi ni _____ __ _____. (*there is someone in the house*)
2 Uchi ni _____ __ _____. (*there is no one in the house*)
3 Sankai ni ____ __ _____ ka. (*is there anything on the third
floor?*)
4 Iie, _____ __ _____. (*no, there isn't anything*)
5 Ano jimusho ni ____ __ _____ ka. (*is there anyone in that
office?*)
6 Hai, _____ __ _____. (*yes, there is somebody*)

How to read hiragana (2)

In this section you will learn:

- the middle 15 hiragana symbols
- ideas to help you remember the symbols
- how to read some simple words

Start reading

Look back to the pronunciation guide in the introduction to
this book, focus on the middle 15 sounds (**ta–ho**), listen to the
recording if you have it and say each sound out loud.

Here are those 15 hiragana symbols with their pronunciation
underneath. Look at them and say each sound out loud. Use the
recording again to reinforce the sounds:

た	ち	つ	て	と
ta	chi	tsu	te	to
な	に	ぬ	ね	の
na	ni	nu	ne	no
は	ひ	ふ	へ	ほ
ha	hi	fu	he	ho

How to remember hiragana symbols

Try to think of some more mnemonics (sound and picture associations) to help you remember these new symbols. Focus on the sounds of the words you choose, not the spellings. Here are a few ideas to get you started:

た (**ta**) looks like the letters **t** and **a**

ち (**chi**) is a *che*erleader

と (**to**) is the *to*e of a shoe

ね (**ne**) Loch *Ness* Monster

ふ (**fu**) Mount *Fu*ji (Japan's highest mountain)

Here are some other ideas that might work for you:

つ **(tsu)** looks like a nose and someone sneezing 'a-tsu!'

て **(te)** looks like a *ta*ble (pronunciation not spelling)

な **(na)** is a *na*nny pushing a pram

に **(ni)** is a *kn*ee

ぬ **(nu)** looks like two chopsticks picking up *noo*dles

の **(no)** is a *kn*ot

は **(ha)** could be made to look like a *hou*se

ひ **(hi)** looks like a mouth laughing – *he*e hee

へ **(he)** turn into a *he*licopter

ほ **(ho)** make it look like a thermometer – *ho*t

Other ideas to help you remember

- Add the new hiragana to your flashcards. Mix them in with the first 15 symbols and keep testing yourself. Then try this game: spread all the cards out, hiragana side up. Collect 'families' as follows (say the sounds out loud):
  1 all symbols ending in 'a'
  2 all symbols ending in 'i'
  3 continue this for 'u', 'e' and 'o'
  4 you can then spread the cards out again and try families beginning with 'k', 's', 't', 'n', and 'h'
- Add the next 15 hiragana symbols to your chart. It should now look like the grid opposite.

Similar looking hiragana

The following hiragana symbols look quite similar and you may find this confusing at times. Here are some clues to help you tell them apart:

ぬ, ね   ぬ **(nu)** has two 'vertical' lines at the top and two loops whereas ね **(ne)** has only one of each

あ	い	う	え	お
か	き	く	け	こ
さ	し	す	せ	そ
た	ち	つ	て	と
な	に	ぬ	ね	の
は	ひ	ふ	へ	ほ

さ, ち	さ (**sa**) leans to the left; ち (**chi**) looks like the number 5 (the top has slipped!)
け, は, ほ	け (**ke**) has no loop at the bottom; は (**ha**) has one horizontal line; ほ (**ho**) has two horizontal lines

Note that you may come across this alternative way of writing **fu** especially when it is hand written: ふ.

Reading activity 3.1

◀ **CD1, TR 39**

First of all, you are going to try reading some hiragana words containing the new hiragana symbols only. These are also on the recording so you can either listen and repeat as you look at the words or try reading them yourself first and then checking your answers with the recording:

1	たて *vertical*	**9**	へた *poor at*
2	なに *what*	**10**	ぬの *cloth*
3	ふね *ship*	**11**	ほね *bones*
4	ちち *father*	**12**	て *hand*
5	ひとつ *one item*	**13**	なつ *summer*
6	ふたつ *two items*	**14**	はな *nose*
7	ななつ *seven items*	**15**	ひと *person*
8	はは *mother*		

Reading activity 3.2

◀ **CD1, TR 40**

Now see if you can read the following hiragana words which contain combinations of all the hiragana symbols you have learned so far. You can also listen to the words on the recording:

1	とけい *clock*	**11**	おはし *chopsticks*
2	へそ *navel*	**12**	おさけ *rice wine*
3	かた *shoulders*	**13**	ほうほう *cheeks*
4	さいふ *purse*	**14**	せなか *back*
5	あに *older brother*	**15**	たいてい *generally*
6	あね *older sister*	**16**	ふつう *usual*
7	おとうと *younger brother*	**17**	いつつ *five items*
8	うち *house*	**18**	ここのつ *nine items*
9	かない *wife*	**19**	とう *10 items*
10	あした *tomorrow*	**20**	いくつ *how many items?*

Reading activity 3.3: The odd one out

Each of the following rows of hiragana symbols has an odd one out. Can you find it and replace it with the correct symbol? Read each symbol out loud to reinforce your learning:

Correct symbol

1	あ	か	し	た	な	は
2	け	ひ	ふ	へ	ほ	
3	ほ	の	と	そ	こ	あ
4	か	さ	く	け	こ	
5	う	く	す	つ	ね	ふ
6	ひ	に	ち	し	き	こ
7	た	さ	つ	て	と	

Reading challenge

Here, in random order, are the 30 hiragana symbols that you have learned so far. Can you read them all? Speak out loud:

た	ぬ	か	ひ	し	つ
う	ほ	く	な	さ	ち
き	へ	そ	て	あ	ふ
お	と	け	え	に	す
は	い	の	こ	ね	せ

End-of-unit challenge

How well have you remembered everything you have learned in this unit? Use this challenge to assess your progress. Read the 10 Japanese sentences and match them with their English meanings. If you score 8 or more, give yourself a pat on the back! If you score less, have a read through the explanations again and try the challenge again before you progress on to Unit 4:

Japanese sentences
1 Kaban o mittsu kudasai.
2 Nikai ni nani ga arimasu ka.

3 Ikkai ni sensu ya yukata nado ga arimasu.
4 O-sake o utteimasu ka.
5 Kono o-sake wa ikura desu ka.
6 Sumimasen, hagaki ga arimasu ka.
7 Ano ningyō o misete kudasai.
8 Uchi ni dare ka imasu ka.
9 Haha mo chichi mo kono kaisha de hatarakimasu.
10 Nikai ni nani mo arimasen.

English meanings
a *May I see that doll over there?*
b *Is there anyone at home?*
c *There is nothing on the second floor.*
d *There are fans, cotton kimono etc. on the first floor.*
e *Both my Mum and Dad work in this company.*
f *May I have three bags?*
g *Do you sell rice wine?*
h *What is there on the second floor?*
i *Excuse me, do you have any postcards?*
j *How much is this rice wine?*

There is a second challenge in this unit – to keep on counting! This time set yourself the following tasks to do as you drive/clean/try to fall asleep! Or whenever you have some 'empty' time.

1 Count in blocks of 100s from 100 to 900
2 Count in blocks of 1000s from 1000 to 10,000
3 Try both of these backwards

Insight

Set yourself the task of reading bigger numbers in Japanese – any numbers will do such as your pin number, numbers and prices on receipts, the year you or family members were born in – the aim is to get your brain tackling and revisiting Japanese numbers.

4

....

Eigakan wa doko ni arimasu ka
Where is the cinema?

In this unit you will learn
- *how to give the location of places, items and people*
- *how to give and follow directions*
- *how to arrange to meet someone*
- *how to speak in the past* (I did, I didn't)
- *how to talk about what you want to do*
- *days of the week and more on telling the time*

Getting started

The main focus of this unit will be to talk about the precise location of people, places and things.

Opening activity

◀) **CD1, TR 41**

You learned in Unit 3 how to say *there is* and *there are* using **arimasu** and **imasu**. Now you are going to use **arimasu** with the question word **doko** to ask 'Where is _____ located ?':

Eigakan wa doko ni arimasu ka   *Where is the cinema* (located)?

Use these 10 place words then the phrase '. . . wa doko ni arimasu
ka' to ask where places are. Check your answers at the back and
by listening to the recording. The recording will also help you with
learning the pronunciation of the new words so listen carefully,
pause and repeat out loud:

resutoran	*restaurant*
eigakan	*cinema*
kaisha	*company*
gakkō	*school*
yūbinkyoku	*post office*
ginkō	*bank*
depāto	*department store*
bijutsukan	*art gallery*
hakubutsukan	*museum*
gekijō	*theatre*

QUICK VOCAB

Build-up activity

The words for *here*, *there* and *over there* are: **koko, soko, asoko.**
And, as you now know, the word for *where* is **doko.** Use these
words and the word for *near here*: **kono chikaku** to explain where
places are:

Example: The cinema is *over there*   Eigakan wa *asoko* ni
                                                  arimasu

1 The restaurant is there.
2 The company is here.
3 The school is near here.

4 The post office is over there.
5 The art gallery is there.

Opening dialogue

Katie Mears, an American English teacher in Tokyo, has become friendly with Rie Franks and has arranged to meet her after work at the hotel where Rie works. First, listen to (read) and *repeat out loud* the 10 new words to improve your pronunciation and confidence. Then listen to the opening dialogue as Katie asks for directions to the hotel and see if you can pick out the 10 new words and also the words and phrases you learned in the opening activity.

Insight

Don't underestimate the power of repeating out loud. Saying words in your head just does not have the same effect. Saying words out loud helps you to focus on pronouncing them correctly and helps you to remember them better too. It also helps to build your confidence. Try saying the words in high, low, quiet and loud voices to make the activity more interesting.

◄))) **CD1, TR 42**

Nyū Tōkyō hoteru	*New Tokyo Hotel* (hoteru = hotel)
gozonji desu ka	*do you know?* (respectful)
shitteimasu	*I know*
ne	*isn't there, isn't it, right?* (used when you expect agreement from other person)
ushiro	*behind*
___ no ushiro	*behind the ___*
shingō	*traffic lights*
migi ni magatte	*turn right* (migi = right)
massugu itte (kudasai)	*(please) go straight ahead* (massugu = straight ahead)
wakarimashita	*I've understood, I've got it*

QUICK VOCAB

Now over to Katie:

Katie	Ano, sumimasen.
Passer-by	Hai?
Katie	Nyū Tōkyō hoteru wa doko ni arimasu ka. Gozonji desu ka.
Passer-by	Nyū Tōkyō hoteru . . . Hai, shitteimasu. Asoko ni Tōkyō bijutsukan ga arimasu ne.
Katie	Hai.
Passer-by	Nyū Tōkyō hoteru wa bijutsukan no ushiro ni arimasu. Ano shingō o migi ni magatte, massugu itte kudasai.
Katie	Hai, wakarimashita. Arigatō gozaimasu.
Katie	*Hey, excuse me.*
Passer-by	*Yes?*
Katie	*Where is the New Tokyo Hotel? Do you know?*
Passer-by	*The New Tokyo Hotel . . . yes, I know. Over there is the Tokyo Art Gallery, right?*
Katie	*Yes.*
Passer-by	*The New Tokyo Hotel is behind the art gallery. Turn right at those traffic lights and go straight ahead.*
Katie	*Right, I've got it. Thank you.*

Key sentences

There are lots of new words and phrases needed for Unit 4's key sentences so listen to the vocabulary first and when you are familiar with it, read through the key sentences and as in previous units see how much meaning you can work out before you read the translations.

Insight

Translation tips:

- Remember that Japanese sentences are often 'backwards' to English ones, so once you have found the subject marked by **wa** (if there is one) start from the end of the sentence and work back
- Divide sentence 3 into two sections, the first section ends with to – translate this first
- Remember also that a preposition (in front of, next to ...) is said after the place it is attached to (**hoteru no tonari** means next to the hotel) There is more on this in Explanation 4.1

1 Massugu itte kudasai.
2 Shingō o migi ni magatte kudasai.
3 Kōsaten o hidari ni magaru to ginkō wa migigawa ni arimasu.
4 Bijutsukan wa hoteru no **tonari** ni arimasu.
5 Kono chikaku ni yūbinkyoku ga arimasu ka.
6 Depāto no **mae** ni **basu-tei** ga arimasu.
7 Bīru o nomimasen ka.
8 Bīru o nomitai desu.
9 Yūbe bīru o zenzen nomimasen deshita.
10 Senshū Katie-san to eiga o mimashita.

◀》 **CD1, TR 44**

kōsaten	*crossroads*
hidari (gawa)	*left (side)*
magaru to	*if you turn*
migi (gawa)	*right (side)*
tonari	*next to*
mae	*in front of*
basu-tei	*bus stop*
nomimasen ka	*won't you/would you like to drink?*
nomitai desu	*I want to drink*
yūbe	*last night*
zenzen	*not at all (+ negative)*
nomimasen deshita	*I didn't drink*

QUICK VOCAB

senshū		*last week*
eiga		*movie, film*
mimashita		(I) *watched*

English translation of the key sentences

1 *Go straight ahead please.*
2 *Turn right at the traffic lights please.*
3 *If you turn left at the crossroads, the bank is on the right side.*
4 *The art gallery is next to the hotel.*
5 *Is there a post office near here?*
6 *Near the department store, there is a bus stop.*
7 *Would you like to drink a beer?*
8 *I want to drink a beer.*
9 *Last night I didn't drink any beer at all.*
10 *Last week I watched a movie with Katie.*

Language explanations

Here is a list of the grammar and language points you will learn in Unit 4:

1 giving the location of places, items and people
2 answering the questions **doko, nani** and **dare** (*where, what, who*)
3 giving and following directions
4 differences between **arimasu** and **desu**
5 arranging to meet someone, making, accepting and refusing suggestions
6 past tense and past negative of verbs (**mashita, masen deshita**)
7 saying I want to (verb stem + **tai**)
8 more time expressions – days of week
9 hobbies and leisure activities
10 telling the time (2)

Explanation 4.1

In this unit so far, you have seen several ways of explaining more precisely where something (or someone) is. Here are those sentences altogether:

Nyū Tōkyō Hoteru wa bijutsukan no ushiro ni arimasu	*The New Tokyo Hotel is behind the art gallery*
Bijutsukan wa hoteru no tonari ni arimasu	*The art gallery is next to the hotel*
Depāto no mae ni basu-tei ga arimasu	*In front of the department store there is a bus stop*

By using words such as *behind*, *in front of* and *next to* you can give more precise locations. However, the order in Japanese is different from English and you need to get used to this. Here is how it works:

behind the hotel = hoteru no ushiro

Insight

In English, you say first the location word (*in front, behind* etc.) then the point/place, whereas in Japanese you do the reverse: point/place of location *then* location word.

Now it's your turn. Say these location points out loud using **ushiro** (behind) and **mae** (in front of):

1 in front of the hotel
2 behind the department store
3 in front of the bank
4 behind the art gallery
5 behind the restaurant

◀ **CD1, TR 45**

Now let's expand your collection of location words (known as *prepositions*). Here's a useful list of 10 words. Listen to the recording and practise saying them:

ushiro	*behind*
mae	*in front (of)*
tonari	*next to, next door*
soba	*alongside, by*
yoko	*beside, side*

ue	*above, on top*
shita	*below, under*
chikaku	*near to*
naka	*inside, in*
mukaigawa	*opposite*

Using these preposition words and the list of place words from the opening activity try saying the following points of location:

6 next door to the restaurant
7 to the side of the bank
8 by the school
9 above the museum
10 below the department store
11 in the theatre
12 opposite the post office

You will probably find that you need to revisit this section to remind yourself of both the new words and the order in which you give a point of location but let's look now at how you say a complete sentence:

Ginkō wa resutoran no tonari ni arimasu	*The bank is next door to the restaurant*

The place (or item or person) whose location you are describing is followed by particle **wa**, then you give the point of location followed by particle **ni** and **arimasu** (**imasu** for people and animals). Look at these sentences:

Basu-tei wa ginkō no yoko ni arimasu	*The bus stop is to the side of the bank*
Watashi no uchi wa gakkō no soba ni arimasu	*My house is by the school*
Rie-san wa gekijō no naka ni imasu	*Rie is inside the theatre*

Can you work out what these sentences mean in English?

13 Hoteru wa yūbinkyoku no mukaigawa ni arimasu.
14 Resutoran wa hakubutsukan no ue ni arimasu.
15 Watashi no kamera wa sono kaban no naka ni arimasu.
16 Katie-san wa watashi no soba ni imasu.

Insight

Did you wonder about when you use **naka** (*inside*)? You could say either of the following to describe where someone (or something) is:

Rie-san wa gekijō <u>no naka ni</u> imasu   *Rie is in the theatre*
Rie-san wa gekijō <u>ni</u> imasu   *Rie is <u>at</u> the theatre*

Using **naka** makes the location more specific: she is *inside*. It is not always necessary to make this clear and then you don't need to use **naka**:

Rie-san wa uchi ni imasu   *Rie is at home/in the house*

Now let's pull together everything you have learned in Explanation 4.1. Can you say these sentences out loud in Japanese?

17 The post office is opposite the bank.
18 The bank is next to the supermarket.
19 The supermarket is behind the school.
20 The school is near the museum.
21 The teacher is in the school.
22 My business card is inside my bag.

One final point: you can often replace **ni arimasu/ni imasu** with **desu**, which gives the meaning 'is' rather than 'is located'. So, for example, to say *The post office is opposite the bank* you can say either of these:

Yūbinkyoku wa ginkō no mukaigawa ni arimasu
Yūbinkyoku wa ginkō no mukaigawa desu

The first one literally says *The post office is located opposite the bank* but the meaning of both sentences is very similar. However, the purpose of this unit is to build your skills in using **arimasu** and **imasu** and so we will focus on using these in location sentences.

Explanation 4.2

Now you are going to focus on three question words: **doko, nani, dare** (*where, what, who*). As you know from the opening activity, if you want to ask where a place, item or person is located you say **doko ni arimasu ka/doko ni imasu ka**:

Yūbinkyoku wa doko ni arimasu ka	*Where is the post office (located)?*
Rie-san wa doko ni imasu ka	*Where is Rie?*

You can ask the same question using **desu**:

Yūbinkyoku wa doko desu ka
Rie-san wa doko desu ka

And when you answer you might say:

Yūbinkyoku wa ginkō no tonari ni arimasu	*The post office is next door to the bank*

Or you don't have to repeat the word post office; you could just reply:

Ginkō no tonari ni arimasu	*(It's) next door to the bank*

When you use **nani** and **dare** (*what, who*) you are asking a different type of question. You have already used these question words in Explanation 3.7. Now look at these examples:

Ni-kai ni nani ga arimasu ka	*What is (there) on the second floor?*
Ginkō no tonari ni nani ga arimasu ka	*What is (there) next to the bank?*

| Ginkō no mae ni dare ga imasu ka | *Who is in front of the bank?* |

So you are not asking *where* a particular place, person or item is, instead you are asking *what there is* at a particular place or location. You have already learned how to construct this type of sentence in Explanations 3.5, 3.6, 3.7. When you add a preposition word such as *in front of*, *behind* and so on, you follow this with particle **ni** (*in, on, at* when using **arimasu** and **imasu**) and then the question **nani ga arimasu ka** or **dare ga imasu ka** (*what is there, who is there* – Explanation 3.7). Now you try by saying these sentences out loud in Japanese:

1 Who is on the second floor?
2 What is there behind the bank?
3 What is there by the school?
4 What is opposite the post office?
5 Where is the supermarket?

As you know from Explanation 3.7, to reply you replace the question word (**nani, dare**) with the information required. So, in reply to **1** above, you can say:

| Ni-kai ni Rie-san ga imasu | *Rie is on the second floor* |

Or simply:

| Rie-san ga imasu | *Rie is there/It is Rie/Rie is* |

Explanation 4.3

Here is a step-by-step guide for giving and following directions. First of all, listen to the recording and read through the key words.

◄» **CD1, TR 46**

shingō	*traffic lights*
kōsaten	*crossroads*
hashi	*bridge*

hodōkyō	*footbridge*
ōdan hodō	*pedestrian crossing*
kado	*corner*
dōro	*street, road*
michi	*road, way*
hitotsu me	*first*
futatsu me	*second*
tsugi	*next*

To give directions you use a special form of verb, which, in this book, is called the te form. You will learn about this in detail in Unit 9 – you will use it in this unit for the purpose of giving directions.

◀ CD1, TR 46, 00:57

Now listen to the recording as you read and say out loud the new phrases and the build-up practice that follows:

massugu	*straight ahead*
massugu itte	*go straight ahead*
massugu itte kudasai	*go straight ahead, please*
magatte kudasai	*please turn*
migi ni magatte kudasai	*please turn (to the) right*
hidari ni magatte kudasai	*please turn (to the) left*

kōsaten o migi ni
  magatte kudasai
	*please turn right at the
	  crossroads*

shingō o migi ni
  magatte kudasai
	*please turn right at the
	  traffic lights*

watatte kudasai	*please cross*
hashi o watatte kudasai	*please cross the bridge*
hodōkyō o wattate kudasai	*please cross the footbridge*
michi o watatte kudasai	*please cross the road*

hitotsu-me no shingō o
  hidari ni magatte kudasai
	*please turn left at the first
	  traffic lights*

tsugi no shingō o hidari
  ni magatte kudasai
	*please turn left at the next
	  traffic lights*

Insight

Points to notice:

- The sentence order and use of particle **o** remains the same – *object* **o** *verb*
- The commands end in **kudasai** (*please*) unlike English commands when we just say 'go', 'turn', 'cross'. So in the English examples that follow 'please' isn't always used where **kudasai** would normally be used in Japanese
- You use particle **ni** after the direction words **migi, hidari** – 'turn *to* the left/right'
- You use particle **no** after saying 'first', 'second', 'next'

If you want to give more than one direction in a sentence you save **kudasai** until the end:

Massugu itte, shingō o migi ni magatte kudasai	*Go straight ahead then turn right at the traffic lights*

Now you try. Say these sentences out loud in Japanese:

1 Go straight ahead.
2 Turn left at the crossroads.
3 Cross at the pedestrian crossing.
4 Turn right at the first traffic lights.
5 Cross the footbridge then turn left at the corner.

Explanation 4.4

You learned in Explanation 4.1 that sometimes **desu** and **arimasu/ imasu** are very close in meaning when you are giving the exact location of something:

Yūbinkyoku wa ginkō no mukaigawa ni arimasu	*The post office is (located) opposite the bank*
Yūbinkyoku wa ginkō no mukaigawa desu	*The post office is opposite the bank*

However, when you want to say 'there is' or 'there are' you must use **arimasu/imasu**:

Uchi ni shinbun ga arimasu   *There is a newspaper*
                                                        in the house

In this case, using **desu** would make no sense:

Uchi ni shinbun desu   *In the house, it is newspaper*

Explanation 4.5

You already know (Explanation 2.8) how to make a suggestion using the verb ending **mashō ka** (the particles are underlined here to remind you of their meanings and purpose):

Resutoran <u>de</u> tabemashō ka   *Shall we eat <u>at</u> a restaurant?*
Issho ni eigakan <u>ni</u>   *Shall we go <u>to</u> the cinema*
  ikimashō ka   *together?*

And if you say **mashō** without **ka**, you are saying 'let's':

Resutoran de tabemashō!   *Let's eat at a restaurant!*
Eigakan ni ikimashō!   *Let's go to the cinema!*

If you want to ask 'where shall we go?' or 'where shall we meet?' (meet = **aimasu**), you use **doko** (*where*) and say:

Doko <u>ni</u> ikimashō ka   *Where shall we go (<u>to</u>)?*
Doko <u>de</u> aimashō ka   *Where shall we meet (<u>at</u>)?*

Similarly, if you want to ask *what time* you use **nanji ni**:

Nan ji <u>ni</u> ikimashō ka   *(<u>At</u>) what time shall we go?*
Nan ji <u>ni</u> aimashō ka   *(<u>At</u>) what time shall we meet?*

And if you want to simply say 'what shall we do?' you use **nani** and say:

Nani o shimashō ka

You can also use the negative of the verb + **ka** – *masen ka* – to ask more tentatively 'would you like to?' ('won't you?'):

Resutoran <u>de</u> tabemasen ka	*Would you like to eat <u>at</u> a restaurant?*
Eigakan <u>ni</u> ikimasen ka	*Would you like to go <u>to</u> the cinema?*

If you want to suggest a particular time, venue or activity you can use the phrase **dō desu ka** (how about … ?) with the particle **wa** to express this:

Ashita wa dō desu ka	*How about tomorrow?*
Eigakan wa dō desu ka	*How about the cinema?*
Gorufu wa dō desu ka	*How about golf?*

To accept, say: **Ii desu ne** (*That'll be great*).

To refuse politely, say: **Zannen desu ga, gorufu (ashita/eigakan) wa chotto …** (*It's a shame but golf (tomorrow/the cinema) is a bit …).

Insight
This way of refusing gives an insight into the Japanese psyche because you don't openly turn someone down – you imply that you don't want to or can't make it by trailing off at the end of the sentence.

◀) **CD1, TR 47**

Let's put this all together. Listen to the conversation between Rie and her friend Miki Sugihara, a Japanese teacher, and see if you can work out the meaning and answer these questions: Where do they decide to go and what time do they decide to meet? The translation is at the back of the book:

Miki	Ashita doko ka issho ni ikimasen ka.
Rie	Hai, doko ni ikimashō ka.
Miki	Eigakan wa dō desu ka.
Rie	Ē, eigakan ni ikimashō!
Miki	Nan ji ni aimashō ka.
Rie	Shichiji wa dō desu ka.
Miki	Ii desu ne. Mata ashita!

Explanation 4.6

The past tense (*did, didn't*) is very simple in Japanese, you simply change **masu** to **mashita** to say *did* and to **masen deshita** to say *didn't*. That's it! Have a look at the following table.

ate	**tabemashita**	*didn't eat*	**tabemasen deshita**
drank	**nomimashita**	*didn't drink*	**nomimasen deshita**
listened	**kikimashita**	*didn't listen*	**kikimasen deshita**
saw	**mimashita**	*didn't see*	**mimasen deshita**
met	**aimashita**	*didn't meet*	**aimasen deshita**

Now see if you can say these sentences in Japanese:

1 I ate breakfast.
2 I didn't drink any coffee.
3 I listened to the news.
4 He didn't watch TV.
5 We met at 7 o'clock at the restaurant.

Explanation 4.7 Saying *I want to*

Now you are going to learn how to manipulate verbs to say *I want to*. To do this, you use the stem of the verb. This is simple – it is the verb without **masu**. Here are a few stems.

stem	English	stem	English
nomi	*drink*	iki	*go*
tabe	*eat*	mi	*see*
kiki	*listen*		

To say *I want to*, you add **tai desu** to the stem. Here are some examples:

Bīru o nomitai desu	*I want to drink beer*
Sushi o tabetai desu	*I want to eat sushi*
Nihon ni ikitai desu	*I want to go to Japan*

Sometimes the particle **ga** is used in place of the particle **o** but both are correct. Now you try saying these 'want to' sentences out loud:

1 I want to go to France next week.
2 I want to listen to the news at home.
3 I want to eat rice <u>with</u> (**de**) chopsticks.
4 I want to buy a Japanese camera.
5 I want to drink sake with my neighbour.

Explanation 4.8 More time expressions: Days of the week

You are now going to learn how to say the days of the week. All the days of the week end in **yōbi** (*day*). Each day is named after elements of the natural world. Read through the following table. You will have the opportunity to learn to read the kanji in Unit 7 and so they are included here for cross-reference later.

English	Japanese	meaning	kanji
Sunday	**nichiyōbi**	*sun* (day)	日
Monday	**getsuyōbi**	*moon*	月
Tuesday	**kayōbi**	*fire*	火
Wednesday	**suiyōbi**	*water*	水

Thursday	**mokuyōbi**	*tree*	木
Friday	**kinyōbi**	*gold*	金
Saturday	**doyōbi**	*earth*	土

Explanation 4.9 Hobbies and leisure activities

Belonging to clubs and having a variety of interests and hobbies is an important element of Japanese society and you may well be asked: **Shumi wa nan desu ka** (*What is your hobby?*). To answer this question you say simply: **Shumi wa _____ desu** (*My hobby is ___*). Here are some popular Japanese sports and hobbies.

origami   ikebana   budō

shumi	*hobby*
origami	*paper folding*
ikebana	*flower arranging*
sadō	*tea ceremony*
shodō	*calligraphy*
koto	*Japanese harp*

QUICK VOCAB

budō	*martial arts*
yakyū	*baseball*
sakkā	*soccer, football*
niwa shigoto	*gardening*

Insight

The word **budō** covers all the many types of martial art practised in Japan, some of the more well-known being **jūdō**, **kendō** (fencing with bamboo swords), **kyūdō** (archery) and karate. The word **dō** by itself means *path* or *way* and it is a Buddhist term attached to arts that help you to achieve a meditative and harmonious state of mind. Other examples are **sadō** (*way of tea* or *tea ceremony*) and **aikidō** (a martial art with spiritual emphasis).

Explanation 4.10

You have already learned (Unit 2) to say the time on the hour. Here's a quick recap:

ichiji = 1 o'clock
jūichiji = 11 o'clock

You also learned that three numbers change when telling the time. They are:

yoji = 4 o'clock
shichiji = 7 o'clock
kuji = 9 o'clock

To say 5 past, 10 past and so on requires some practice but it is logical. First, you need to know these words:

gofun = 5 minutes
juppun = 10 minutes

In Japanese, you give the hour first (as you have learned) and then the minutes. Here's how it works:

1.05 = ichiji gofun (1 o'clock and 5 minutes)
1.10 = ichiji juppun (1 o'clock and 10 minutes)

To say 15 minutes you say 15 (**jūgo**) and add **fun** to the end. To say 20 minutes you say 20 (**nijū**) and add **pun** to the end (the sound 'squashes' to **juppun**).

> **Insight**
>
> When telling the time all multiples of 5 end in **fun**, all multiples of 10 end in **pun**.

Now can you work out these times? Speak out loud and check the answers in the back before continuing:

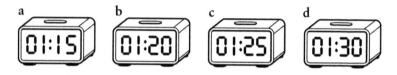

As well as saying 30 minutes past (**sanjuppun**) you can also say half past using **han**:

ichiji **han** = ichiji **sanjuppun** = 1.30 (half past one)

To say times to the hour you keep everything in the same order but add the additional word **mae**. You learned that this means *in front of* or *before* so in the context of time it adds the meaning *before the hour* or simply *to*:

1.35 = 25 to 2 = niji nijū gofun *mae*

You can also say 1.35 as in *one thirty-five*: **ichiji sanjū gofun**. In which case, of course, you don't need **mae**.

◀) **CD1, TR 48**

Here is a table summarizing how to tell the time in 5-minute segments. Listen to the recording, pause and repeat out loud to really make these your own.

English time	Japanese time	alternative
1.05 (5 past 1)	ichiji gofun	
1.10 (10 past 1)	ichiji juppun	
1.15 (quarter past 1)	ichiji jū gofun	
1.20 (20 past 1)	ichiji nijuppun	
1.25 (25 past 1)	ichiji nijū gofun	
1.30 (half past 1)	ichiji sanjuppun	ichiji han
1.35 (25 to 2)	ichiji sanjū gofun	niji nijū gofun mae
1.40 (20 to 2)	ichiji yonjuppun	niji nijuppun mae
1.45 (quarter to 2)	ichiji yonjū gofun	niji jū gofun mae
1.50 (10 to 2)	ichiji gojuppun	niji juppun mae
1.55 (5 to 2)	ichiji gojū gofun	niji gofun mae

Finally, if you want to distinguish between morning and afternoon (am and pm) you can use **asa** and **gogo** (*morning, afternoon*) or the more formal equivalent of *am* which is **gozen**. Say the *am/pm* word *before* the time:

1.30 am = gozen (asa) ichiji han
1.30 pm = gogo ichiji han

Main dialogue

◆) **CD1, TR 49**

The main purpose of this dialogue is to develop your listening skills. If you have the recording and have read the questions then, without looking at the printed dialogue, listen through several times and see if you can answer the questions. If you don't have the recording then read through the dialogue and try to answer the questions. (Ignore the underlining for now.)

Rie Franks has been doing a bit of matchmaking between two of her friends – Miki Sugihara, who teaches Japanese in a Tokyo language school, and Roger Wilson, an Australian who is spending a year in Tokyo as part of his Japanese degree. Listen as Miki and Roger arrange by phone to have an evening out.

Miki	**Konshū** doko ka ni ikimasen ka.
Roger	Ii desu ne. Doko ni ikimashō ka.
Miki	Sō desu ne. <u>**Kissaten** de kōhī to kēki o</u> <u>tabemashō</u> ka.
Roger	<u>Kissaten</u> desu ka. <u>Kissaten</u> wa chotto … **Bōringu** wa dō desu ka.
Miki	<u>Bōringu</u> desu ka. Watashi wa **bōringu ga heta** desu ga <u>bōringu</u> o shimashō!
Roger	Jā, ashita wa dō desu ka.
Miki	Ashita wa <u>suiyōbi</u> desu ne. <u>Suiyōbi</u> wa chotto … <u>Mokuyōbi</u> wa dō desu ka.
Roger	<u>Mokuyōbi</u> wa **ii desu**. Nanji ni aimashō ka.
Miki	<u>Shichiji han</u> wa dō desu ka.
Roger	Hai, <u>shichiji han</u> ni **'Gurīn rando' bōringu jō** no mae de aimashō.
Miki	Ano, sumimasen. <u>'Gurīn rando' bōringu jō</u> wa doko ni arimasu ka.
Roger	<u>Nyū Tōkyō gekijō</u> o gozonji desu ka.
Miki	Hai, shitteimasu.
Roger	<u>Gekijō</u> no mae ni <u>shingō</u> ga arimasu. Sono <u>shingō</u> o <u>migi</u> ni magatte, massugu itte kudasai. <u>Hidarigawa</u> ni <u>eigakan</u> ga arimasu. <u>Eigakan</u> no <u>ushiro</u> ni 'Gurīn rando' bōringu jō ga arimasu.
Miki	<u>Eigakan</u> no <u>ushiro</u> desu ne. Wakarimashita. **Jā mokuyōbi ni**. Sayōnara.
Roger	Sayōnara.

QUICK VOCAB

konshū	*this week*
kissaten	*coffee shop*
bōringu	*bowling* (ten pin)
(bōringu) ga heta desu	*I'm no good at (bowling)*

ii desu	it's ok, it's fine
'Gurīn rando'	Greenland
bōringu jō	bowling alley
jā mokuyōbi ni	right, till Thursday

Questions

1 What does Miki suggest they do?
2 How does Roger react?
3 When does Roger suggest meeting?
4 On which day and at what time do they agree on meeting up?
5 Summarize the directions given to the bowling alley

Learn to say

This time, rather than memorizing, you are going to revisit the main dialogue but change some of the information given. The information you have to change is underlined in the dialogue. You will play both parts and you will say the dialogue out loud with the new changes. Here is the information you will need to include:

- Miki suggests going to the theatre but Roger isn't keen and suggests playing tennis instead
- Tomorrow is Friday, which isn't good for Miki so she suggests Saturday instead
- They agree to meet at 6.30 in front of Roppongi tennis courts (**roppongi tenisu jō**)
- Directions: The landmark is Tokyo museum. In front of this is a bus stop. Turn left here and go straight on. On the right is Mitsukoshi department store. Opposite here are the tennis courts

Activities

Activity 4.1

Look at the map of a town centre. There is a person X standing at the end of the main street. Give him directions and the precise locations of the five places numbered 1–5 on the map. Start by saying the question he would ask you. Speak out loud and check your answers with those at the back – but note that these are only sample answers; yours may be different but equally correct. The first one is done for you.

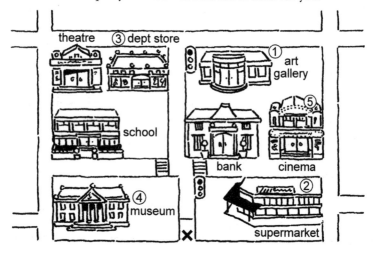

1 Sumimasen, bijutsukan wa doko ni arimasu ka.

Massugu itte, ōdan hodō o watatte kudasai. Bijutsukan wa ginkō no ushiro ni arimasu.

Activity 4.2

◀) **CD1, TR 50**

This is a gap-filling activity. Select the correct words from the box and complete the sentences 1–10 by putting the number of each word in the brackets, then jot down their English meanings. Listen to the recording to check if you have selected the correct words.

1 Resutoran wa ( ) ni ( ).
2 Ano shingō ( ) migi ni ( ), massugu itte kudasai.
3 Watashi no ( ) wa gakkō ( ) soba ni arimasu.
4 Watashi no ( ) wa kaban no ( ) ni arimasu.
5 Yūbinkyoku no ( ) ni ( ) ga arimasu ka.
6 Hodōkyō o ( ), kado o ( ) ni magatte kudasai.
7 Eigakan ni ( ) ka.
8 Shichiji ( ) resutoran ( ) aimashita.
9 Kōhī o ( ).
10 Kinjo no hito ( ) o-sake o ( ) desu.

1 mukaigawa	**2** o	**3** arimasu
4 ni	**5** hidari	**6** de
7 nomimasen deshita	**8** to	**9** magatte
10 nomitai	**11** soko	**12** ikimasen
13 meishi	**14** watatte	**15** uchi
16 no	**17** nani	**18** naka

Activity 4.3

You now know the four **masu** tenses – present, present negative, past, past negative (**masu, masen, mashita, masen deshita**). You have also learned to say 'I want to' (stem + **tai** desu). Complete these sentences with the correct tense/ending:

1 Yūbe terebi o mi _____. (yesterday I watched TV)
2 Raishū bōringu ni iki _____. (next week I want to go bowling)
3 Asa itsumo rokuji ni oki _____. (I always get up at 6 in the mornings)
4 O-sake o zenzen nomi _____. (I never drink sake)
5 Senshū terebi o zenzen mi _____. (I didn't watch TV at all last week)
6 Raishū Amerika ni iki _____. (I am not going to America next week)

7 Rie-san to ai _____. (I want to meet up with Rie)

8 Rainen kuruma o kai _____. (next year I want to buy a car)

Activity 4.4

◀ **CD1, TR 51**

This listening activity is designed to improve your understanding of the time. Listen to the recording as you look at the clocks and decide which clock matches with the times you hear. When you have finished this activity (also if you don't have the recording), try saying the times out loud.

Activity 4.5

How well have you remembered the days of the week (Explanation 4.8)? Test yourself by matching the English meanings to the Japanese words and meanings. Write the correct number and letter in the brackets next to the English meanings:

1 Sunday ( ), ( ).

2 Monday ( ), ( ).

3 Tuesday ( ), ( ).

4 Wednesday ( ), ( ).

5 Thursday ( ), ( ).

6 Friday ( ), ( ).
7 Saturday ( ), ( ).

---

1 kayōbi **2** mokuyōbi **3** nichiyōbi **4** doyōbi
5 suiyōbi **6** getsuyōbi **7** kinyōbi
a sun **b** tree **c** earth **d** water **e** fire **f** gold **g** moon

---

How to read hiragana (3)

In this section you will learn:

- the final 16 hiragana symbols
- more ideas to help you remember the symbols
- how to read some more words

Start reading

Look back to the pronunciation guide in the introduction to this book, focus on the final 16 sounds (**ma–n**), listen to the recording if you have it and say each sound out loud.

Here are those 16 hiragana symbols with their pronunciation underneath. Look at them and say each sound out loud. Use the recording again to reinforce the sounds:

ま	み	む	め	も
ma	mi	mu	me	mo
や		ゆ		よ
ya		yu		yo
ら	り	る	れ	ろ
ra	ri	ru	re	ro
わ				を
wa				(w)o
ん (n)				

How to remember hiragana symbols

Here are some more ideas for mnemonics to help you remember the new symbols:

ま (**ma**) *ma*mmon the god of wealth

む (**mu**) a '*moo*' cow

や (**ya**) shouts the cowboy as he throws his lasso

よ (**yo**) practising *yo*ga

ら (**ra**) is half a *ra*bbit

を (**o**) *Australian sat by a lake

Here are some other ideas that might work for you:

み (**mi**) looks like number 4 '*me* when I was 4'

め (**me**) a *me*ssy knot – ends showing

も (**mo**) she has a *mo*dern hairstyle (looks like し (**shi**) with two hair clips)

ゆ (**yu**) looks like an un*u*sual fish

り (**ri**) the flow of a *ri*ver

る (**ru**) the loop is a *ru*by whereas ろ (**ro**) has no ruby because there's been a *ro*bbery

れ (**re**) can you see a *re*indeer?

わ (**wa**) a baby's wide-open mouth crying '*wa*aaah'

ん (**n**) like a simplified version of え (**e**), which put together almost spell 'the e*nd*'!

Other ideas to help you remember

Add the new hiragana to your flashcards. Mix them in with the other 30 symbols (you now have a complete set of the 46 basic symbols) and keep testing yourself. Then try this game: spread all the cards out, hiragana side up. Can you pick out the symbols that spell the following words (most of which you have learned in this or previous units). Say the words out loud as you pick them up:

あかい *red*
あおい *blue*
しろい *white*
くろい *black*
おかあさん *mother*
おとうさん *father*
むすこ *son*
むすめ *daughter*
うえ *above*
した *below*

うしろ *behind*
まえ *in front*
となり *next to*
なか *inside*
よこ *beside*
ちかく *near*
ここ *this place*
そこ *that place*
あそこ *that place over there*
どこ *where*

Add the final 16 hiragana symbols to your chart. It should now look like this:

あ	い	う	え	お
か	き	く	け	こ
さ	し	す	せ	そ
た	ち	つ	て	と
な	に	ぬ	ね	の
は	ひ	ふ	へ	ほ
ま	み	む	め	も
や		ゆ		よ
ら	り	る	れ	ろ
わ				を
ん				

The symbol ん (**n**) is traditionally put in its own row but don't worry if you don't have room for this.

Similar looking hiragana

Here are some more hiragana symbols which look similar and some clues to help you tell them apart:

い, り　　　い (i) the left stroke is slightly longer than the right whereas in り (ri) the right stroke is much longer than the left (hand written ri looks like this: **リ** – two separate strokes)

ほ, ま　　　the top horizontal line in ほ (ho) rests on top of the vertical line whereas in ま (ma) both horizontal lines cut through

ぬ, め　　　both ぬ (nu) and め (me) have two 'vertical' lines at the top but ぬ (nu) has a loop (the '*noo*dles') whereas め (me) has none

す, む　　　さ (su) curves to the left; む (mu) curves to the right and has an extra 'dash' (hand-written version: **む**)

る, ろ　　　you've been given the story of 'the ruby and the robbery' for this but also remember that る (ru) has a loop and ろ (ro) looks like number 3

ね, れ, わ　　ね (ne) has a loop, れ (re) curves out at the end, わ (wa) curves in (hand-written versions: **れ** (re), **わ** (wa); other hand-written versions are: **も** (mo も), **や** (ya や), **ら** (ra ら)

Reading activity 4.1

◆ CD1, TR 52

Here are some hiragana words containing the new hiragana symbols only. Try reading them out loud both with and without the help of the recording:

1　むら *village*
2　よる *evening*
3　ゆめ *dream*
4　ゆり *lily*
5　やま *mountain*
6　もも *peach*
7　もり *forest*
8　みみ *ear*
9　もん *gate*
10　われわれ *we*
11　わん *bowl*
12　まる *circle*

Reading activity 4.2

◄》 CD1, TR 53

Now see if you can read the following hiragana words which contain combinations of all the 46 basic hiragana symbols. You can also listen to the words on the recording. Try saying each word out loud first then playing it on the recording. All the words are ones you have learned in the first four units:

1 ほん *book*
2 かいもの *shopping*
3 わたし *I*
4 なまえ *name*
5 おはよう *good morning*
6 すみません *excuse me*
7 おやすみ なさい *good night*
8 のみます *drink*
9 します *do*
10 かきます *write*
11 かいます *buy*
12 ききます *listen*
13 かえります *return*
14 おきます *get up*
15 ねます *go to bed*
16 みます *look*
17 よみます *read*
18 はなします *talk*
19 つくります *make*
20 はたらきます *work*

Reading activity 4.3

◄》 CD1, TR 54

Now you are going to try reading some simple sentences using objects, time expressions, ます and ました (**masu/mashita**) verbs and particle を (**o**). You can either listen to the recording as you read the sentences or, if you are really ready for a challenge, read the sentences first then listen to the recording. When you have read each sentence successfully, work out the English meaning:

1 とけい を かいました。
2 はなし を ききました。
3 はやく おきました。
4 おそく ねました。
5 ほん を よみました。

6 まいにち はたらきます。
7 おそく うち に かえりました。
8 あした はは と かいもの を します。
9 わたし の なまえ を かきました。
10 よる たいてい おさけ を のみます。

Reading challenge

Here, in random order, are all 46 hiragana symbols. Can you read them all? Speak out loud:

1 な ん り ひ あ き る そ も わ に ふ
2 ぬ へ う こ ま ろ し を お ほ と ゆ
3 や た れ ね つ さ み は す い か
4 の て ら く む よ け え め せ ち

End-of-unit challenge

Your challenge this time is to say times in 5-minute segments out loud. Say the following times in Japanese using both methods you have learned (note that, in some cases, they will be the same). Then check your answers against the table in Explanation 4.10. **Gambatte!**

Challenge 1	Challenge 2
7.05	5 past 7
7.10	10 past 7
7.15	quarter past 7
7.20	20 past 7
7.25	25 past 7
7.30	half past 7
7.35	25 to 8
7.40	20 to 8
7.45	quarter to 8
7.50	10 to 8
7.55	5 to 8

5

....

Ano hito wa yūmei desu yo!
That person is famous you know!

In this unit you will learn
- *all about adjectives (describing words)*
- *how to describe people*
- *how to give an opinion and express your hopes*
- *some useful illness phrases*

_____

Getting started

In this unit you are going to focus on adjectives. These are 'describing' words, such as *beautiful*, *small*, *good*, which tell you what a noun (person, place, object, idea) is like.

Opening activity

🔊 **CD1, TR 55**

Here are seven useful adjectives for describing personality. Listen to them on the recording and repeat them out loud.

yūmei	*famous*
utsukushii	*beautiful*
akarui	*bright, cheerful*
yasashii	*kind, gentle*
otonashii	*quiet, shy*
hazukashii	*embarrassed, ashamed*
ii	*good, nice*

Following the sentence structure of the title you are going to make comments about 'that person' as follows:

Ano hito wa yūmei desu   *That person is famous*

Now you try. Say:

1 That person is beautiful.   **4** That person is quiet.
2 That person is cheerful.   **5** That person is embarrassed.
3 That person is kind.   **6** That person is nice.

Build-up activity

Now you are going to try linking two adjectives to say sentences such as 'that person is beautiful and famous'. You can't use the word you have already learned for *and* – **to** – because this is only used between two nouns. Instead, you change the first adjective like this:

utsukushii *beautiful* → utsukushi**kute** *beautiful and*

You take off the final 'i' sound and add the adjective *and* word **kute**. In other words, the adjective itself has an *and* form rather than using a separate *and* as we do in English.

Insight

Pronunciation tip: When you have a **shi** sound before the **kute**, this reduces down to a 'sh' sound – the 'i' becomes unvoiced.

Now you try. Following the example, say the sentences in Japanese:

**Ano hito wa utsukushikute   *That person is beautiful
yūmei desu   and famous***

1 That person is cheerful and kind.
2 That person is quiet and embarrassed.
3 That person is gentle and beautiful.

4 That person is quiet and nice.
5 That person is kind and nice.

___

Opening dialogue

Miki and Roger have had their first date at the bowling alley and are now, separately, telling Rie what they thought of one another. First, listen to (read) and *repeat out loud* the 10 new words to improve your pronunciation and confidence. Then listen to the opening dialogue as Rie speaks first to Roger and then to Miki and see if you can pick out the 10 new words and also the words and phrases you learned in the opening activity.

◀) **CD1, TR 56**

dēto *date*	
dō deshita ka	*How was it?*
sukoshi	*a little*
hazukashigari de	*shy and*
sonna ni	*(not) especially* (+ negative)
hazukashigari ja nai	*not shy*
(da) to omoimasu	*I think that*
mata *again*	
(shi)tai to omoimasu	*I hope to (do)*
totemo jōzu	*very good at*

◀) **CD1, TR 57**

First, here is Rie catching up with Roger.

Rie	Nē, Roger-san, Miki san to **dēto** wa **dō deshita ka.**
Roger	Kanojo wa ii hito desu ne. **Sukoshi hazukashigari de** otonashii hito desu ga utsukushii desu ne.
Rie	**Sonna ni hazukashigari ja nai to omoimasu** yo. **Mata** aitai desu ka.
Roger	Hai, raishū issho ni tenisu o **shitai to omoimasu**

Next, Rie gets Miki's side of the story.

Rie	Roger-san wa ii hito desu ne.
Miki	Sōdesu ne. **Totemo** akarukute yasashii hito da to omoimasu. Kare wa bōringu mo totemo **jōzu** desu. Watashi wa supōtsu ga chotto . . .
Rie	Mata aitai desu ka.
Miki	Hai, raishū eigakan de eiga o **mitai to omoimasu**.
Rie	[*Sounds surprised*] Eiga desu ka.
Rie	*Hey, Roger, how was the date with Miki?*
Roger	*She is a nice person, isn't she? She's a little shy and quiet but she's beautiful, isn't she?*
Rie	*I think she's not especially shy, you know. Do you want to meet again?*
Roger	*Yes, I hope to play tennis together next week.*
Rie	*Roger's a nice person isn't he?*
Miki	*Yes, indeed. I think he's a very cheerful and kind person. He's also very good at bowling. Me and sports are a bit . . .*
Rie	*Do you want to meet again?*
Miki	*Yes, next week I hope to see a movie at the cinema.*
Rie	[*Sounds surprised*] *A movie?*

Did you manage to pick out the new words and phrases? Now listen again and this time see if you can answer these questions:

1 How does Roger describe Miki?
2 What part of this doesn't Rie agree with?
3 What is Roger hoping to do on their second date?
4 How does Miki describe Roger?
5 Why is Rie surprised at the end?

◀) **CD1, TR 58**

majime (na)	*serious, conscientious*
hiroi	*spacious, big* (of places)
nigiyaka (na)	*lively, busy*
tokoro	*place*
heya	*room, bedroom*

QUICK VOCAB

amari	*not very* (+ negative)
kirei	*beautiful; clean*
da	*is* (informal of desu)
atama	*head*
itai	*hurts*
se ga takai	*tall* (lit. back is tall)
me	*eyes*
ōkii	*big* (objects)

Insight

Make sure you lengthen the first sound when you say ōkii (big). Each sound of the word has one 'beat' and your voice smoothly moves from one to the next: o-o-ki-i

---

Key sentences

◀) CD1, TR 59

Remember to listen to and practise saying the vocabulary first and then, when you are familiar with it, listen to and read through the key sentences and see how much meaning you can work out before you read the translations.

Insight

Translation tips:

- Remember that you link two adjectives together by dropping the final i and replacing it with **kute**

- **to omoimasu** at the end of a sentence means *I think that*. So, when you are translating into English, this is your starting point – *I think that . . .* – then find the subject (marked with **wa**) and the verb or a version of **desu** (*is* – **dewa arimasen, ja nai** . . .), and then the rest should fall into place

1 Kanojo wa totemo yasashii desu ga sukoshi **majime** desu.

2 Tokyo wa **hirokute nigiyakana tokoro** desu.

3 Watashi no **heya** wa **amari kirei** dewa arimasen.
4 Miki-san wa sonna ni hazukashigari ja nai to omoimasu.
5 Roger-san wa akarui hito **da** to omoimasu.
6 Rainen mata Nihon ni ikitai to omoimasu.
7 Haha wa **atama** ga **itai** desu.
8 Haha wa **se ga takakute me** ga ōkii desu.

English translation of the key sentences

1 *She is very kind but a bit serious.*
2 *Tokyo is a big and busy place.*
3 *My room is not very clean.*
4 *I think that Miki is not especially shy.*
5 *I think that Roger is a cheerful person.*
6 *Next year I hope to go to Japan again.*
7 *My mother has a headache (her head hurts).*
8 *My mother is tall and has big eyes.*

Language explanations

Here is a list of the grammar and language points you will learn in this unit:

1 introduction to **i** and **na** adjectives
2 different types of sentence using adjectives
3 describing people
4 connecting adjectives using **kute, de, ga**
5 giving an opinion using (**da**) **to omoimasu**
6 saying *I hope to* using **tai** + **to omoimasu**
7 how to form the negative of **i** adjectives (including **tai**)
8 how to form the negative of **na** adjectives
9 some useful illness phrases using adjectives

Explanation 5.1 Japanese adjectives (i and na)

You have met the following adjectives so far in this unit.

utsukushii	*beautiful*
akarui	*bright, cheerful*
yasashii	*kind, gentle*
otonashii	*quiet* (person)
hazukashii*	*embarrassed*
ii	*good, nice*
itai	*hurts*
ōkii	*big* (objects)
hiroi	*spacious, big* (places)
se ga takai	*tall* (lit. back is tall)
hazukashigari* (na)	*shy, seems shy*
nigiyaka (na)	*lively, busy*
kirei (na)	*beautiful; clean*
yūmei (na)	*famous*
majime (na)	*serious, conscientious* (person)
jōzu (na)	*good at, skilful*
heta (na)	*bad at, poor* (in Unit 4)

Insight

Hazukashigari is linked to **hazukashii** and they carry overlapping meanings of *shy, embarrassed* and *ashamed*. However, when you are making observations about someone else's shyness you use **hazukashigari** (*seems shy*).

You may have wondered why the word **na** is written in brackets after some adjectives. This is because there are two types of adjective in Japanese, often referred to as **i** and **na** adjectives. They follow different rules when you change the tense or form – you will learn more about these rules in Explanations 5.4 and 5.7.

Another important difference is that when the noun you are describing follows immediately after a **na** adjective you must put **na** at the end of the adjective. Look at these two sentences:

Ano hito wa *yūmei* desu yo!	*That person is famous you know!*
Are wa *yūmeina* hito desu yo!	*That is a famous person you know!*

The best way to understand this is to try doing it yourself. Six sentences follow with brackets after the **na** adjective. Decide whether **na** is needed or not and work out the English meanings:

1 Miki-san wa kirei ( ) hito desu ne.
2 Roger-san wa bōringu ga jōzu ( ) desu ne.
3 Tōkyō wa nigiyaka ( ) desu ne.
4 Koko wa nigiyaka ( ) tokoro desu ne.
5 Hondo Tatsuya-san wa majime ( ) hito da to omoimasu.
6 Kore wa kirei ( ) heya desu ne.

By contrast, **i** adjectives remain the same in both types of sentence:

Ano hito wa *utsukushii* desu yo	*That person is beautiful you know!*
Are wa *utsukushii* hito desu yo	*That is a beautiful person you know!*

Insight

How do you know whether an adjective is **i** or **na**? It's not always obvious but the following points will help you:

- The majority of adjectives are **i** adjectives
- All **i** adjectives end in **i** (and this is always written in hiragana)
- Some **na** adjectives end in **i** but if this is preceded by an 'e' sound then it must be a **na** adjective (e.g. kir**ei**, yūm**ei**)
- Adjectives that don't end in **i** can't be **i** adjectives! (e.g. majime, jōzu)
- Some dictionaries (e.g. learner dictionaries) list when an adjective is **na**
- If the word is only made up of kanji with no hiragana **i** at the end, it must be a **na** adjective – you can see this in all dictionaries that include kanji

The main objective of this unit is not to overburden you with lists of adjectives but to get you using them and understanding how they work so you can apply this knowledge to new adjectives as you come across them.

Explanation 5.2 Sentence structures

All the sentences you have been reading and saying so far have followed the basic pattern of: noun **wa** adjective (noun) **desu**. Here are two examples:

Miki-san wa kireina hito desu   *Miki is a beautiful person*
Kono heya wa hiroi desu   *This room is spacious*

However, there have also been two examples of sentences with a different structure:

Roger-san wa bōringu ga jōzu desu   *Roger is good at bowling*
Haha wa atama ga itai desu   *My mother's head hurts*

Here the sentence pattern is: noun 1 **wa** noun 2 **ga** adjective **desu**. In both these sentences, we are learning more information about the *overall subject* which is noun 1 and so this noun takes **wa**.

> ### Insight
> Remember I said that **wa** can sometimes be thought of as meaning *as for*? It fits well in this scenario where you have two nouns and an adjective:
>
> Roger-san **wa** bōringu **ga** jōzu desu   *As for Roger, his bowling is skilful*
>
> Haha **wa** atama **ga** itai desu   *As for my mother, her head hurts*

Particle **ga** is used after noun 2 and relates directly to the adjective: the bowling is *skilful*, the head *hurts*. You will gradually learn and understand more about the differences of use between **wa** and **ga** as you work through this book so don't panic at this stage – have a go instead at saying these sentences in Japanese using the adjectives from the table in Explanation 5.1 (there are some explanations in brackets to guide you):

1 This place is a busy place.
2 Tokyo is very busy, isn't it!
3 This is a spacious and clean room. (this is = **kore wa**)
4 My mother has big eyes. (as for my mother, the eyes are big)
5 My eyes hurt. (as for me, the eyes hurt)
6 Roger is tall with big eyes. (as for Roger, height tall and eyes big)
7 Naoe is good at origami. (as for Naoe, her origami is skilful)
8 Miki is bad at bowling. (as for Miki, her bowling is poor)

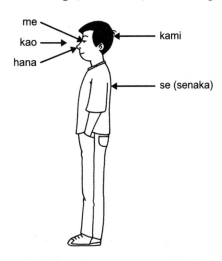

Explanation 5.3 Describing people

Now let's look in more detail at how to describe people. You will need more words in order to do this but they are given in chart form so you can easily refer back to them.

part of body	description 1	description 2	description 3
me *eyes*	**ōkii** *big*	**chiisai** *small*	**marui** *round*
se *height/back*	**takai** *high/tall*	**hikui** *low/short*	**futsū** *average*
hana *nose*	**takai** *tall/big*	**chiisai** *small*	**ōkii** *wide*
kami *hair*	**nagai** *long*	**mijikai** *short*	**kata gurai** *mid-length*

part of body	description 1	description 2	description 3
kao *face*	nagai *long/narrow*	shikakui *square*	marui *round*
eye colour	aoi *blue*	kuroi *black/dark brown*	chairo *brown*
hair colour	kinpatsu *blonde*	kuroi	chairo

Insight

Points to note when describing physical attributes:

- In Japanese, you talk about people's heights as high/tall or low/short rather than big or small
- **mijikai** (*short*) refers to length *not* height
- Noses are not big in Japanese but high (**takai**); also wide (**ōkii**)
- Very dark eyes are referred to as black (**kuroi**) rather than brown (**chairo**)
- Average length hair is shoulder length (**kata gurai**)

Now let's try putting this together. You should use the pattern you learned in Explanation 5.2:

> Noun 1 **wa** noun 2   **ga** adjective **desu**
> →   Person **wa** body part   **ga** description **desu**

You can leave out noun 1 when it is clear who is being talked about.

Here's an example:

I am short →	**Watashi wa se ga**		**hikui desu**
	Noun 1	noun 2	adjective
	Person	body part	description

If you want to make longer sentences you can use **kute** (*and*) with i adjectives *only* to link together two descriptions as follows:

I am short with brown hair → (Watashi wa) se ga hikukute, kami ga chairo desu

Did you notice that you only use **desu** once, at the end of the sentence?

◀) **CD1, TR 60**

Now you are going to try saying out loud some descriptions that gradually increase in length. By the way, the only adjectives in the chart that are not **i** adjectives are those not ending in **i**. Once you have tried saying the sentences out loud you can check with the correct version on the recording. Here are your sentences:

1 I am tall.
2 I am tall with blue eyes.
3 I am tall with blue eyes and blonde hair.
4 My mother has a round face.
5 My mother has a round face and a high nose.
6 My mother has a round face, a high nose and brown eyes.
7 She has long, black hair. (you don't need to repeat the word for hair)

Explanation 5.4 Linking adjectives with *and*

You are probably fairly familiar now with the connector **kute** (*and*). It can only be used for i adjectives and to use it you drop the final **i** and add **kute**:

akaru*kute* utsukushii desu	*bright* (cheerful) *and beautiful*
naga*kute* kuroi desu	*long and black*

Na adjectives work differently. For these you use another *and* word – **de** – which is used exclusively with **na** adjectives. This is how it works:

yūmei de utsukushii hito desu	*a famous and beautiful person*
kirei de hiroi heya desu	*a clean and spacious room*

Remember that the final adjective isn't in the *and* form. Now you try:

1 (He is) a serious and quiet person.
2 Tokyo is lively and big (spacious).

You can also use **ga** (*but*) when giving contrasting descriptions. In this case, use **desu** both before **ga** and at the end of the sentence:

Kare wa majime desu ga yasashii desu   *He's serious but kind*

If you use **ga** (but) in this way, then the second item being described (and sometimes the first item, too) takes particle **wa** (to emphasize contrast) rather than **ga**:

Supōtsu ga heta desu ga   *I'm poor at sports but I'm good at*
origami *wa* jōzu desu   *origami*

Explanation 5.5 Giving an opinion

When you want to say what you think about something, you use the expression **to omoimasu**:

Kono heya wa hiroi   *I think that this room is*
  to omoimasu   *spacious (large)*
Roger-san wa akarui hito   *I think that Roger is*
  da to omoimasu   *a cheerful person*

Insight

With **i** adjectives (this includes **tai desu** – *I want to*), you simply replace **desu** with **to omoimasu**: hiroi desu → hiroi to omoimasu.

With **na** adjectives and nouns, you replace **desu** with its informal form **da** then add **to omoimasu**: akarui hito desu → akarui hito da to omoimasu; kirei desu → kirei da to omoimasu.

Now you try:

1 I think that he is famous.
2 I think that it is a big (spacious) place.
3 I think that she is shy.

Explanation 5.6 I hope to

You have learned that by adding **tai desu** to the stem of the verb (Explanation 4.7) you can say 'I want to do'. By adding **tai to omoimasu,** you can say 'I hope to'. You try:

1 I hope to go to Japan next year.
2 I hope to eat sushi in Japan.
3 And I hope to see Mount Fuji (**Fujisan**).

Explanation 5.7 Saying it is not (1)

To form the negative of **i** adjectives you take off **i** and add **kunai desu** (*it is not*):

ōkii desu → ōkikunai desu	*it isn't big*
chiisai desu → chiisakunai desu	*it isn't small*

There is one adjective which changes slightly:

ii desu (good) → yokunai desu	*it isn't good*
Also note → yokute *good and . . .*	

Explanation 5.8 Saying it is not (2)

Rie-san used the negative of a **na** adjective when she said about Miki:

Sonna ni hazukashigari ja	*I don't think she's*
nai to omoimasu	*especially shy*

The negative of **na** adjectives and nouns follows the same rule as in English – the **desu** (*is*) changes to the negative (*is not*). You learned this in Explanation 1.9.

Explanation 5.9 Useful illness phrases

You've met the phrase **itai desu** for describing what hurts:

Me ga itai desu	*My eyes hurt/are sore*
Atama ga itai desu	*I have a headache*

◀) **CD1, TR 61**

Here is a table with a short list of useful symptoms. Listen to the recording and practise saying the phrases out loud.

<table>
<tr><td rowspan="9" style="writing-mode: vertical">QUICK VOCAB</td></tr>
<tr><td>dō shita n desu ka</td><td>what's wrong?</td></tr>
<tr><td>nodo ga itai desu</td><td>my throat is sore</td></tr>
<tr><td>kata ga itai desu</td><td>my shoulders ache</td></tr>
<tr><td>senaka ga itai desu</td><td>I've got backache</td></tr>
<tr><td>onaka ga itai desu</td><td>I've got stomach ache</td></tr>
<tr><td>kibun ga warui desu</td><td>I feel bad/ill</td></tr>
<tr><td>kaze o hiiteshimaimashita</td><td>I've caught a cold</td></tr>
<tr><td>kaze</td><td>a cold</td></tr>
</table>

Insight

The Japanese phrase for *I've caught a cold* might look rather daunting at first. Try breaking it down like this:

hi-i-te
hi-i-te shi-ma-i
hi-i-te shi-ma-i ma-sh(i)-ta

Main dialogue

◆) **CD1, TR 62**

Listen to the recording (or read the dialogue) as Robert complains to Miki and Rie of not feeling well. Refer back to the table in Explanation 5.9 for support with illness phrases and listen out for them.

Miki	Robāto-san, dō shita n desu ka.
Robert	Chotto . . . kibun ga warui desu.
Miki	Kaze o hiiteshimaimashita ka.
Robert	Atama ga itai desu. Onaka mo itai desu.
Miki	Sō desu ka. Nodo ga itai desu ka.
Robert	Chotto itai desu. Kata mo itai desu.
Miki	Jā, kaze desu ne.
Rie	Kaze dewa arimasen. **Futsuka yoi** desu yo!

Questions

1 List the five symptoms Robert is suffering from.
2 What conclusion does Miki come to?
3 What alternative conclusion does Rie come to?

futsuka yoi   *hangover*

Learn to say: Description of myself

◄) CD1, TR 63

Before Miki met Roger she wrote this description of herself for a computer dating agency. Read it through, check your understanding, then try listening to the recording and saying it in chunks until you can do it off by heart:

> Watashi wa Sugihara Miki desu. Se ga futsū de kami ga kurokute nagai desu. Me ga kurokute marui desu. Kao mo marui desu ga hana wa shikakui desu. Watashi wa otonashii desu ga yasashii to omoimasu. Eiga ga **suki** desu ga supōtsu wa suki ja arimasen.

suki	I like

Activities

Activity 5.1

To make the new describing language your own you are going to write and learn your self-description. Use Miki's computer dating description as your model (speech) and alter it to describe yourself. Use the information in the opening activities and in Explanations 5.1–5.4 to help you do this. Once you have written it, learn it off by heart and say it out loud in a confident manner!

Activity 5.2

How well have you understood the rules for making the negative and connectors of adjectives? A table of 10 adjectives follows. See if you can convert them correctly (the first two are done for you) and also write in the English meaning. There is a mix of **na** and **i** adjectives so be careful.

adjective	English	negative	connector (and)
hazukashii	*embarrassed*	hazukashikunai	hazukashikute
kirei	*beautiful; clean*	kirei dewa arimasen	kirei de
1 otonashii			
2 majime			
3 yūmei			
4 akarui			
5 itai			
6 jōzu			
7 ii			
8 ōkii			

Activity 5.3

How well have you remembered the illness phrases? See if you can match the Japanese phrases with the English meanings, then label the picture.

1 Kata ga itai desu		**A**	*What's wrong?*
2 Kaze o hiiteshimaimashita		**B**	*My throat is sore*
3 Onaka ga itai desu		**C**	*My shoulders ache*
4 Kibun ga warui desu		**D**	*I've got backache*
5 Senaka ga itai desu		**E**	*I've got stomach ache*
6 Dō shita n desu ka		**F**	*I feel bad/ill*
7 Nodo ga itai desu		**G**	*I've caught a cold*

How to read hiragana (4)

In this section you will learn:

- how to alter the basic 46 hiragana symbols to make new sounds
- how to read some more words

Start reading

Rule 1: Changing the sounds of single hiragana symbols

You are going to learn how to change the sounds of some hiragana symbols by adding the marks " (**tenten**) and ° (**maru**). First, review those particular symbols before you learn the new rules:

か	き	く	け	こ
ka	ki	ku	ke	ko
さ	し	す	せ	そ
sa	shi	su	se	so

た	ち	つ	て	と
ta	chi	tsu	te	to
は	ひ	ふ	へ	ほ
ha	hi	fu	he	ho

By adding the **tenten** mark, these symbols change their sounds as follows:

1 k sounds become g sounds (hard g as in *get*)

か	き	く	け	こ	→	が	ぎ	ぐ	げ	ご
ka	ki	ku	ke	ko		ga	gi	gu	ge	go

2 s sounds → z sounds

さ	し	す	せ	そ	→	ざ	じ	ず	ぜ	ぞ
sa	shi	su	se	so		za	ji*	zu	ze	zo

* じ is pronounced **ji** (not **zi**)

3 t sounds become d sounds

た	ち	つ	て	と	→	だ	ぢ	づ	で	ど
ta	chi	tsu	te	to		da	(ji	zu)*	de	do

* ぢ (**ji**) and づ (**zu**) are not normally used because they create the same sounds as じ (**ji**) and ず (**zu**) [See 2.]

4 h sounds become b sounds

は	ひ	ふ	へ	ほ	→	ば	び	ぶ	べ	ぼ
ha	hi	fu	he	ho		ba	bi	bu	be	bo

5 In addition, **h** sounds become **p** sounds when a small circle ° (**maru**) is added:

は	ひ	ふ	へ	ほ	→	ぱ	ぴ	ぷ	ぺ	ぽ
ha	hi	fu	he	ho		pa	pi	pu	pe	po

These five rules cover all the sound changes for single hiragana symbols. Practise reading them while listening to the recording from the pronunciation guide then try the following reading activities to help you practise and learn these rules.

Reading activity 5.1

Can you read the sequences of symbols that follow? Speak out loud:

1 が ざ だ ば ぱ   **4** ざ じ ず ぜ ぞ
2 が ぎ ぐ げ ご   **5** げ ぜ で べ ぺ
3 ご ぞ ど ぼ ぽ   **6** び ぶ ぴ ぷ

Reading activity 5.2

Here are the days of the week written in hiragana. Say them out loud and convert them into English. Check your answers in Explanation 4.8:

にちようび
げつようび
かようび
すいようび
もくようび
きんようび
どようび

Reading activity 5.3

Here are some words you learned in Units 1–5 which have **tenten** and **maru** symbols. Can you read them and what do they mean in English?

1 かぞく   **3** ぎんこう
2 しんぶん   **4** ご

5 にほんご   13 いちがつ

6 あさごはん   14 ごぜん

7 ばんごはん   15 ごご

8 たまご   16 えいがかん

9 でんわ   17 はくぶつかん

10 しごと   18 おはようございます

11 ときどき   19 ありがとうございます

12 ぜんぜん

Rule 2: Contracted sounds

◀ CD1, TR 3, 01:46

These new sounds are made by combining the hiragana symbols that end in an 'i' sound (き，し，ち，に，ひ，み，り) with a small version of や，ゆ or よ. Each of these new sounds is pronounced as a single syllable or 'beat'. Look at the following, listen to the recording (from the introduction) and practise saying the sounds as you read them:

き →	きゃ (kya)	きゅ (kyu)	きょ (kyo)
し →	しゃ (sha)	しゅ (shu)	しょ (sho)
ち →	ちゃ (cha)	ちゅ (chu)	ちょ (cho)
に →	にゃ (nya)	にゅ (nyu)	にょ (nyo)
ひ →	ひゃ (hya)	ひゅ (hyu)	ひょ (hyo)
み →	みゃ (mya)	みゅ (myu)	みょ (myo)
り →	りゃ (rya)	りゅ (ryu)	りょ (ryo)

Insight
When saying a word, try to move smoothly from one sound to the next – it shouldn't sound disjointed. Be especially careful of this when う (u) follows a sound

Reading activity 5.4

◆ CD1, TR 65

Here are some words from Units 1–5 that contain these contracted sounds. Can you read them? What do they mean in English?

1 しゃちょう
2 かいしゃ
3 じむしょ
4 しゅふ
5 しょくじ
6 きょうだい
7 りょこう
8 ちゅうごく
9 とうきょう
10 きょうと
11 でんしゃ
12 ゆうびんきょく
13 べんきょう
14 ひゃく
15 らいしゅう

Rule 3: Contracted sounds with tenten and maru

Do you remember the rules you learned for hiragana symbols that change their sound (rule 1)? These rules also apply to the contracted sounds (rule 2) beginning with **k**, **s** and **b**. Can you work out how to say these sounds? Cover up the rōmaji given on the right and see if you can say each sound out loud then uncover and see if you were right (remember: each sound is one syllable/beat):

ぎゃ	ぎゅ	ぎょ	gya, gyu, gyo
じゃ	じゅ	じょ	ja, ju, jo
びゃ	びゅ	びょ	bya, byu, byo
ぴゃ	ぴゅ	ぴょ	pya, pyu, pyo

Reading challenge

Here, in sequences of random order, is a selection of changed and contracted sound hiragana that you have learned in this unit. Can you read them all? Speak out loud:

1 が きゃ ぎゃ
2 じ しゃ じゃ ちゃ
3 ひょ びょ ぴょ
4 で ぎ ざ ぺ
5 ぎゅ じゅ びゅ ぴゅ
6 ちょ にょ ひょ みょ りょ
7 りゃ みゅ ひゅ ぴゅ
8 ぎょ じょ びょ ぴょ
9 ず ぐ ぶ りゅ
10 ぱ ぴ ぷ ぺ ぽ

End-of-unit challenge

◀) CD1, TR 64

Here are 10 useful phrases in English that you have learned
in this unit. Can you say each one in Japanese? Speak out loud
then listen to the recording and repeat out loud again, focusing
on the pronunciation. (You can also check your answers at the
back.)

1 I hope to go to Japan next year.
2 I don't think she's especially shy.
3 Tokyo is lively and big (spacious).
4 This department store is very busy, isn't it!
5 I am tall with blue eyes and blonde hair.
6 My mother is tall and has big eyes.
7 I think he's a very cheerful and kind person.
8 That person is serious but kind.
9 I am poor at sports but I am good at origami.
10 Miki is a beautiful person, isn't she?

6

....

Ryokō wa dō deshita ka
How was your trip?

In this unit you will learn
- *more about adjectives and descriptions*
- *more about describing past events*
- *weather phrases and reports*
- *about the Japanese seasons*
- *about transport and travel*

Getting started

In this unit you are going to learn to use adjectives to describe past events and experiences.

Opening activity

◆) **CD2, TR 1**

Here are five useful **i** adjectives for describing events:

QUICK VOCAB

tanoshii desu	*enjoyable, pleasant*
omoshiroi desu	*interesting, funny, fun*
ii desu (yoi desu)	*good, nice*
subarashii desu	*wonderful, great*
tsumaranai desu	*boring*

To change these into the past tense (it *was* enjoyable) you drop the last i and add **katta desu: tanoshii desu → tanoshikatta desu.**

Insight

Notice that when you change Japanese **i** adjectives into the past tense it is the adjective itself that changes form: **tanoshii desu, tanoshikatta desu.** This is different from English when it is the verb 'to be' which changes: *it is enjoyable, it was enjoyable.*

Now you try. Say the past tense of all five adjectives in the table then listen to the recording to check your pronunciation. For **ii desu** (*good*) use **yoi** and change it into the past.

Build-up activity

You learned how to link two adjectives in Unit 5 by using the connector **kute** (for **i** adjectives) and **de** (for **na** adjectives). This remains the same when talking about past events – only the final adjective of the sentence is in the past tense:

tanoshikute omoshirokatta desu *it was enjoyable and fun*

Now you try. Say the following sentences in Japanese out loud:

1 interesting and enjoyable
2 interesting and good
3 wonderful and fun
4 nice and enjoyable

Key sentences

Practise saying the vocabulary first and when you are familiar with it, read through the key sentences and see how much meaning you can work out before you read the translations.

1 **Ryokō** wa omoshirokute tanoshikatta desu.
2 Eiga wa omoshirokatta desu ga chotto nagakatta desu.
3 Kono hon wa tsumaranakute **fuyukai** deshita.
4 Senshū Ōsaka ni **shutchō shimashita. Omoshirokunakatta** desu.

5 Hondō-san wa **shinkansen** de Ōsaka ni ikimashita.
6 **Mō sugu natsu ni narimasu. Dandan atsuku narimasu.**
7 Ashita no **tenki** wa **kumori nochi ame deshō.**
8 Ōsaka-**yuki** no **kippu** o nimai kudasai.

Insight

- Remember when you see the ending **katta** it is the past tense of an adjective (*it was*) and when you see **kunakatta** it is the past negative (*it was not*)
- When you see **kute** this is an *and* link between two adjectives
- **deshita** is the past tense of **desu** (*is, was*)

ryokō	*travel, trip* (ryōko shimasu)
fuyukai (na)	*unpleasant, disagreeable*
shutchō shimashita	*did a business trip* (shutchō = business trip)
omoshirokunakatta	*it wasn't interesting*
shinkansen de	*by bullet train* (de = by)
mō sugu	*soon* (sugu = at once)
natsu	*summer*
(ni) narimasu	*become, get, will be*
dandan	*gradually*
atsuku	*hot* (atsui = hot)
tenki	*weather*
kumori	*cloudy*
nochi	*later*
ame	*rain*
deshō	*it will probably*
-yuki	*bound for*
kippu	*ticket*

English translation of the key sentences

1 *The trip was interesting and enjoyable.*
2 *The film was interesting but a bit long.*
3 *This book was boring and disagreeable.*
4 *Last week I did a business trip to Osaka. It wasn't interesting.*

5 *Mr Hondo went to Osaka by bullet train.*
6 *Soon it will be summer. It will gradually get hotter.*
7 *Tomorrow's weather will probably be cloudy, later rain.*
8 *Please may I have two tickets for Osaka.*

Language explanations

Here is a list of the grammar and language points you will learn in Unit 6:

1 past tense of adjectives
2 past negative of adjectives
3 review of past and past negative of **masu** verbs and **desu**
4 introduction of adverbs
5 using adverbs with **narimasu** (*to become*)
6 weather phrases and reports
7 Japanese seasons
8 types of transport and use of particle **de**
9 buying tickets to travel

Explanation 6.1 Saying *it was*

You already know about the past tense of **i** adjectives from the opening activity. To recap: drop **i**, add **katta desu**.

Example: omoshiroi desu → omoshirokatta desu

For **na** adjectives, you simply change **desu** (*is*) to **deshita** (*was*):

kirei desu → kirei deshita   *it was clean/she was beautiful*

To help you make this new information your own, try saying these sentences in Japanese and out loud:

1 It was good.
2 It was enjoyable.
3 It was disagreeable.
4 He was famous.

Explanation 6.2 Saying *it wasn't*

Now for the past negative (*it wasn't*) of i and **na** adjectives. This is how i adjectives form the past negative:

1 take the present negative: **omoshiro*kunai* desu**
2 drop the final i and add the past **katta: omoshirokuna*katta* desu**

In other words, you are using **katta** to make the negative into the past. You may simply find it easier to think of the process like this: Drop i and add **kunakatta: omoshiroi desu → omoshiro*kunakatta* desu.**

Now you try. Change the following adjectives into their past negative and give the English meaning:

1 tanoshii desu
2 ii desu
3 subarashii desu
4 tsumaranai desu

For **na** adjectives you need to change **desu** into its past negative. Look at the following table.

am, is, are	was not, were not (formal)	was not, were not (informal and more so)
desu	dewa arimasen deshita	ja arimasen deshita (ja nakatta desu)

Example: yūmei desu → yūmei dewa (ja) arimasen deshita

Insight

You can use either **dewa arimasen deshita** or **ja arimasen deshita** to form the past negative. **Ja** is simply a more informal ('squashed') version of **dewa**. Even more informal is **ja nakatta desu** – you will hear this a lot in everyday Japanese speech and can use it yourself outside formal/polite situations.

You try:

5 She wasn't beautiful.
6 He wasn't serious.
7 It wasn't disagreeable.

Explanation 6.3 Summary of tenses

You have now been introduced to four main **masu** and **desu** tenses. Here they are summarized in a table for you to recap and refer back to as necessary.

English	present (*is*) future (*will be*)	past (*was*)	negative (*isn't*)	past negative (*wasn't*)
eat	tabemasu	tabemashita	tabemasen	tabemasen deshita
big	ōkii desu	ōkikatta desu	ōkikunai desu	ōkikunakatta desu
famous	yūmei desu	yūmei deshita	yūmei ja (dewa) arimasen	yūmei ja (dewa) arimasen deshita
is	desu	deshita	ja (dewa) arimasen (ja nai desu)	ja (dewa) arimasen deshita (ja nakatta desu)

Explanation 6.4 Describing actions (adverbs)

The function of adverbs is to describe or give more information about the verb. Here are some English sentences in which the adverb is underlined:

He talks <u>quickly</u>
She writes <u>beautifully (neatly)</u>

They are playing <u>happily</u>

In Japanese, as in English, adjectives can be turned into adverbs:

hayai *quick* – hayaku *quickly*
kirei *beautiful; clean* – kirei ni *beautifully*

You have already come across some adverbs in previous units:

hayaku	*early* (also: *quickly*, *fast*)
osoku	*late*
chikaku	*nearby*
yoku	*often* (also: *well*)

This is how it works. For **i** adjectives you drop **i** and add **ku**:

omoshiroi → omoshiroku *interestingly*
tanoshii → tanoshiku *enjoyably*

For **na** adjectives, you add **ni** after the adjective:

fuyukai → fuyukai ni *disagreeably*
jōzu → jōzu ni *skilfully*

Read these Japanese sentences and see if you can work out their English meanings. The adverbs are underlined:

1 Miki-san wa <u>jōzu ni</u> kanji o kakimasu.
2 Robāto-san wa <u>yoku</u> nihongo o hanashimasu.
3 Hondō-san wa <u>majime ni</u> shigoto o shimasu.
4 Naoe-san wa <u>kirei ni</u> sōji o shimasu.
5 Katie-san wa <u>yasashiku</u> eigo o hanashimasu.

Explanation 6.5 Narimasu *to become*

The verb **narimasu** means *to become, be, get* in English. For example:

Mō sugu natsu ni narimasu   *Soon it will be summer*

Ashita roku-sai ni narimasu	*Tomorrow I will be(come) 6 years old*
Rokuji ni narimashita	*It has become 6 o'clock (6 o'clock has come)*

Narimasu can be used with adverbs to talk about things becoming hot, cold, happy etc. You use the past tense – **narimashita** – to say things 'have become'. Here are examples of its use:

Dandan atsuku narimasu	*It gradually gets hotter*
Kono heya wa kirei ni narimashita	*This room has become cleaner*
Miki-san wa bōringu ga jōzu ni narimashita	*Miki has got good at bowling*

Insight
The weather

Weather is an important subject in Japan – people are more likely to make comments about the weather when they meet up than ask casually after someone's health. A useful phrase to remember for good days is:

Ii tenki desu ne!	*It's nice weather, isn't it?*

Explanation 6.6

The following chart gives a short list of types of weather. You can either use **desu** (*it is/it will be*) where the weather is definite or is happening or, when making a prediction, the Japanese use **deshō** – *it probably will be*.

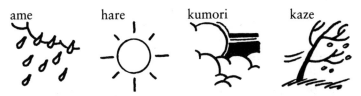

ame	hare	kumori	kaze

kiri kaminari yuki

QUICK VOCAB

desu	*it is*
deshō	*it will probably*
ame	*rain*
hare	*sun*
kumori	*cloudy/dull*
kaze	*wind, windy*
kiri	*fog*
kaminari	*lightning*
yuki	*snow*

Three other useful words are:

nochi	*later*
tokidoki	*sometimes*
ichinichi	*all day*

Here is how you put it all together:

Kumori nochi ame deshō	*It will probably be cloudy, later rain*
Kumori tokidoki ame deshō	*It will probably be cloudy, sometimes rainy*
Ichinichi ame deshō	*It'll rain all day*

Now you try. Say these weather conditions out loud. All are predictions (use **deshō**):

1 Rainy later fine.
2 Cloudy sometimes snow.
3 Fine all day.
4 Dull sometimes foggy.

Insight

The Japanese seasons

Japanese life and customs are traditionally closely linked to the four distinct seasons (**kisetsu**). These are:

haru   *spring*
natsu   *summer*
aki   *fall/autumn*
fuyu   *winter*

Explanation 6.7

We can use the adverbs and **ni narimasu** you learned in Explanations 6.4 and 6.5 to talk about the seasons using the phrase: **mō sugu** *season* **ni narimasu** (*soon it will be [season]*) and four new adjectives:

adjective	adverb	English
atsui	atsuku	*hot*
samui	samuku	*cold*
atatakai	atakaku	*warm*
suzushii	suzushiku	*cool/fresh*

Here's how you do it:

Mō sugu haru ni narimasu   *Soon it will be spring*
Dandan atatakaku narimasu   *It will gradually get warm(er)*

Now read these sentences and see if you can work out the meaning:

1 Mō sugu natsu ni narimasu. Dandan atsuku narimasu.
2 Mō sugu fuyu ni narimasu. Dandan samuku narimasu.
3 Mō sugu aki ni narimasu. Dandan suzushiku narimasu.

Explanation 6.8

As you know (Explanation 2.5) the word for *go* in Japanese is **ikimasu**. When you want to talk about the type of transport you *go by* you need the particle **de** after the mode of transport. Look at these examples:

shinkansen de	*by bullet train*
densha de	*by train*
shinkansen de ikimashita	*I went by bullet train*
Ōsaka ni shinkansen de ikimashita	*I went by bullet train to Osaka*
shinkansen de Ōsaka ni ikimashita	*I went by bullet train to Osaka*

Insight

The last two examples show that the meaning is the same whether you say 'to Osaka' first or 'by bullet train' first. The important thing is to use the particles correctly, the order is less important but always say the verb at the end.

To ask '*how did* you go (there)?' you say **dō yatte** ikimashita ka.

Now you try. Using the transport words for train, bus (**basu**) and car (**kuruma**), say these sentences:

1 I went by bus.
2 I went to town (**machi**) by bus.
3 I went to my mum's house by car.
4 I went to New York (**Nyū Yūku**) by train.

Explanation 6.9

Key sentence 8 introduced how to buy tickets:

Ōsaka-yuki no kippu o nimai kudasai	*Two tickets to Osaka please*

You know (Explanations 3.2, 3.3 and 3.4) about shopping and asking for numbers of items already. The word for ticket is **kippu** and the counter is **mai** for flat items (**ichi-mai, ni-mai** etc.). You may also be asked:

Katamichi desu ka. Ōfuku desu ka   *Is it one way or return?*

You can reply:

Katamichi desu (Ōfuku desu)   *It's one way (It's return)*

Main dialogue

◆ **CD2, TR 2**

Hondo Tatsuya-san has become friendly with Ian Ferguson, a New Zealander, through work. (Ian gives corporate English lessons at Hondo-san's company.) He meets up with Ian at a bar following a business trip to Osaka. Listen to the recording several times then use your pause button to practise repeating chunks of dialogue to help you improve your pronunciation. Then see if you can answer the questions.

Insight

From now on there will not be a complete English translation but there will be English questions so that you can check your general understanding and Japanese questions for you to answer in Japanese so that you can practise structuring sentences. Write the Japanese answers down in a notebook then check against the answers in the back.

Tatsuya	Senshū Ōsaka ni shutchō shimashita. Omoshirokunakatta desu.
Ian	Sō desu ka. Ōsaka ni ikitai desu. Omoshirokunai tokoro desu ka.

Tatsuya	Ōsaka wa subarashii tokoro desu ga shigoto wa tsumaranakatta desu.
Ian	Dō yatte ikimashita ka.
Tatsuya	Ōsaka **made** shinkansen de ikimashita. Katamichi no kippu o kaimashita. **Dōryō** no kuruma de kaerimashita. Sore mo **tanoshikunakatta** desu. **Tōsugimashita**.
Ian	O-tenki wa dō deshita ka.
Tatsuya	Mō sugu haru ni narimasu ga sonna ni **atatakakunakatta** desu. Mokuyōbi wa ichinichi yuki deshita. Fuyukai deshita.
Ian	Tōkyō no tenki **yohō** o kikimashita ka.
Tatsuya	Iie, **mada desu**.
Ian	Ashita wa samuku narimasu. Ame nochi yuki deshō.
Tatsuya	**Iya** desu ne!

QUICK VOCAB

made	*until, to*
dōryō	*colleague*
tanoshikunakatta	past negative of tanoshii
tōsugimashita	*it was too far*
atatakakunakatta	past negative of atatakai
yohō	*forecast*
mada desu	*not yet*
iya (na)	*awful*

English questions

1 What does Tatsuya-san think of Osaka?
2 How did he get there, how did he return and how was the return journey?
3 What was the weather like?
4 What is the weather forecast for Tokyo?

Japanese questions

5 Shutchō wa omoshirokatta desu ka
6 Tatsuya-san wa Ōsaka made ōfuku no kippu o kaimashita ka
7 Mokuyōbi no tenki wa dō deshita ka
8 Ashita wa atatakaku narimasu ka

Learn to say: The seasons in my country

◀ CD2, TR 3

Listen to the recording as Ian explains briefly about the weather
and seasons in New Zealand. Check your understanding then
practise saying it in chunks out loud.

> **Insight**
>
> This is a good activity to do while you are driving, cleaning
> or jogging with ear phones.

Nyū Jīrando wa kisetsu ga yottsu arimasu. Haru wa kugatsu **kara**
jūichigatsu **made** desu. Tenki wa hare tokidoki ame desu. Dandan
atatakaku narimasu. Natsu wa jūnigatsu kara nigatsu made desu.
Dandan atsuku narimasu. Aki wa sangatsu kara desu. Tenki wa
hare, kaze, ame … Fuyu wa rokugatsu kara desu. Totemo samui
desu. Yuki ga **ippai furimasu**.

New Zealand has four seasons. Spring is from September to
November. The weather is fine sometimes rainy. It gradually gets
warm. The summer is from December to February. It gradually
gets hot. Autumn is from March. The weather is fine, windy,
rain … Winter is from June. It is very cold. It snows a lot.

Nyū Jīrando	*New Zealand*
ippai	*plenty, full, a lot*
kara . . . made	*from . . . to* (placed after the noun)
furimasu	*falls* (rain, snow)

QUICK VOCAB

Activities

Activity 6.1

On the recording, you will hear a weather forecast. As you listen
see if you can fill in the chart with the weather for each city,

temperature and any additional information where given (e.g. 'it will be hot'). The word for 'degree' is **do** and this is said after the number: **jū do** = 10°.

◀ CD2, TR 4

city	weather	temperature	additional
1 Sapporo			
2 Sendai			
3 Tōkyō			
4 Ōsaka			
5 Fukuoka			
6 Okinawa			

Activity 6.2

The following Japanese sentences (with English translations) are incomplete. Your task is to complete them by adding the correct tense ending – the tense is indicated in brackets (see the table in Explanation 6.3 to remind yourself of these). Then translate them into English:

1 Kono eiga wa omoshirokute yokatta _____. (*past*)
2 Senshū no shutchō wa tsumaranakute fuyukai _____. (*past*)
3 Ashita no tenki wa kumori nochi ame _____. (*future/ probability*)
4 Ashita sanjū ni-sai ni nari _____. (*future*)
5 Kono heya wa kirei ni nari _____. (*past*)
6 Watashi wa amari shinbun o yomi _____. (*negative*)
7 Kinjo no hito wa me ga ōki ____ (*link, 'and'*) se ga taka _____ (*negative*)
8 Ryokō wa zenzen tanoshi _____. (*past negative*)
9 Anata no heya wa kirei _____. (*negative*)
10 Yūbe atama ga ita _____ (*past*). Nani mo tabe _____. (*past negative*)

Activity 6.3

Look back to Ian's speech in the 'learn to say' section and write out a similar speech that describes the seasons in your own country. (Or if you are a New Zealander, choose a country in the northern hemisphere.) Use as much of the vocabulary and as many of the structures for months, seasons and weather as you can and try to give your speech some variety. Write it out and try recording yourself. Keep listening to it and see how much you can eventually say from memory.

Activity 6.4

You have learned a lot about particles (**wa, ga, o, de, ni, mo, no, kara, made, to**). The following sentences are all about the characters and events you have learned about in this book. Can you put the missing particles into the brackets?

1 Naoe-san ( ) asa hayaku asagohan ( ) tabemasu.
2 Miki-san ( ) bōringu ( ) amari jōzu dewa arimasen.
3 Hondō-san ( ) dōryō ( ) kuruma ( ) Tōkyō ( ) kaerimashita.
4 Rokuji ( ) bōringu-jō ( ) aimashō.
5 Rie-san ( ) Miki-san ( ) eigakan ( ) ikimashita.
6 Hondō-san ( ) mainichi asa hayaku ( ) yoru osoku ( ) shigoto ( ) shimasu.
7 Miki-san ( ) bōringu ( ) tenisu ( ) heta desu.
8 Robāto-san ( ) se ( ) futsū de me ( ) aoi desu.
9 Nyū Tokyo hoteru ( ) bijutsukan ( ) ushiro ( ) arimasu.
10 Ōsaka ( ) subarashii tokoro desu ( ) shigoto ( ) tsumaranakatta desu.

Insight

At this stage in your learning you will probably feel there is a huge amount of remembering to do! By now you have learned or at least been exposed to a large number of Japanese words, phrases and structures. Unless you are lucky enough to have a photographic memory, you are not going to be able to recall everything! But you can help yourself greatly by keeping a *vocabulary book*. You can keep words alphabetically but remember this is already done for you in the back of the book. You might want to arrange words instead by themes such as food, travel, places, dates and numbers. You could also try keeping a list of structures by theme, too – i adjectives, **na** adjectives, verbs – and jot down rules as you learn them with one example. Look at this book regularly, test yourself by covering up either the Japanese or English side and see if you can remember the words.

How to read hiragana (5)

In this section you will learn:

- how sounds are lengthened (two beats) using う (**u**)
- how the small つ (**tsu**) is used to create a pause in a word
- how to write particles in Japanese
- how to read sentences

Start reading

Rule 1: Lengthened sounds

◆ **CD2, TR 5**

Here are some words you have already learned in Units 1–6, written in hiragana. These words all contain う (**u**). Listen to how they are pronounced on the recording and repeat each word out loud. Alternatively try saying the words out loud keeping your pronunciation smooth and flowing: (answers in the key)

1 きょうだい *siblings*
2 べんきょう *study*
3 ゆうびんきょく *post office*
4 ぎんこう *bank*

5 きゅうしゅう *Kyushu*
6 とうきょう *Tokyo*
7 らいしゅう *next week*
8 りょこう *travel*

You learned in the pronunciation guide that these long syllables (double length) are written with a macron over the vowel to indicate that it is a long sound. When written in hiragana, most commonly う (**u**) is used but you will also come across: あ (**a**), い (**i**), え (**e**) and お (**o**) used to lengthen sounds. Read and listen to how you say these words:

9 おおきい *big*
10 おねえさん *older sister*
11 おにいさん *older brother*
12 おかあさん *mother*

Rule 2: Using つ (tsu) to create a short pause

◀» **CD2, TR 5, 00:57**

You also learned about double consonants in the pronunciation guide – words such as:

jussai (*10 years old*); kitte (*stamp*); gakkō (*school*); kissaten (*coffee shop*); shutchō (*business trip*) and kippu (*ticket*). Here are how these words are written in hiragana:

じゅっさい (jussai) きって (kitte) がっこう (gakkō)
きっさてん (kissaten) しゅっちょう (shutchō) きっぷ (kippu)

Notice that the pause (glottal stop) is represented by a small つ (**tsu**). Listen and read as the words are spoken on the recording.

Rule 3: Writing particles in hiragana

An important function of hiragana is to represent the grammar parts of Japanese sentences. The various particles you have learned (**o, ga, de, ni, wa, e**) are all written in hiragana. Here they are:

o = を (you have already met this)   ni = に
ga = が   wa = は
de = で   e = へ

They are all as expected except:

- particle **wa** (は), which is normally pronounced **ha** when part of a word but as **wa** when a particle
- particle **e** (へ), which is normally pronounced **he** when part of a word but as **e** when a particle

Rule 4: Punctuation marks

Here is a short selection of Japanese punctuation marks:

- full stop = 。
- comma = 、
- speech marks = 「　」

In addition, rules about spaces between words are different in Japanese, for example it is all right for words to split over two lines and the particle normally follows a word without a space in between. However, to help you learn to read, the words have been spaced out so that you can easily identify words and particles.

Reading activity 6.1

◀ᴼ **CD2, TR 6**

Now that you have learned all the main rules for reading hiragana you are going to try reading some sentences. All of these are taken from the key sentences in Units 1–6 and are also recorded so that you can listen as you read if you wish to. Check the English meanings and readings by looking back at the key sentences in each unit (sentence number given in brackets).

Unit 1

1 かない の なまえ は りえです。 (2)
2 かぞく は ごにん です。 (3)
3 むすめ は じゅっさい です。 (5)

Unit 2

4 かぞく と あさごはん を たべます。 (1)
5 あさ そうじ を します。 (5)
6 きんじょ のひと とにほんごをはなします。(4)

Unit 3

7 この しんぶん は いくら ですか。 (1)
8 にかい に なにも ありません。 (5)
9 あの じむしょ に おとうさん が います
か。 (6)

Unit 4

10 まっすぐ いって ください。 (1)
11 しんごう を みぎ に まがって くださ
い。 (2)

Unit 5

12 とうきょう は ひろくて にぎやかな とこ
ろ です。 (2)
13 わたし の へや は あまり きれい で は
ありません。 (3)

14 りょこう は おもしろくて たのしかった
です。 (1)
15 おおさか ゆき の きっぷ を にまい くだ
さい。 (8)

Final words on reading

You have now learned the tools for reading hiragana. You will
continue to have the chance to read hiragana passages in the
reading sections that follow so that you can reinforce and keep
practising what you have learned. There will also be passages
available on the Teach Yourself website.

Reading challenge

Here are the opening dialogues from Units 1 and 2 written in
hiragana (katakana words are written in rōmaji). Can you read
them? You can use the recordings from these units as you follow
the text to support you. This is also a great opportunity to review
your learning in the first two units.

Unit 1

◄) **CD1, TR 6**

*Robert Franks, a British journalist working for a Japanese
newspaper company in Tokyo, is about to interview Tatsuya
Hondo who works for an electronics company.*

Robert	はじめまして、 Robert Franks と　もう します。どうぞよろしく。

Hondō-san	はじめまして、ほんどう たつや と もうします。よろしく おね がいします。
Robert	わたし の めいし です。どうぞ。
Hondō-san	ありがとう ございます。わたし の です。どうぞ。
Robert	ああ、ほんどうさん は かいし ゃ の えいぎょう ぶちょうです ね。おいそがしい でしょう ね。
Hondō-san	そう です ね。

Unit 2

🔊 **CD1, TR 19**

Listen to Naoe Hondo as she explains her morning routine.

あさ はやく おきます。かぞく と あさごは ん を たべます。いつも terebi nyūsu を みます。 そして kōhī を のみます。ときどき きんじょ のひと と はなします。それから そうじ を します。

End-of-unit challenge

Your challenge for this unit is a vocabulary challenge. Can you link these Japanese words with their English meanings?

Food and drink
1 asagohan ( )
2 bangohan ( )
3 hirugohan ( )
4 kōhī ( )
5 o-sake ( )
6 shokuji ( )

People
1 kyōdai ( )
2 eigyō buchō ( )
3 musuko ( )
4 shachō ( )
5 tsuma ( )
6 dōryō ( )

Directions
1 migi ( )
2 tonari ( )
3 soba ( )
4 hidarigawa ( )
5 shingō ( )
6 ōdan hodō ( )

Time expressions
1 ashita ( )
2 senshū ( )
3 raigetsu ( )
4 mainen ( )
5 gogo ( )
6 kayōbi ( )

Places
1 ginkō ( )
2 bijutsukan ( )
3 uchi ( )
4 kaisha ( )
5 gakkō ( )
6 gekijō ( )

Verbs
1 aimasu ( )
2 tsukurimasu ( )
3 benkyō shimasu ( )
4 kaimono o shimasu ( )
5 omoimasu ( )
6 hanashimasu ( )

---

a son **b** speak **c** colleague **d** Tuesday **e** meal **f** theatre
g think **h** right **i** alongside **j** brothers and sisters
k every year **l** coffee **m** tomorrow **n** pm **o** sales manager
p home **q** lunch **r** pedestrian crossing **s** rice wine **t** meet
u next to **v** make **w** wife **x** next month **y** company
z left side **aa** study **bb** director **cc** school **dd** do shopping
ee last week **ff** traffic lights **gg** art gallery **hh** breakfast
ii bank **jj** dinner/evening meal

7

....

Uchūhikōshi ni naritai desu!
I want to be an astronaut!

In this unit you will learn:
- *to talk about likes, dislikes and desires*
- *how to say what you are good and bad at*
- *how to use the verb stem to say more*
- *some useful work phrases*

_____

Getting started

A main theme of this unit will be work and types of job.

Opening activity

◀) CD2, TR 7

You can see from the title that to say what you want to be you use this phrase:

[*job title*] **ni naritai desu**   *I want to be a 'job title'*

The following list is of 10 common (and one uncommon!) jobs. Practise saying 'I want to be …' for each of the jobs then listen to the pronunciation on the recording. The first one is done for you.

shigoto	*job*
kaisha-in	*company employee*
ginkō-in	*bank worker*

shachō	company president, director
isha	doctor
sakka	writer
jānarisuto	journalist
kameraman	photographer
keisatsukan	policeman
bengoshi	lawyer
uchūhikōshi	astronaut

1 Kaisha-in ni naritai desu. *I want to be a company employee.*

Build-up activity

Maybe your childhood ambitions of a future occupation were different from today's reality! (Or maybe not?) Here is a selection of occupations that children talk about doing. You are going to say for each one: 'When I was a child I wanted to be a . . . '

You learned in Unit 6 how to put **i** adjective endings into the past – you drop **i** and add **katta desu**. Treat **naritai** in the same way: **naritai desu** → **naritakatta desu** (*I wanted to be*).

Here is the vocabulary you will need. The first one is done for you. Say each sentence out loud.

kodomo no koro	when (I was) a child
eiga sutā	film star
haiyū	actor
nō gekai	brain surgeon
kashu	singer
shōbōshi	firefighter
roketto kagakusha	rocket scientist
kangoshi	nurse, medical carer

1 Kodomo no koro, eiga sutā ni naritakatta desu. *When I was a child I wanted to be a film star.*

Key sentences

Practise saying the vocabulary first and when you are familiar with it, read through the key sentences and see how much meaning you can work out before you read the translations:

1 Ian-san wa o-sake o **nomitakunakatta** desu.
2 Miki-san wa bīru ga amari **suki** ja arimasen.
3 **Maiasa** Naoe-san wa kōhī o nomi**nagara** shinbun o yomimasu.
4 Roger-san wa Miki-san ni bōringu no **shikata** o **oshiemashita**.
5 Katie-san wa **machi** e Rie-san ni **ai ni ikimashita**.
6 Kono eiga wa **omoshirosō** desu ne.
7 Roger-san wa supōtsu ga **ichiban** suki desu.
8 Hondō Yuki-san wa **shōrai** isha ni naritai desu.
9 Robāto-san wa **mainichi** osoku made shigoto o shimasu.

nomitakunakatta	*didn't want to drink*
suki	*like*
maiasa	*every morning*
nagara	*while*
shikata	*how to do/play*
oshiemashita	*taught*
machi	*town*
e = ni	*to (a place)*
(ni) ai ni ikimashita	*went to meet (up with/to)*
omoshirosō	*looks interesting*

QUICK VOCAB

ichiban	*most, -est, number one*
shōrai	*in the future*
mainichi	*every day*

English translation of the key sentences

1 *Ian didn't want to drink rice wine/alcohol.*
2 *Miki doesn't like beer very much.*
3 *Every morning Naoe reads the paper while drinking her coffee.*
4 *Roger taught Miki how to do bowling.*
5 *Katie went to town to meet up with Rie.*
6 *This film looks interesting, doesn't it?*
7 *Roger likes sports best.*
8 *Yuki Hondo wants to be a doctor in the future.*
9 *Robert works every day until late.*

Language explanations

Here is a list of the grammar and language points you will learn in Unit 7:

1 saying *I want to, I don't want* and their past structures
2 saying what you are good and bad at
3 saying what you like and dislike

Using the verb stem to say:
4 while doing one thing I do another (**nagara**)
5 how to do something (**kata**)
6 go to a place to do something (**ni ikimasu**)
7 how something appears, seems to be (**sō desu**)

Also:
8 saying what you like best (**ichiban suki desu**)
9 useful work phrases

Explanation 7.1 The four tenses of *I want to*

You learned how to say *I want to* in Explanation 4.7. Look back to this now if you want to refresh your memory. To say the four main tenses of *I want to* you follow the same rules as for **i** adjectives (see Explanation 5.7 and Explanations 6.1 and 6.2). Look at the following table.

present	past	present negative	past negative
tai desu	takatta desu	takunai desu	takunakatta desu
I want to eat	*I wanted to eat*	*I don't want to eat*	*I didn't want to eat*
tabetai desu	tabetakatta desu	tabetakunai desu	tabetakunakatta desu

Insight

Remember: you take the stem of any verb (drop **masu**) then add **tai desu**. To change the tense, you first drop **i** then add **katta** (past), **kunai** (negative) or **kunakatta** (past negative). As with verbs, sometimes the particle **wa** is used instead of **o** (or **ga**). In particular, if you don't mention the subject of the sentence, **wa** sounds more natural in negative sentences.

Look at these examples:

| Robāto-san wa sushi o tabetakunai desu | *Robert doesn't want to eat sushi* |
| Sushi *wa* tabetakunai desu | *He doesn't want to eat sushi* |

Now try this build-up activity. You don't need to say the word for 'I'. Say in Japanese:

1 I want to eat.
2 I want to eat a banana.
3 I don't want to eat toast.
4 I don't want to drink coffee.
5 I didn't want to drink rice wine.
6 Last night I didn't want to drink beer.

Explanation 7.2 *Good at* **and** *bad at*

In previous units you have met the words **jōzu** (*good at*) and **heta** (*bad at*). For example:

Kare wa bōringu mo totemo jōzu desu	(Unit 5)	*He is also very good at bowling*
Watashi wa bōringu ga heta desu	(Unit 4)	*I am bad at bowling*

Notice the structure: *person* **wa** *activity* **ga jōzu/heta desu.**

You can also use the negative – *I am not good at/not bad at* – by changing **desu** to **ja arimasen** (**ja nai desu**): *person* **wa** *activity* **ga jōzu/heta ja arimasen.**

Insight

Jōzu and **heta** are used to talk about skills and practical activities that you are good at or bad at, for example, sports, crafts, arts – 'hands-on' activities. If you want to talk about your strong (or weak) point or your talents (including academic or professional skills), you use **tokui** (*good at*) and **nigate** (*poor at*). The structure remains the same: *person* **wa** *subject* **ga tokui/nigate desu.**

Here are two short lists of words you have already met, one of more practical skills or sports and the other of more academic skills. However, there can be overlap – for example, speaking Japanese or playing baseball can be both a practical skill and your strong point:

jōzu/heta		**tokui/nigate**	
bōringu	*bowling*	eigo	*English*
supōtsu	*sports*	benkyō	*studying/learning*
gitā	*guitar*	nihongo	*Japanese*
sakkā	*football*	sūgaku	*maths*

gorufu	*golf*
kaimono	*shopping*
kompyūtā	*computer*
bijutsu	*art*
yakyū	*baseball*
ryōri	*cooking*

Can you make five sentences about your own skills and good and weak points using these words? Start with **watashi wa**, follow the structure and examples given and don't worry if the limited vocabulary prevents you from being truthful – it's the 'out-loud' practice that is important. Here is an example to start you off:

Watashi wa kaimono ga   *I'm very good at shopping!*
totemo jōzu desu!

By the way, in situations where you want to be modest, use **tokui** rather than **jōzu**.

Explanation 7.3 Likes, dislikes and hates

Using the **na** adjectives **suki** (*like*) and **kirai** (*hate*) you can also use the structure from Explanation 7.2 to talk about likes and dislikes: *person* **wa** *noun* **ga suki/kirai desu** (*a person likes/hates something*).

Insight

Kirai is a strong word – don't use it about people. In any case, it's better to say you don't like something very much using **amari** (*not very*) and the negative of **desu**: **person wa noun ga amari suki ja arimasen** (*a person doesn't like something very much*).

And if you really like something use **totemo suki desu.**

Following the example, can you say these sentences out loud in Japanese?

Example: I don't like bananas very much. **Watashi wa banana ga amari suki ja arimasen**

1 Miki doesn't like sports very much.
2 Roger really likes tennis.
3 Rie likes shopping.
4 Miki really likes films.
5 Ian hates the rain.

Explanation 7.4 Verb stem + nagara *while*

The next four explanations are going to explore ways of using the verb stem (drop **masu**) to say more. Before you start, check you understand what the verb stem is by saying the stems of the following verbs:

Example: tabemasu (eat) → tabe

1	kaimasu (buy)	**6**	mimasu (watch)
2	kakimasu (write)	**7**	ikimasu (go)
3	kikimasu (listen)	**8**	hatarakimasu (work)
4	yomimasu (read)	**9**	shimasu (do)
5	nomimasu (drink)	**10**	hanashimasu (talk)

First, we'll look at **nagara** (*while*):

Maiasa Naoe-san wa kōhī
o nominagara shinbun
o yomimasu

Every morning Naoe reads the paper <u>while drinking coffee</u>

The underlined part is where you use the verb stem with **nagara**. The order is: verb stem + **nagara** followed by main verb (**masu/ mashita**).

Now you try. Follow the example and say the sentences out loud. Write them down if it helps you to remember better:

Example: Roger drinks beer <u>while watching football</u> → Roger-san wa sakkā o minagara bīru o nomimasu

11 Katie drinks green tea (**ocha**) <u>while listening to the news.</u>
12 Naoe talks to Yuki <u>while she makes the meal.</u>
13 Robert writes kanji <u>while he listens to music.</u>
14 Ian reads a book <u>while eating breakfast.</u>
15 Mr Hondo eats his lunch <u>while working.</u>

To describe past actions, you simply change the final verb to **mashita**. Try this now with the sentences 11–15.

Insight

By the way, you cannot use **nagara** if you are describing the actions of two different people, only when it is the same person doing both actions.

Explanation 7.5 Verb stem + kata *how to*

This is when you want to say how something is done:

Roger-san wa Miki-san ni *bōringu no shikata* o oshiemashita
Roger taught Miki *how to bowl*

In technical or grammar terms, by adding **kata** to the stem you are changing the verb (action or doing word) into a noun (a word you can put *a* or *the* in front). If there is a noun in front of the **kata** word, you link the two using particle **no**: bōringu no shikata → how to bowl.

Try saying these 'how-to' phrases:

1 how to eat sushi
2 how to make sushi
3 how to write kanji
4 how to read Japanese
5 how to speak English

Now turn these phrases into full sentences by talking about what Rie taught Katie to do (1–4) then what Katie taught Rie to do (5). The first is done for you:

Rie-san wa Katie-san ni sushi no tabekata o oshiemashita

Explanation 7.6 Go to a place in order to do something

Katie-san wa machi e Rie-san ni ai ni ikimashita
Katie went to town to meet up with Rie

When you use this structure, the place you go to normally takes particle **e** (*to* – alternatively you can use **ni**) and the action you are going to do is in the stem form followed by **ni ikimasu** (*go in order to*). Look at the examples then you try:

> go (in order) to buy → kai ni ikimasu
> go to town in order to buy → machi e kai ni ikimasu
> go to town to buy some CDs → machi e shii dii o kai ni
>   ikimasu
> I went to town to buy some CDs → Watashi wa machi e shii
>   dii o kai ni ikimashita

Now you try:

1 go (in order) to eat
2 go to a restaurant in order to eat
3 go to a restaurant in order to eat Japanese food (washoku)
4 I went to a restaurant to eat Japanese food.
5 I went with Katie to a restaurant to eat Japanese food.

Explanation 7.7 Expressing a personal opinion using *sō desu*

To express a personal opinion based on looking at something or at a situation you use the stem + **sō desu** (*it looks, it appears to be*). You can also use the stem of adjectives with this structure – for the stem of **i** adjectives you drop the final **i**, for **na** adjectives you use the full adjective without **na**:

Omoshirosō desu	*It looks interesting*
Jōzusō desu	*He looks good at it*
Ame ga furisō desu	*It looks like it will rain*

Now you try:

1 He looks famous.
2 This film looks boring.
3 He looks like he's got a headache.
4 She looks very beautiful, doesn't she?
5 He looks like he speaks Japanese.

Insight

Here is a summary of how to form the stem:

verbs – drop **masu**	tabemasu → tabe
i adjectives – drop final **i**	omoshiroi → omoshiro
na adjectives – drop the **na**	jōzuna → jōzu

Explanation 7.8 Saying what you like best

To say the equivalent of 'most' or 'least' in Japanese – e.g. saying what you like best – you use **ichiban** (number one) + adjective:

Roger-san wa supōtsu ga ichiban suki desu	*Roger likes sports best*
Roger-san wa bōringu ga ichiban jōzu desu	*Roger is most skilful at bowling*

Now use **heta, jōzu, suki, kirai** and **tsumaranai** to say these things about Miki (you can only use each adjective once):

1 Miki likes films the best.
2 (She) is most skilful at art.

3 She is least skilful ('most bad') at sports.
4 She hates tennis most of all but . . .
5 Baseball is the most boring.

Explanation 7.9 Useful work phrases

◀» CD2, TR 8

There are a number of Japanese phrases that you will find useful in work or business situations. Here are some listed in a table for you to refer to and learn as needed. You can practise saying them with the recording.

moshi moshi	*hello* (on the telephone – in all situations)
shitsurei shimasu	*excuse me for interrupting* (used especially when entering a work room/ office or end of phone call)
shitsurei shimashita	*as above but used when leaving a room*
o-saki ni	*I'm leaving before you* (used when leaving work at the end of the day – an acknowledgement that other people are still hard at work!)
gokurō-sama desu/deshita	*thanks for your hard work* (said by those left behind when you leave or to thank someone for working on a project/doing some thing for you)
otsukare-sama desu/deshita	similar to the above but can be used between equals as well as to people 'below' you
yoroshiku onegaishimasu	*I'm indebted to you* – said in antici pation of someone helping you/do ing you a favour; can be used at the end of a business phone call if future collaboration is anticipated

QUICK VOCAB

arigatō gozaimasu	*thank you very much*
arigatō gozaimashita	*thank you very much for something you have done for me*
sumimasen	*excuse me, sorry*
shōshō omachi kudasai	*please wait a minute* (very polite)

Insight
Japanese language in the workplace

From the phrases in Explanation 7.9 you can see that the politeness that runs through the Japanese language is also part of work life. Women, who traditionally are often in the inferior roles such as OL (office lady – clerical, making the tea) use the most polite and humble language. However, in situations where you don't know people well (which is usually the case for foreigners working on short-term or new projects with Japanese companies) you should keep to polite Japanese phrases and language (**masu/desu**) so that you don't sound disrespectful regardless of whether you are male or female. As you become more familiar with the people you work with then you can begin using more informal language but be led by your peers in this. Even if a superior speaks to you very informally you should still show respect to them through your language and use polite Japanese – this is the normal order of things. However, it would seem that the Japanese language is changing in response to the new demands and expectations of an increasingly global society to such an extent that some Japanese companies are having to teach young people how to use respect and polite language in the workplace. Only one generation ago this would have been totally unthinkable.

Main dialogue

◆》 CD2, TR 9

Mr Hondo is phoning Robert at work to invite him to play golf at the weekend. Listen to the recording several times then use your pause button to practise repeating chunks of dialogue to help you improve your pronunciation. Then see if you can answer the questions.

> **Insight**
>
> As explained in Unit 6 there will not be a complete English translation but there will be English questions so that you can check your general understanding and some true/false Japanese questions as well as some for you to answer in Japanese so that you can practise structuring sentences. Write the Japanese answers down in a notebook then check against the answers in the back.

Hondō-san	Moshi moshi, Robāto Furankusu-san **wa irasshaimasu ka.**
Female voice	Hai, shōshō o-machi kudasai.
[*Pause*]	
Robert	Moshi moshi?
Hondō-san	Robāto-san, konnichiwa. **Hondō desu ga . . .**
Robert	Ā, Hondō-san, **o-genki desu ka.**
Hondō-san	**Okagesama de.** Ano, Robāto-san, konshū no nichiyōbi ni issho ni gorufu o shimasen ka.
Robert	Gorufu desu ka. Boku wa amari jōzu dewa arimasen ga **yattemimashō!**
Hondō-san	Jā, **boku** wa gorufu no shikata o oshiemasu.
Robert	Ii desu ne. Yoroshiku onegaishimasu. Gorufu jō wa doko desu ka.
Hondō-san	Boku no kuruma de ikimashō. Jūniji ni Robāto-san no **apāto** e **mukae** ni ikimasu.
Robert	Jūniji desu ne. Wakarimashita.
Hondō-san	Jā, nichiyōbi ni. Shitsurei shimasu.

person **wa irasshaimasu ka**	*is [person] there?* (respectful)
Hondō desu ga . . .	*this is Hondo (speaking)* – used on the phone
o-genki desu ka	*how are you?* (used if you haven't spoken to the person for a while)
okagesama de	*I'm fine thank you* (said in response)
yattemimashō	*let's try/I'll give it a try*
boku	= watashi (used by men)
apāto	*apartment*
mukae (mukaemasu)	*to meet, receive, collect* (someone)

English questions

1 What is Robert's response when Mr Hondo invites him to play golf? (two parts)

2 What two things does Mr Hondo offer to do for Robert?

3 When and at what time will they set off to play golf?

True or false?

Write either O (**maru** = true) or X (**batsu** = false) next to these statements:

4 Hondō-san wa Robāto-san ni gorufu no mikata o oshiemasu.
5 Nichiyōbi ni isshō ni gorufu o shimasu.
6 Hondō-san wa gorufu-jō e mukae ni ikimasu.

Japanese questions

Write your answers in Japanese:

7 Nanji ni mukae ni ikimasu ka.
8 Basu de gorufu-jō ni ikimasu ka.
9 Robāto-san wa gorufu ga jōzu desu ka.

Learn to say: Plans for the future

◀》 **CD2, TR 10**

Listen as Robert talks about his job and his plans for the future. Check your understanding then try saying it out loud in chunks. When you have done this, see if you can make a speech about yourself by changing the underlined parts. If you don't know a word in Japanese simply substitute the English word for now and don't worry about being entirely truthful – the main purpose of this activity is to get you using the structures in a more personal context:

Kodomo no koro shōbōshi ni naritakatta desu ga **jitsu wa** jānarisuto ni narimashita. Mainichi yoru osoku made hatarakimasu ga shigoto wa totemo tanoshii desu. Tabitabi uchi de shokuji o shinagara shigoto o shimasu ga **shikata ga arimasen**. Shōrai Amerika de hatarakitai desu. Amerika no **seikatsu** wa omoshirosō desu ga Tōkyō no **seikatsu** ga ichiban suki desu.

*When I was a child I wanted to be a firefighter but, in fact,
I became a journalist. Every day I work until late in the evening
but the work is very enjoyable. Many times I do my work at home
while having a meal but it can't be helped. In the future I want to
work in America. The American lifestyle looks interesting but I like
the Tokyo lifestyle best of all.*

jitsu wa	*in fact*
shikata ga arimasen	*it can't be helped*
seikatsu	*lifestyle*

Activities

Activity 7.1

You have learned how to use the stem of the verb with **nagara**
(*while*), **kata** (*how to*), **sō** (*it looks like*), **tai desu** (*I want to*) and
ni ikimasu (*go to do*). The following sentences have one of these
words missing – decide which is needed to make sense of the
sentence and write out the English meaning, too:

1 Hondō-san wa Robāto-san ni gorufu no shi_____ o
oshiemashita.
2 Naoe-san wa asagohan o tabe_____ terebi o mimasu.
3 Ashita Katie-san to issho ni machi e eiga o mi _____.
4 Eiga sutā no seikatsu wa fuyukai_____ desu ne.
5 Rainen Nihon e iki _____.
6 Kēki no tsukuri_____ ga wakarimasen.
7 Miki-san wa sono sushi o tabe _____ desu ne.

Activity 7.2

Look at the pictures of Katie trying different activities and say
whether she is good or bad at it, likes it or doesn't like it or
whether it's her strong or weak point. Speak out loud.

Activity 7.3

🔊 **CD2, TR 11**

Listen as Ian talks about his childhood and on the following statements write a circle (**maru**) if it is true and a cross (**batsu**) if it is false:

1 As a child Ian wanted to be a rocket scientist.
2 He liked football but hated tennis.
3 At school he was very good at maths but useless at Japanese.
4 His mother really liked shopping but was no good at cooking.
5 His father used to make dinner while watching the football.

....

Insight
End of Part 1 – keep reviewing

Congratulations! You have completed Part 1 of *Complete Japanese* and are halfway through the whole course. You can keep returning to Part 1 at any time – try and find a balance between recapping on learning and moving on to new learning.

Use the recording to refresh your memory and to work towards perfect pronunciation. You can also refer to the grammar index at the back when you want to look up any particular grammar point. And keep returning to the activities in Part 1 to recap on your learning.

Introduction to kanji 漢字 (1)

In this section you will learn:

- how simple kanji developed from pictures
- how simple kanji are used to form more complex kanji
- how two or more kanji form new words
- more hiragana reading practice

Introduction

You learned in the Unit 1 reading section that kanji are ideographs that convey a specific meaning, word or idea. The simplest and earliest of these were pictographs, which were pictures drawn by the Chinese of the world around them and gradually standardized into the kanji used today.

Start reading

You have already looked at these kanji – do you remember their meanings?

日　月　木

Look back to the kanji section in Unit 1 for the answers.

Now you are going to look at a further 15 simple pictograph kanji. The pictures they are derived from are numbered a–o. Can you match them with their standardized kanji (1–15) which follow?

a gold **b** root **c** wood **d** forest

c mountain **f** child **g** fire **h** water

i power **j** ground/earth **k** woman **l** rice field

m stone **n** bamboo **o** river

1 山   **2** 川   **3** 金   **4** 田   **5** 竹   **6** 火

7 本   **8** 林   **9** 森   **10** 水   **11** 土   **12** 石

13 力   **14** 女   **15** 子

Now here is an artist's impression of how the pictures developed into standard kanji:

1 山

2 川

3 金

4 田

5 竹

6 火

木

7 本

8 林

9 森

10 水

11 土

12 石

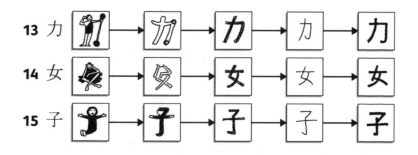

13 力

14 女

15 子

Reading activity 7.1

How familiar do you now feel with the 18 kanji you have learned so far? Here they are again – what do they mean in English? (cover up the preceding pictures)

1 山　　**2** 川　　**3** 竹　　**4** 女　　**5** 子　　**6** 森

7 石　　**8** 本　　**9** 日　　**10** 月　　**11** 林　　**12** 火

13 田　　**14** 力　　**15** 土　　**16** 水　　**17** 木　　**18** 金

Complex kanji

Pictograph and simple kanji are used as components of more complex kanji. You have already learned three examples of this:

木 + 木 = 林　　two trees make a **wood**

木 + 木 + 木 = 森　　three trees make a **forest**

木 + 一 = 本　　the line through the trunk represents the tree's **root** or **origin**

Here are some more examples using the kanji you have learned so far. The new meanings are in bold:

女 + 子 = 好　woman + child = **love** – a woman's **love** for her child

田 + 力 = 男　a **man** uses his power in the rice field

日 + 月 = 明　the sun and moon out together are **bright**

Kanji compounds

Kanji compounds are words made up of two, three or four kanji. For example 日本 means *Japan* (**Nihon**) and is made up of *sun* and *root*. This is because Japan is known as *the land of the rising sun* – it is in the east from where the sun has its root or origin.

Reading activity 7.2

Here are some more compound kanji words. Can you match them with their English meaning?

1 水力　　**a** girl

2 水田　　**b** boy

3 火山　　**c** water power

4 男子　　**d** volcano

5 女子　　**e** paddy field (wet rice growing)

Days of the week

You learned how to say the days of the week in Explanation 4.8. The kanji used for writing them are simple pictorial kanji and you have learned them already. Here they are:

kanji	meaning	day of week
日	sun	*Sunday*
月	moon	*Monday*

kanji	meaning	day of week
火	fire	*Tuesday*
水	water	*Wednesday*
木	tree	*Thursday*
金	gold, money	*Friday*
土	ground	*Saturday*

Insight

Hints for remembering:

- Sunday and Monday are easy – they are the same as in English (Monday was originally moon day in English too)
- Wednesday and water both begin with W; Thursday and tree begin with T
- Friday is money day – many people get paid on Fridays
- Saturday is earth day – you might do the gardening on this day!
- Tuesday in English derives from Tiw who was the Norse god of war. Connect fire day with war day and you have Tuesday!

As well as meaning 'sun', 日 also means 'day' because a day is defined by the rising and setting of the sun. When the days of the week are written in full they are written with three kanji, the first is one of the seven you have just learned and the second two are the kanji for *week* and for *day*. Here is an example:

日曜日 is Sunday, made up of *sun*, *week* and *day*

Reading activity 7.3

You are now going to match the kanji days of the week with their English meaning and Japanese reading (look back to Explanation 4.8 if you need to review these):

Sunday	1 水曜日	a nichiyōbi
Monday	2 木曜日	b kayōbi
Tuesday	3 日曜日	c doyōbi
Wednesday	4 土曜日	d getsuyōbi
Thursday	5 火曜日	e kinyōbi
Friday	6 月曜日	f mokuyōbi
Saturday	7 金曜日	g suiyōbi

Reading challenge

◀ **CD2, TR 9**

Here is the main dialogue of this unit, but this time it is written in hiragana and 'Sunday' is written in kanji. This kanji word has its reading written above in small hiragana known as **furigana**. All katakana words are written in rōmaji. You can set yourself the challenge of reading it straight off or you can listen to the recording as you read it:

Mr Hondo is phoning Robert at work to invite him to play golf at the weekend.

Hondō-san	もしもし、Robāto Furankusu さん は いらっしゃいますか。
Female voice	はい、しょうしょう おまち ください。
Robāto-san	もしもし？
Hondō-san	Robāto さん、こんにちは、ほんど うですが...
Robāto-san	ああ、ほんどうさん、おげんき ですか。

Hondô-san	おかげさまで。あの、Robâto さん、こん しゅうの

<ruby>日曜日<rt>にちようび</rt></ruby>に いっしょに gorufu をし ませ んか。

Robâto-san	Gorufu ですか。ぼくは あまり じょうず では ありませんが やってみましょう！
Hondô-san	じゃあ、ぼくは gorufu の しかたを おしえます。
Robâto-san	いい ですね。よろし く おねが いします。Gorufu じょう はどこ ですか。
Hondô-san	ぼくの くるま で いきましょ う。じゅうに じに Robâto さ んの apâto へ むかえに いきま す。
Robâto-san	じゅうに じ ですね。わかりま した。
Hondô-san	じゃあ、<ruby>日曜日<rt>にちようび</rt></ruby>に。しつれい します。

Final words

You have learned 18 simple kanji in this unit as well as three complex kanji and 13 kanji compound words. Review these before you move on to the reading section in the next unit.

Part two

Extending and manipulating the language

Introduction to Part 2

In Part 1 of this book (Units 1–7), you have learned the basics of the Japanese language and have under your belt a large number of relatively simple but very important structures. In Part 2, you are going to learn to manipulate the language further so that you can begin to speak using more complex and sophisticated structures. The first important step in this process is to learn how to manipulate and change verbs in order to be able to say more and to make longer sentences.

Insight

Remember that a verb is an action word such as *run*, *eat* and *play* and is a word that you can put a pronoun in front of such as I, *s/he*, *we*, *it*, *you* and *they* (*I run*, *she eats*, *you play*). We shall start, in Unit 8, with a grammar process often referred to as the '**te**' form.

8

....

Doyōbi ni jūji goro okite ...
On Saturdays I get up at about 10 ...

In this unit you will learn
- *all about the te form*
- *how to talk about daily routine in longer sentences*
- *how to ask someone to do something*
- *how to ask, give and refuse permission*

Getting started

Opening activity

◀》 **CD2, TR 12**

If you want to ask someone to do something for you in Japanese (simple commands) you use the **te** form of the verb followed by **kudasai** (meaning *please* in this context but we don't always use *please* when we use English commands). You have actually met this structure already when you gave directions in Unit 4 (**migi ni magatte kudasai** – *turn right*, **massugu itte kudasai** – *go straight ahead*). You haven't learned how to form the **te** form yet but here are 10 verbs in the **te** form. Can you use them to make simple commands as in the example? Say out loud, then listen to the recording, pause and repeat out loud:

tabete	please eat (it) → tabete kudasai
kaite	please write (it) →

kiite	please listen →
nonde	please drink (it) →
mite	please look →
misete	please show me →
katte	please buy (it) →
yonde	please read (it) →
hanashite	please speak →
okite	please get up →

Build-up activity

◀) **CD2, TR 13**

Now try saying longer sentences using the additional vocabulary that follows and following the example given. Then listen to this activity on the recording and repeat it to improve your pronunciation:

asagohan	eat your breakfast → asagohan o tabete kudasai
sakubun	(please) write an essay →
nyūsu	(please) listen to the news →
mizu	(please) drink water →
sensei	(please) look at the teacher →
sakubun	(please) show me your essay →
dejikame	(please) buy a digital camera →
sakubun	(please) read the essay →
Nihongo	(please) speak Japanese →

Key sentences

As you are now used to, practise saying the vocabulary first and when you are familiar with it, read through the key sentences and see how much meaning you can work out before you read the translations:

1 Rokuji ni okite, asagohan o tabete, shichiji ni **dekakemasu**.
2 Yoru bangohan o **tabete kara** kompyūta de **e-mēru** o **dashimasu**.
3 Bangohan o tabete kara, **shukudai** o shite kudasai.
4 Terebi o mite **mo ii desu ka**.

5 Koko de tabete **mo ii desu.**
6 Koko de tabete **wa ikemasen.**
7 Yūbinkyoku wa kuji kara goji made desu.

> ## Insight
> *Translation tip*:
>
> Treat sentence 1 as a string of events – *I get up, then I eat …* – the function of the **te** form here will be covered in Explanation 8.2.

dekakemasu	*go out, set off*
tabete kara	*after eating*
e-mēru	*email*
dashimasu	*send, submit*
shukudai	*homework*
mo ii desu ka	*may I (is it ok?)*
mo ii desu	*you may (it is ok)*
wa ikemasen	*you may not (it is not allowed)*

English translation of the key sentences

1 *I get up at 6, eat breakfast then set off at 7 o'clock.*
2 *In the evening after eating dinner I send emails on my computer.*
3 *After eating dinner, please do your homework.*
4 *May I watch the TV?*
5 *You may eat here.*
6 *You are not allowed to eat here.*
7 *The post office is (open) from 9 until 5.*

Language explanations

Here is a list of the grammar points you will learn in Unit 8:

1 how to form the **te** form – introduction to group 1 and 2 verbs + irregular verbs

2 using the **te** form when talking about sequence of events

3 **te kara** – after doing something

4 **te kudasai** – asking someone to do something

5 **te mo ii desu (ka)** – giving permission/asking if you may do something

6 **te wa ikemasen** – refusing permission/you are not allowed to

Explanation 8.1 How to form the *te* form

To understand how verbs work in Japanese, it helps to think of two types of verb, which we shall refer to as *group 1* and *group 2*. We will begin with group 2 verbs because these are more straightforward to manipulate than group 1 verbs.

<u>Group 2 verbs</u>: To make the **te** form of group 2 verbs, simply drop **masu** and add **te**:

dekakemasu → dekakete
tabemasu → tabete
okimasu → okite

Group 1 verbs, by way of contrast, follow one of four different rules. These four rules follow, but you may find it easier at this stage simply to remember each **te** form. There is also a table for you to fill in at the end of this unit. To apply these rules you need to look at the *stem* of the verb (the verb without the **masu** part – you met this in Unit 7).

<u>Group 1 verbs, rule 1</u> (**ki**): If the last syllable (sound) is **ki**, change it to **i** + **te**:

kikimasu (listen) → ki*ki* → kiite
kakimasu (write) → ka*ki* → ka*ite*

However, if the last syllable is **gi**, change it to **i** + **de**:

oyogimasu (swim) → oyogi → oyoi*de*

<u>Group 1 verbs, rule 2</u> (**i, chi, ri**): If the last syllable is **i, chi** or **ri**, change it to **tte**:

kaimasu (buy) → ka*i* → ka*tte*
tsukurimasu (make) → tsuku*ri* → tsuku*tte*
machimasu (wait) → ma*chi* → ma*tte*

Group 1 verbs, rule 3 (mi, bi, ni): If the last syllable is **mi**, **bi** or **ni**, change it to **nde**:

nomimasu (drink) → no*mi* → no*nde*
asobimasu (play) → aso*bi* → aso*nde*
shinimasu (die) → shi*ni* → shi*nde*

Group 1 verbs, rule 4 (shi): Add **te** (similar to group 2 rule):

hanashimasu (speak) → hanashi → hanashite

Irregular verbs:

(There are only three irregular verbs in Japanese!)

shimasu (do) → shi → shite
kimasu (come) → ki → kite
ikimasu (go) → itte

Insight

It will be useful for you to practise these new rules even
if you find it easier simply to remember each **te** form as
it comes along. At some stage in your learning you will
probably find that the rules fall into place and that you do
find them useful.

Now try this activity: simply convert the verbs into their **te** forms.

English	masu form	group	*te* form
sleep	nemasu	2	
wake up	okimasu	2	
teach	oshiemasu	2	
work	hatarakimasu	1	

understand	**wakarimasu**	1
meet	**aimasu**	1
read	**yomimasu**	1
study	**benkyō shimasu**	3

Explanation 8.2 Making longer sentences using *te*

The title to this unit gives a sequence of events in one long sentence:

Doyōbi ni jūji goro okite, yukkuri asagohan o tabemasu
On Saturdays I get up at about 10 and have a leisurely breakfast

The **te** form is used to say *and* or *then* when you use verbs. So you can change short sequences such as this one:

Jūji goro okimasu	*I get up at about 10*
Asagohan o tabemasu	*I eat breakfast*
Kaimono ni ikimasu	*I go shopping*

into longer sentences like this:

Jūji goro okite, asagohan o tabete, kaimono ni ikimasu
I get up at about 10, then I have breakfast, then I go shopping

You can use the **te** form in this way when the actions you do have an order to them – first you do action 1, then action 2, then action 3 and so on. The last verb in the sequence ends in **masu** (if present) or **mashita** (if past):

Kinō rokuji ni uchi ni kaette, bangohan o tabete, terebi o mite, jūichiji goro nemashita
Yesterday I got home at 6, I ate dinner, then I watched TV and I went to bed at about 11

◀) **CD2, TR 14**

You try. Sentences 1–5 are in Japanese. What do they mean in English? Sentences 6–10 are in English. How do you say them in Japanese? Say them out loud then listen to all 10 sentences on the recording and practise saying them out loud:

1 Mainichi rokuji ni okite, asagohan o tabete, shigoto ni ikimasu.
2 Doyōbi ni kuji goro okite, kōhī o nonde, machi de kaimono o shimasu.
3 Kinō osoku made shigoto o shite, kaisha no hito to resutoran ni ikimashita.
4 Yoru bangohan o tabete, terebi o mite, osoku nemasu.
5 Ashita kinjo no hito to kaimono ni itte, uchi ni kaette, gorogoro shimasu.
6 Every day I get up at 7, I eat breakfast and then I clean the house.
7 Every day I have lunch at 12, then I go to work.
8 Yesterday I got up late, I drank some coffee then I went into town.
9 Tomorrow I will go home at 6, have dinner then watch TV.
10 On Mondays I study Japanese, then I go to a restaurant to eat lunch.

Explanation 8.3 Tabete kara *After I ate*

As well as using **te** to give a sequence of actions, you can also refine what you want to say a little bit more by adding **kara**. This gives the meaning *after*:

Asagohan o tabete kara, shigoto ni ikimashita	*After I'd had breakfast I went to work*
Uchi ni kaette kara, shinbun o yomimasu	*After I get home I read the newspaper*

Now you try. Say these sentence out loud in Japanese:

1 After I had watched TV, I went to bed.
2 After I've had lunch I always listen to the news.
3 After I've studied Japanese I usually relax.
4 After I'd phoned my parents I went to my friend (**tomodachi**)'s house.
5 After reading (after I'd read) the newspaper I cleaned the house.

Explanation 8.4 Giving simple commands using *te kudasai*

You have learned and practised this in the opening and build-up activities so look back to these now to remind yourself how to give commands or ask someone to do something.

Explanation 8.5 Giving and asking for permission

◀) **CD2, TR 15**

To say 'you may do something' ('you are allowed to do something') you use the **te** form like this:

Koko de tabetemo ii desu   *You may eat in here*

Rule: Attach the phrase **mo ii desu** (literally meaning *even that is good*) to the **te** form of the verb.

Now you try. Convert these verbs into 'you may' sentences. The **te** form is given in brackets. Speak out loud then check your answers with the recording and key:

Example: You may drink in here (**nonde**) → koko de nondemo ii desu

1 You may sleep in here. (**nete**)
2 You may read in here. (**yonde**)
3 You may study in here. (**benkyō shite**)
4 You may watch TV in here. (**mite**)

5 You may speak Japanese in here. (**hanashite**)
6 You may listen to music in here. (**kiite**)
7 You may play in here. (**asonde**)

It is simple to convert this structure into the question 'may I?' Just add the question word **ka**:

> Toire ni ittemo ii desu ka   *May I go to the toilet?*

You try now – speak out loud and then listen to and practise with the recording. The underlined parts are new words, given in the brackets along with the **te** form:

8 May I eat in here? (**tabete**)
9 May I read this newspaper? (**yonde**)
10 May I listen to music in here? (**kiite**)
11 May I open the window? (**mado o akete**)
12 May I close the window? (**mado o shimete**)
13 May I enter this room? (**kono heya ni haitte**)
14 May I take (use 'enter') a bath? (**ofuro ni haitte**)

Explanation 8.6 Refusing permission

◀» CD2, TR 16

You also use the **te** form to refuse permission and tell someone they are not allowed to. This is how it works:

Rule: Add **wa ikemasen** (*not allowed to*) to the **te** form:

> Koko de tabete wa ikemasen   *You are not allowed to eat in here*

Here are some sentences for you to try. New words are given in brackets. Say the sentences out loud then listen and practise with the recording:

1 You are not allowed to drink in here.
2 You are not allowed to open the window.

3 You are not allowed to open <u>that door</u>. (**sono doa**)
4 You are not allowed to enter this room.
5 You are not allowed to take a bath.

Insight

There is a more informal version of **ikemasen,** which is **dame desu.** This can sound quite direct and impolite; for example, a teacher might use it with pupils or a parent with their child.

Explanation 8.7 Kara . . . made *From . . . until*

You first met these words in Unit 2. You use them when you want to *say from/to* or *open from/to.* Here are some examples:

jūji kara niji made	*from 10 o'clock to 2 o'clock*
ichigatsu kara sangatsu made	*from January to March*
Tōkyō kara Ōsaka made	*from Tokyo to Osaka*

Make sure that you say the <u>from</u> or <u>to</u> word <u>after</u> the noun (so the other way round to English): **Tōkyō <u>kara</u>** (<u>*from*</u> *Tokyo*); **niji <u>made</u>** (*until 2 o'clock*).

Try saying these sentences using **kara made:**

Example: The bank is (open) from 9 until 3 → Ginkō wa kuji kara sanji made desu

1 This bank is (open) from 10 until 2.
2 The post office (**yūbinkyoku**) is (open) from 9 until 5.
3 The film is from 7.30 until 10.30.
4 I went from Tokyo to Kyoto.
5 I went from Tokyo to Kyoto by bullet train (**shinkansen**).

Main dialogue

Katie and Ian are spending the weekend in Nikkō, a famous Shogun shrine in Japan. They are checking in at the youth hostel and the rather officious receptionist is explaining the hostel rules and opening hours.

Receptionist	Irasshaimase!
Katie	Konnichiwa. Kyō **yoyaku** o shimashita. Katie Mears to Ian Ferguson desu ga.
Receptionist	Hai, wakarimashita. Sukoshi **yūsuhosuteru** no **rūru** o **setsumei shimasu. Nihongo de ii desu ka.**
Katie	Hai, ii desu.
Receptionist	Kono yūsuhosuteru wa gozen jūji made **aiteimasu.** Soshite **mata** gogo yoji kara **aiteimasu. Hiruma** haitte wa ikemasen.
Katie	Yoru yoji kara **aiteimasu** ne.
Receptionist	Hai. Soshite yūsuhosuteru no naka de wa **kutsu o haite** wa ikemasen.
Ian	[*Looking at his shoes*] Ā sumimasen.
Receptionist	Sorekara ofuro no rūru desu. **Dansei** wa goji kara shichiji made **ofuro ni haitte**mo ii desu. **Josei** wa shichiji kara kuji made desu.
Ian	Heya de tabetemo ii desu ka.
Receptionist	Tabetewa dame desu! **Shokudō** de tabete kudasai. **Shokudō** wa kuji made **aiteimasu.**
Katie	Wakarimashita.
Receptionist	Soshite terebi no **heya** wa jūji made **aiteimasu.** Terebi wa jūji made mitemo ii desu.
Ian	Jūji made desu ka. **Demo konban** no eiga wa jūji han made desu. Jūji han made mitemo ii desu ka.

Receptionist	Ikemasen. Terebi no heya wa jūji made desu. Soshite **nerujikan** wa jūji han desu.
Ian	[*Getting annoyed*] Jūji han desu ka. Sore wa . . .
Katie	[*Interrupting*] Wakarimashita. **Heya** wa doko desu ka.
Receptionist	**Josei** no **heya** wa **kono kai** desu. **Dansei** no **heya** wa nikai desu.
Ian	**Heya** wa **betsubetsu** desu ka. **Shinjirarenai!**
Receptionist	Koko wa **yūsuhosuteru** desu yo!
Katie	[*Quickly*] Hai, hai, wakarimashita. Arigatō.

yoyaku (shimasu)	*reservation, booking (make)*
yūsuhosuteru	*youth hostel*
rūru	rules
setsumei shimasu	*explain*
Nihongo de ii desu ka	*is Japanese alright?*
aiteimasu	*is open*
mata	*again*
hiruma	*daytime, during the day*
kutsu o haite	*wear shoes* (kutsu = shoes)
dansei	*men, male*
ofuro ni haitte	*take a bath*
josei	*women, female*
shokudō	*dining room, canteen*
heya	*room*
demo	*but*
konban	*tonight, this evening*
nerujikan	*sleep time*
kono kai	*this floor*
betsubetsu	*separately*
shinjirarenai!	*I can't believe it!*

QUICK VOCAB

True or false?

Write either **O** (**maru** = true) or **X** (**batsu** = false) next to these statements:

1 Katie-san to Ian-san wa yoyaku o shimasen deshita.
2 Josei no ofuro wa 7 ji kara 9 ji made desu.
3 Hiruma jūji kara yoji made yūsuhosuteru ni haittewa ikemasen.
4 Ian-san wa konban jūji han made eiga o mimasu.
5 Katie-san to Ian-san wa konban heya de shokuji o shimasu.

Japanese questions

Write your answers in Japanese:

6 Terebi no heya wa nanji made aiteimasu ka.
7 Dansei no heya wa doko ni arimasu ka.
8 Dansei no ofuro wa nanji kara nanji made desu ka.
9 Yūsuhosuteru de wa kutsu o haitemo ii desu ka.
10 Doko de tabetemo ii desu ka.

English questions

11 At what time does the youth hostel close in the morning and when does it re-open?
12 What are the bath time rules?
13 What time is the dining room open until?
14 Why is Ian annoyed about the TV room rules?
15 For what other two reasons is Ian annoyed?

_____

Learn to say: Daily routine

◀) CD2, TR 18

You learned to say Katie's daily routine in Unit 2. (Look back at this if you want to refresh your memory.) Now you are going to say this routine again, applying the new knowledge you have acquired about sentence structure. Listen to the recording then use the pause button to listen line by line and repeat. Focus on good pronunciation and speaking confidently. When you have tried this a few times see if you can produce a personalized version about yourself.

Shichiji ni okite, asagohan ni itsumo kōhī o nomimasu. Asa tabitabi **tomodachi** to depāto de kaimono o shite, resutoran de shokuji o shimasu. Gogo tokidoki sūpā ni itte, soshite uchi ni kaerimasu. Uchi ni kaette kara tama ni uchi o sōji shimasu. Sorekara terebi o mite, bangohan o tsukutte, yoru shichiji kara shigoto o shimasu.

tomodachi   *friend*

Activities

Activity 8.1 Japanese school rules

◀) **CD2, TR 19**

You are going to listen to a short recording listing 'dos' and 'don'ts' for Japanese school students. Match each rule to a picture by writing the rule number in the box. If you don't have the recording, the script is printed in the answers section. Remember: you are not expected to understand every word, the skill you are developing is to pick out the *key* information.

Activity 8.2 Daily routine

◀) CD2, TR 20>

Takeshi Ishibashi, a student at Tokyo University and guitarist in a boy band, is describing his daily routine. Listen to the recording (the script is with the answers) and put the sequence of pictures into the right order by writing in the number 1 to 7 (1 is done for you).

Activity 8.3 Using the *te* form rules

This activity will give you the opportunity to practise and manipulate the rules you were introduced to in Explanation 8.1. (Look back to these if you need help.) The following table lists verbs you have not used before. Can you convert them into their correct **te** form?

Group 1 verbs	English	*te* form
mochimasu	*hold, possess*	1
keshimasu	*switch off, rub out*	2
utaimasu	*sing*	3
erabimasu	*choose*	4

hikimasu	*play* (an instrument)	5
yasumimasu	*rest*	6
nugimasu	*take off* (clothes)	7
Group 2 verbs	**English**	*te* **form**
kimemasu	*decide*	8
demasu	*leave, exit*	9
tsukemasu	*switch on, attach*	10

Activity 8.4 Giving and refusing permission

Use the verbs from Activity 8.3 to say out loud these sentences using **te mo ii desu (ka)**, **te wa ikemasen** and **te kudasai**:

1 Please hold this camera.
2 May I switch on the lights? (**denki**)
3 Please switch off the lights.
4 You are not allowed to sing in here.
5 Please choose one (item).
6 You may play your guitar (**gitā**) in this room.
7 May I take a rest?
8 Please take off your shoes.
9 Please decide quickly.
10 You are not allowed to go out in the evening.

Activity 8.5 Gap-filling exercise

There follows a mixture of sentences based mainly on information in Unit 8. Fill in the gaps from the selection of phrases in the box (you can only use each word or phrase once) to complete the sentences and write out an English translation:

1 Yūsuhosuteru no naka de wa kutsu o _____.
2 Gakkō de wa kutsu o _____.
3 Dansei no ofuro wa _____ desu.
4 Takeshi-san wa _____, jūichiji goro okimasu.

5 Katie-san wa asa depāto de _____, resutoran de shokuji o shimasu.

6 Soshite _____ tama ni uchi o sōji shimasu.

7 Hiruma yūsuhosuteru ni _____.

8 Yoru bangohan o tabete kara kompyūtā de _____.

9 Yūbinkyoku wa _____ aiteimasu.

10 Hondō-san wa _____ shinkansen de ikimashita.

a haitte wa ikemasen	**b** nuide kudasai
c Tōkyō kara Ōsaka made	**d** kaimono o shite
e osoku made nete	**f** kuji kara goji made
g goji kara shichiji made	**h** uchi ni kaette kara
i haite wa dame desu	**j** e-mēru o dashimasu

Introduction to kanji 漢字 (2)

In this section you will learn:

- more simple kanji developed from pictures
- kanji used for parts of the body and description
- kanji radicals
- more kanji compound words

Start reading

Can you match the following 11 simple pictograph kanji with their standardized kanji (1–11)?

foot   ear   person   above

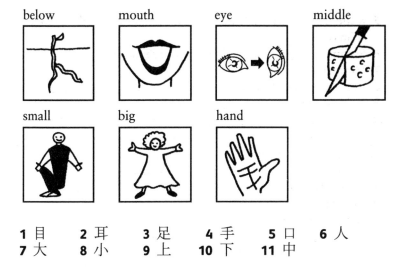

1 目   **2** 耳   **3** 足   **4** 手   **5** 口   **6** 人
7 大   **8** 小   **9** 上   **10** 下   **11** 中

Here are some stories to help you remember these new kanji (meanings are in bold):

1 目 if you turn this on its side you can see a square-shaped *eye*
2 耳 can you see the folds of skin that make up the *ear*?
3 足 you can see a mouth, an outstretched hand and a big *foot*
4 手 you may have to work hard to see four fingers and a thumb on this skeletal *hand* but they are there!
5 口 this round *mouth* or *opening* has been simplified into a square
6 人 this *person* has long legs
7 大 a person stretching out their arms and legs to be *big*
8 小 a person squeezing in their arms and legs to be *small*
9 上 can you see a plant growing *above* the ground?
10 下 now can you see its roots *below* the ground?
11 中 a line running through the *middle* of a box

Reading activity 8.1

How familiar do you now feel with these 11 kanji? Here they are again – what do they mean in English?

1 大	**2** 耳	**3** 耳	**4** 下	**5** 中	**6** 上
7 口	**8** 目	**9** 目	**10** 足	**11** 手	

Complex kanji

Here are some more complex kanji made up of elements of simpler ones:

少   this means *few, a little* and uses *small* plus a dash below

白   this means *white* and uses *sun* plus a speck to represent a ray of sun. The ancient Chinese saw the sun's colour as white

青   this means *blue/green*. You can see moon at the bottom, above it a plant is growing in the earth. Plants are **green** and we have the phrase *once in a blue moon*!

黒   this means *black*. You can see *rice field* and *earth* kanji and below it is the shortened version of *fire* (火). *Fire* is used to burn the stubble of the *rice* plant and the colour it burns to is *black*

Kanji radicals

You have already learned that simple kanji can become components of more complex ones. One of these components can give a *general* meaning to the whole kanji. This type of component is called the **radical**. The most common location of a radical is on the left side of a kanji. Other locations include on top, below or surrounding. Here are two kanji you have learned already:

青   *blue/green*: the radical is *moon* and is below the kanji (think of *blue* moon)

黒   *black*: the radical is *fire* (also below) – fire burns things to *black*

Insight

Kanji radicals will be pointed out to you as they appear in new kanji. They are useful to help you home in on the general meaning of a kanji but won't give you the exact meaning.

Kanji compounds

As you know, kanji compounds are words made up of two, three or four kanji. Here are two examples from the new kanji of this unit:

上手   **jōzu** this means *good at*, *skilful* – the above (upper) hand means you are skilled at something

下手   **heta** this means *poor/bad at* – and is represented by the below (lower) hand

Reading activity 8.2

Here are some more compound kanji words using kanji from this and the previous unit. Can you match them with their English meaning? Some have hiragana の between them but simply focus on the kanji meanings:

1	人口	**a**	girl
2	日本人	**b**	boy
3	男の人	**c**	man (person) power
4	女の人	**d**	population
5	女の子	**e**	Japanese person
6	男の子	**f**	in the public eye
7	人力	**g**	man
8	人目	**h**	woman

Insight

There are some interesting new meanings here: *population* focuses on 'mouths to feed'; *in the public eye* is literally that – the people's eyes.

Reading activity 8.3

You have now learned 36 single kanji. Can you remember them all? Here they are grouped into themes – can you give their English meanings?

1 position: 上 下 中
2 body parts: 口 耳 目 足 手
3 people: 人 女 男 子 力
4 description: 小 大 少 青 黒 白 明 好
5 nature: 山 川 木 森 林 竹 田 日 月 本
6 minerals and elements: 水 火 金 土 石

Reading challenge

Here is the *learn-to-say* passage from Unit 5 reproduced in hiragana with kanji words as appropriate. All katakana words are written in rōmaji. As with the previous unit try reading it with or without the recording to help you:

Before Miki met Roger she wrote this description of herself for a computer dating agency.

わたし は すぎはら みき です。せ が ふつ
う で かみ が 黒くて ながい です。目 が
黒くて まるい です。 かお も まるい で
す が はな が しかくい です。わたし は お
となしい です が やさしい と おもいます。
えいが が 好きです が

supōtsu は 好き じゃありません。

Final words on reading

You have learned 15 simple kanji in this unit as well as 10 kanji compound words. Review these before you move on to the reading section in the next unit.

End-of-unit challenge

You have been exposed to a lot of verbs in this unit. Here they are in a table. Can you write down the English meaning first and then see if you can fill in the **te** form.

masu form	English meaning	*te* form
Group 1		
dashimasu		
kakimasu		
kikimasu		
nomimasu		
kaimasu		
yomimasu		
hanashimasu		
oyogimasu		
machimasu		
asobimasu		
shinimasu		
hatarakimasu		
wakarimasu		
aimasu		
mochimasu		
tsukurimasu		
keshimasu		
utaimasu		
erabimasu		
hikimasu		
yasumimasu		
nugimasu		
Group 2		
tabemasu		
mimasu		
misemasu		
okimasu		

nemasu
dekakemasu
kimemasu
demasu
Irregular
ikimasu
shimasu
setsumei shimasu
yoyaku shimasu
kimasu

Check your answers against Explanation 8.1 and use the verb
tables at the back for English meanings.

9

Ima nani o shiteimasu ka

What are you doing at the moment?

In this unit you will learn
- *to talk about what you are or were doing*
- *to describe routines and habitual actions*
- *to say I am trying to*
- *to talk about what you want*
- *more about family*

Getting started

Opening activity

◀) **CD2, TR 21**

You learned about the **te** form in Unit 8. Now you are going to learn how to say 'I am do*ing* something' using **te** + **imasu**:

Ima asagohan o tabe*teimasu*   *At the moment I am eating breakfast*

Rule: Use the **te** form and add **imasu**.

Now you try. Say the following sentences out loud in Japanese then listen to and practise with the recording. Look back at the end-of-unit challenge for Unit 8 if you want to check any **te** forms:

Example: I am drinking coffee now → Ima kōhī o nondeimasu

1 I am listening to music now.
2 I am listening to the news at the moment.
3 I am watching TV.
4 I am reading a Japanese (language) newspaper.
5 I am having a meal with my family.
6 I am cleaning the house now.
7 I am writing a *letter* to my friend. (**tegami**)
8 I am talking *with my friends*. (**tomodachi to**)
9 I am buying a camera at the department store.
10 I am resting now.

Build-up activity

You can also talk about what you were doing (past actions) by changing **imasu** into **imashita**:

Asagohan o tabeteimashita   *I was eating breakfast*

Practise this by putting the sentences from the opening activity into the past 'I was doing ...':

Example: I was drinking coffee → **Kōhī o nondeimashita**

Key sentences

Remember to practise saying the vocabulary first and when you are familiar with it, read through the key sentences and see how much meaning you can work out before you read the translations:

> ### Insight
>
> *Translation tip*: Remember that the ending **te imasu** means *am (do)ing* and the ending **te imasen** means *am not (do)ing*.

1 Ima kazoku to bangohan o tabeteimasu.
2 Gitā o **naratteimasu**.

3 Daigaku de Nihongo o benkyō shiteimasu.
4 **Ane** wa **kekkon** shiteimasu.
5 Chichi wa ima Amerika ni itteimasu.
6 Kono sushi o **tabetemimashō**!
7 Terebi o keshite **hoshii** desu.
8 **Mō** asagohan o tabemashita ka.
9 Iie, **mada** tabeteimasen.

naratteimasu (naraimasu)	*learn*
ane	*older sister*
kekkon (shimasu)	*marriage (get married)*
temimashō (te + mimasu)	*have a go at, try*
hoshii (te + hoshii)	*want to (want you to do)*
mō	*already (no longer)*
mada	*not yet (still)*

English translation to the key sentences

1 *At present I am eating dinner with the family.*
2 *I am learning the guitar.*
3 *I am studying (study) Japanese at university.*
4 *My older sister is married.*
5 *My Dad has gone to (and is in) America at the moment.*
6 *Let's try this sushi!*
7 *I want you to switch off the TV.*
8 *Have you already eaten breakfast?*
9 *No, not yet. (I haven't eaten it yet/I am not eating it yet)*

Language explanations

Here is a list of the grammar points you will learn in Unit 9:

1 **te** form + **imasu** (1) – present and past continuous (*is/was ... ing*)
2 **te** form + **imasu** (2) – in the process of ... ing
3 **te** form + **imasu** (3) – habitual actions (*I usually do ...*)
4 **te** form + **imasu** (4) – existing state (*I have done and still am doing*)

5 te form + **imasu** (5) – with verbs of motion (**ikimasu, kimasu** etc.)
6 te form + **mimasu** – have a go at, try to do, try for the first time
7 te form + **hoshii desu** – I want you to …
8 **mada** (*not yet, still*) and **mō** (*already, no longer*)
9 more family words

Explanation 9.1 Ima tabeteimasu *I am eating at the moment*

You have already met the continuous form (*I am doing, I was doing*) in the opening and build-up activities. You can also use this form in the negative to say what you are not or were not doing. Here are some more examples:

Ima kompyūtā o tsukatteimasu	*I am using a computer now*
Senshū kompyūtā o tsukatteimashita	*I was using a computer last week*
Ima kompyūtā o tsukatteimasen	*I am not using a computer now*
Senshū kompyūtā o tsukatteimasen deshita	*I wasn't using a computer last week*

Compare the four continuous sentences you have just read with the following simple present and past sentences and look at the difference in meaning:

Insight

The simple present in English is *I do, I eat* etc. In Japanese, this is **shimasu, tabemasu**. The simple past is *I did, I ate* etc. and in Japanese it is **shimashita, tabemashita**.

Kompyūtā o tsukaimasu	*I use a computer*
Senshū kompyūtā o tsukaimashita	*I used a computer last week*
Kompyūtā o tsukaimasen	*I don't use a computer*
Senshū kompyūtā o tsukaimasen deshita	*I didn't use a computer last week*

Explanation 9.2 Gitā o naratteimasu *I am learning the guitar*

The **teimasu** form is also used to describe something you are in the process of doing even if you are not actually doing it at the moment, for example, learning an instrument, reading a book, watching a TV series. It can be translated as *I am ... ing* or *I have been ... ing*. Here are some examples:

Ima kaisha de Eigo o benkyō shiteimasu	*I am presently studying English at my company*
Ima totemo ii hon o yondeimasu	*I'm reading a really good book currently*
Kugatsu kara piano o naratteimasu	*I've been learning the piano since September*

Explanation 9.3 Daigaku de Nihongo o benkyō shiteimasu *I study Japanese at university*

You also use the **teimasu** form when talking about *habitual actions* – things you do on a regular or daily basis, things you are *in a habit* of doing. There is some overlap here with the simple present form, for example:

Mainichi kazoku to bangohan o tabemasu	*I eat dinner with my family every day*
Mainichi kazoku to bangohan o tabeteimasu	

Insight

Using **teimasu** puts an emphasis on the number of times or regularity with which you do an action; in other words, it emphasizes that you are in the *habit* of doing it.

Here are some more examples:

Doyōbi ni itsumo karē o tabeteimasu	*I always eat curry on Saturdays*

Hondō-san wa maiban bīru o nondeimasu	*Mr Hondo drinks beer every night*
Mainichi osoku made hataraiteimasu	*I work until late every day*
Shigoto ni densha de kayotteimasu	*I commute to work by train*
Miki-san wa Amerika de Nihongo o oshieteimashita	*Miki taught (was teaching) Japanese in America*

Explanation 9.4 Ane wa kekkon shiteimasu *My sister is married*

You use **teimasu** here to talk about an action that has happened and the result of that action still exists. So the older sister got married and she is still married. Here are some other examples:

Watashi wa dejikame o motteimasu	*I have got a digital camera*
Kinjo no hito wa shindeimasu	*The neighbour has died (is dead) [implies recently]*
Rie-san wa jaketto o kiteimasu	*Rie has got a jacket on (is wearing)*

| Roger-san wa
heya ni haitteimasu | *Roger has entered his room*
(and is still there) |

This explanation also works for an existing state (*I still am*) which might not have had an initial action:

| Ryōshin wa Ōsaka ni
sundeimasu | *My parents live in Osaka* |
| Tōkyō o yoku shitteimasu | *I know Tokyo very well* |

Insight

You will normally find the verbs **sundeimasu** (*live*), **motteimasu** (*have*, *possess*), **shitteimasu** (*know*), **shindeimasu** (*die*) in the **teimasu/teimashita** form (although not when used to talk about future actions). The **teimashita** form puts it further into the past – *I lived, I died, I knew*.

Explanation 9.5 Chichi wa Amerika ni itteimasu *My Dad has gone to America*

The verbs of motion **ikimasu** (*go*), **kimasu** (*come*) and **kaerimasu** (*return, go back*) used with **teimasu** can have meanings similar to Explanation 9.3 (*habitual actions*) or Explanation 9.4 (*I have done and still am*) depending on context and so it is useful to group them together within a separate explanation. Here are some examples:

Mainichi gakkō ni itteimasu	*I go to school every day* (habitual)
Itsumo rokuji ni uchi ni kaetteimasu	*I always return home at* *6 o'clock* (habitual)
Ryōshin wa Nihon ni itteimasu	*My parents have gone to* *Japan (and are still there)* (action and existing state)
Tomodachi ga kiteimasu	*A friend has come (and is still* *here)* (action and existing state)
Hondō-san wa uchi ni kaetteimasu	*Mr Hondo has gone home* *(and is there now)* (action and existing state)

Using words such as **itsumo** (*always*), **mainichi** (*every day*) and **taitei** (*usually*) makes it absolutely clear that you are talking about habitual or repeated actions as you can see with the first two examples in the previous list.

These verbs *never* have the meaning of *doing now* (continuous action). Look at this example to help you understand this:

Ima ryōshin wa Nihon ni itteimasu	*My parents are in Japan now* ✓ correct *My parents are going to Japan* X incorrect

---

Insight

When the meaning is *I have done and still am* the implication is that that the action is temporary – *I am still in America at the moment (but I will be returning)*. If the action is permanent you use **mashita**:

Ryōshin wa Igirisu ni kaerimashita	*My parents have gone back to England (and are staying there)*

◆) **CD2, TR 22**

To help you to consolidate what you have learned in Explanations 9.1–5 there follows 10 sentences for you to work out in Japanese. For all of them use the **teimasu** form – this will help you to understand the different uses of this form. Remember to speak out loud then listen to the recording and repeat to improve your pronunciation. Keep thinking about the meaning too:

1 What are you doing now?
2 I am buying a *digital camera*. (**dejikame**)
3 What was Mr Hondo doing?
4 He was making a phone call.
5 I am currently learning *flower arrangement*. (**ikebana**)
6 I play golf every Sunday. (every week's Sunday)

7 Both Katie and Ian teach English in Japan.
8 My Mum lived in *Sydney*. (**Shidonī**)
9 Katie has returned to America. (for a holiday – temporarily)
10 My parents have gone back to America. (permanently)
11 Robert has come to Japan from England.

Explanation 9.6 Kono sushi o tabetemimashō! *Let's try this sushi!*

When you use the **te** form with **mimasu** (*see*) it means *try, give something a try* and often refers to things you are trying for the first time. Here are some examples:

Ashita sushi o tabetemimasu *Tomorrow I'm going to try sushi*
Yūbe sake o nondemimashita *Last night I tried sake*

Notice that you change the **mimasu** part when you want to talk about past events. In fact, it is always the **mimasu** part you change to say different things. Look at these examples:

Kanji de kaite *mitemo ii* desu ka *May I try writing it in kanji?* (Explanation 9.5)
Kono jaketto o kite *mitai desu* *I want to try on this jacket* (Explanation 5.6)
Omoshiroi DVD o katte *mimashō* *Let's try and buy an interesting DVD* (Explanation 2.8)

Here are some examples for you to try. Speak out loud:

1 I tried on a smart (**sutekina**) jacket.
2 I want to try (drinking) Japanese beer.
3 May I try phoning (to) Mr Hondo?
4 Please try writing it in Japanese.
5 Let's have a go at playing golf.

Explanation 9.7 Terebi o tsukete hoshii desu *I want you to switch off the TV*

You have learned how to say what you yourself want to do using the verb stem with **tai desu**:

Kono jaketto o kaitai desu	*I want to buy this jacket*

If you want someone else to do something for you then you use the te form with **hoshii desu** (*want*):

Shukudai o shite hoshii desu	*I want you to do your homework*
Tamago o katte hoshii desu	*I want you to buy some eggs*
Miki-san ni Nihongo o oshiete hoshii desu	*I want Miki to teach me Japanese*

Insight

The person whom you want to do something takes particle **ni** as you can see in the last example (**Miki-san ni**). This is because the subject is the person who *wants* the action. In English **ni** might translate literally as *for* – I want <u>for</u> Miki to teach me Japanese.

You can also use **hoshii** to talk about things you want. The thing you want is followed by particle **ga**:

Kuruma ga hoshii desu	*I want a car*
Sutekina jaketto ga hoshii desu	*I want a smart jacket*
Nani ga hoshii desu ka	*What do you want?*

Insight

The difference between **hoshii** and **tai** here is that **hoshii** is used for things you *want* whereas **tai** is used to talk about things you want to *do*.

Here are some sentences for you to try:

1 I want you to write it in Japanese.
2 I want Roger to teach me English.
3 I want you to buy an American newspaper. (for me)
4 I want Rie to come to my house.
5 I want a big car.

Explanation 9.8 Mada tabeteimasen *I haven't eaten yet*

You use **mada** with the **teimasu** form when you want to talk about things you haven't done *yet* or things you are *still* in the process of doing. Look at these two examples:

| Mada asagohan o tabeteimasen | *I haven't had breakfast yet* |
| Mada asagohan o tabeteimasu | *I am still eating breakfast* |

Both examples are describing incomplete actions – with the negative (**teimasen**) it means *not yet* whereas with the positive (**teimasu**) it means *still*. Here are some more examples:

Mada shukudai o shiteimasen	*I haven't done my homework yet*
Mada shukudai o shiteimasu	*I'm still doing my homework*
Mada kaisha ni itteimasen	*I haven't gone to work yet*
Hondō-san wa mada kaisha ni imasu	*Mr Hondo is still at work*

As you can see from the last example, when you use **imasu** as a verb by itself or **arimasu** (*there is, is*) you use the simple form and *not* **teimasu**.

The opposite word to **mada** is **mō** (*already, no longer*), which is used when an action is finished. Look at these two examples:

| Mō asagohan o tabemashita | *I have already eaten my breakfast* |
| Mō asagohan o tabemasen | *I no longer eat breakfast* |

In the first example, the action is complete (*I've already eaten*) so the verb is in the simple past (**mashita**). In the second example, the action will no longer be done and so the verb is in the simple negative (**masen**). You can also use **teimasen** when talking about habitual actions you no longer do:

Yuki-san wa mō gitā o naratteimasen	*Yuki no longer learns the guitar*

You can use **mada** and **mō** when asking and answering questions like this:

Mada asagohan o tabeteimasu ka	*Are you still eating your breakfast?*
Iie, mō tabemashita	*No, I've already eaten it*
Mō bīru o nomimashita ka	*Have you already drunk your beer? (have you finished your beer?)*
Iie, mada nondeimasen	*No, I haven't drunk it yet*
Iie, mada desu	*No, not yet*

Now you try. Say these sentences in Japanese:

1 I am still listening to the news.
2 Rie no longer learns the piano.
3 Have you already phoned (to) Mr Hondo? No, not yet.
4 I haven't bought a digital camera yet but (**ga**) I have already bought a new TV.
5 Eri hasn't done her homework yet but Yuki is still doing hers.

Explanation 9.9 More about the family

In Explanation 1.5 you learned various words for your own and other people's families. Here are some more words for you to use and practise with.

English	my family	other family
parents	ryōshin	go-ryōshin
grandmother	sobo	obāsan
grandfather	sofu	ojīsan
older brother	ani, aniki (boys use)	onīsan
older sister	ane, aneki (boys use)	onēsan
younger brother	otōto	otōtosan
younger sister	imōto	imōtosan

Notice the use of **san** to most of these words to add respect when talking about other people's families. **Go** (**go-ryōshin**) works in the same way.

Insight
About Japanese families

There are some interesting cultural differences between English family terms and Japanese family terms. First of all, in English, we don't have separate terms for own family and other's family although we do have ways of showing more respect to other people. For example, we might say 'my Mum' but use 'your mother' rather than 'your mum' in a situation where we were being polite. However the difference is that we choose when to say, for example, 'your mother' or 'your mum' whereas the terms are used fairly rigidly in Japanese.

Secondly, although in Japanese you use humble terms when talking *about* your family to other people, you do something different when *directly* addressing your family. In this situation you use respect words for older family members and informal 'soft' words when addressing younger family members. Look at the following chart.

English	addressing own family	softer words (used by small children)
mum	okāsan	mama (okāchan – used in rural areas)

dad	**otōsan**	**papa** (**otōchan** – used in rural areas)
older brother	**onīsan, aniki** (boys use)	**onīchan, aniki**
older sister	**onēsan, aneki** (boys use)	**onēchan**
younger brother	use first name + **chan**	(e.g. **Takashi-chan**)
younger sister	use first name + **chan**	(e.g. **Eri-chan**)
grandma	**obāsan**	**obāchan**
grandad	**ojīsan**	**ojīchan**

So you can see that the respect words used for other people's family are also used when directly addressing your own, with the use of **chan** to soften the words when used by small children (although children of all ages and adults in front of children tend to say **obāchan** and **ojīchan** to grandparents).

A third interesting point that makes Japan different from the West is that within the family you normally only address brothers and sisters by their name if they are younger than you. Otherwise, you address them as *older brother* or *older sister*. Husbands and wives will call one another *Mum* and *Dad* in front of the children (we often do this, too but not always) and **anata** (*you*) in private rather than using first names. They would use first names, however, to address each other when out, for example, with friends.

Of course, you are more likely to hear these words being used than to use them yourself although if you stayed long term with a Japanese family you would be treated like a family member and begin to use these words.

To help you consolidate your learning, let's look at the situation from the Hondo family's point of view. Can you say the correct family terms for Yuki and Eri?

1 Yuki is 16. How would she address a) her mum, b) her dad, c) her sister, Eri, d) her granddad?
2 Eri is 10. How would she address a) her mum, b) her dad, c) her sister, Yuki, d) her grandma?

Main dialogue

🔊 **CD2, TR 23**

Robert is interviewing Yuki and Eri as he continues to research his article on Japanese family life.

Robert	Yuki-san, Eri-chan, **jibun no ichinichi ni tsuite** oshiete kudasai.
Yuki	Watashi wa mainichi **aruite** gakkō ni itteimasu. Gakkō **no ato de** tenisu **kurabu** ni **sanka** shiteimasu. Soshite maishū **nikai juku** ni itte, sūgaku ya eigo o benkyō shiteimasu. Shichiji goro uchi ni kaette, bangohan o tabete, soshite osoku made shukudai o shimasu.
Eri	Watashi mo **aruite** gakkō ni ikimasu. Gakkō **no ato de** taitei uchi ni kaette, haha to issho ni bangohan o tsukuri-masu. Ima piano o naratteimasu **kara** mainichi **renshū** o shiteimasu. Soshite onēchan to bangohan o tabemasu. Maishū **nikai** gakkō de jūdō o shiteimasu. Jūji goro nemasu.

Robert	**Shūmatsu** ni taitei nani o shiteimasu ka.
Yuki	Doyōbi no asa gakkō de **kurabu** o shimasu. Soshite gogo taitei tomodachi to machi ni itte kaimono o shimasu. Tokidoki eiga o mi ni ikimasu. Nichiyōbi ni tabitabi kazoku to issho ni **doraibu** o shimasu. Tokidoki sofu to **sampo** shimasu.
Eri	Watashi wa doyōbi ni yoku haha to ojīchan to machi ni itte, kaimono o shimasu. Tokidoki gakkō de jūdō no **shiai** ni **sanka** shimasu. Nichiyōbi wa Itsumo kazoku to **sugoshimasu**.
Robert	Eri-chan, **itsu** shukudai o shimasu ka.
Eri	Sō desu ne. Mainichi **sukoshi** shiteimasu ga konshū wa mada shiteimasen!
Yuki	Eri-chan wa shukudai ga amari suki janai desu.
Eri	Onēchan ni shukudai o shite hoshii desu.
Yuki	**Dame** desu yo! **Jibun** de shitemite kudasai.

True or false?

Write either O (**maru** = true) or X (**batsu** = false) next to these statements:

1 Yuki-san wa mainichi densha de gakkō ni itteimasu.
2 Eri-chan wa gakkō no ato de tenisu o shiteimasu.
3 Eri-chan wa ima piano o narattemimasu.
4 Yuki-san wa konshū mada shukudai o shiteimasen.
5 Eri-chan wa shukudai ga amari suki ja arimasen.

Japanese questions

Write your answers in Japanese:

6 Yuki-san wa gakkō no ato de nani o shimasu ka.
7 Yuki-san wa maishū nankai juku ni ikimasu ka.
8 Yuki-san wa itsu ojīsan to sampo shimasu ka.
9 Eri-chan wa gakkō no ato de nani o shimasu ka.
10 Eri-chan wa doko de jūdō o shimasu ka.

English questions

11 Briefly describe Yuki's weekend.
12 Now briefly describe Eri's weekend.
13 When does Yuki do her homework?
14 What is the issue about Eri's homework?
15 What does Yuki study at cram school?

Learn to say: What I am doing now

🔊 **CD2, TR 24**

Naoe is describing her family as they go about their morning routine. Listen to this short passage and practise saying it out loud. Then try adapting it to your own life – use the vocabulary you know even if this means you have to 'bend the truth' a little! The main aim is to make the language your own and to have something to say.

Ima watashi wa nyūsu o kikinagara kōhī o nondeimasu. Soshite Yuki wa asagohan o tabenagara terebi o miteimasu. Eri wa tōsuto o tabenagara shukudai o shiteimasu. Itsumo **osoi** desu! Shujin wa mō kaisha ni dekakemashita ga ojīchan wa mada neteimasu.

At the moment I am drinking coffee while listening to the news. And Yuki is watching TV while eating breakfast. Eri is doing her homework while eating toast. She is always late! My husband has already set off to his company but Grandad is still sleeping.

 osoi *late, slow*

Activities

Activity 9.1

◄) **CD2, TR 25**

The pictures 1–10 show Katie doing various activities. Listen to the recording and match the activities you hear with the pictures. If you don't have the recording, try saying the activities out loud in complete sentences.

8 WELCOME TO ROPPONGI **9** **10** MITSUKOSHI

Activity 9.2

Can you make these sentences complete by inserting either **mada** or **mō** into the gaps and then working out the English meaning? The sentences are based on information you know about the main characters of this book:

1 Roger-san wa _____ Miki-san to tenisu o shiteimasen.
2 Miki-san wa _____ Roger-san to dēto o shimashita.
3 Hondō-san wa ima uchi ni imasen. _____ kaisha ni imasu.
4 Eri-san wa konshū _____ shukudai o shiteimasen.
5 Yuki-san wa konshū ____ shukudai o shimashita.
6 Katie-san no go-ryōshin wa _____ Nihon ni imasu.
7 Takeshi-san wa _____ shigoto o shiteimasen.
8 Naoe-san no chichi wa _____ shigoto o shiteimasen. Mainichi uchi ni imasu.

Activity 9.3

Select the correct words and phrases from the box to complete the sentences 1–7. You can only use each phrase once:

1 Onēchan ni shukudai o _____ desu. (*I want my sister to do my homework for me*)
2 Kono tīshatsu o _____ desu. (*I want to try on this t-shirt*)
3 Ima kodomo wa uchi de asonde_____. (*at the moment the children are playing in the house*)
4 Mō Tōkyō ni sunde_____. (*I no longer live in Tokyo*)
5 Konban doitsu no ryōri o tabete_____. (*let's try German food tonight*)

6 Eri-chan ni shinbun o _____ desu. (*I want Eri to buy a newspaper for me*)

7 Atarashii kuruma ga _____ desu. (*I want a new car*)

8 Kyonen furansugo o naratte_____. (*last year I had a go at learning French*)

| **a** imasu | **b** kattehoshii | **c** kitemitai | **d** hoshii |
| **e** mimashō | **f** mimashita | **g** shitehoshii | **h** imasen |

Introduction to kanji 漢字 (3)

In this section you will learn:

- the kanji for numbers, prices and years
- how to read dates and the Japanese calendar
- more hiragana reading practice

Start reading

You have learned the kanji for *sun* 日 and *moon* 月. These two kanji are also used for dates. 日 represents the days of the month (1st, 2nd, 3rd etc.) and 月 represents the months of the year (months were traditionally measured by the phases of the moon). Here are some examples:

１日１２日 = 1st 12th
１月１２月 = January, December
３月５日 = March 5th

If you need to remind yourself of how the months work in Japanese look back to Explanation 2.10.

....
Insight

When you write month and date you must write it in that order only – first month then date. If you also include the weekday this comes third:

2月１８日 （月曜日） = February 18th (Monday)
or Monday 18th February
５月２日 （日曜日） = May 2nd (Sunday) or Sunday 2nd May

Reading activity 9.1

Here are some important dates in the Japanese calendar. Can you match them to the correct English date? (a and e dates are always the 3rd Monday of the month):

1	１月１日	**a**	Spring Equinox (21st March)
2	３月３日	**b**	7-5-3 (Children's) Festival (11th November)
3	５月５日	**c**	Emperor's birthday (23rd December)
4	７月７日	**d**	Bean-throwing Ceremony (3rd February)
5	１２月２３日	**e**	Greenery Day (29th April)
6	１２月３１日	**f**	New Year's Eve
7	１１月１１日	**g**	New Year's Day
8	２月３日	**h**	Star Festival (7th July)
9	４月２９日	**i**	Girls' Day (3rd March)
10	３月２１日	**j**	Boys' Day (5th May)

Kanji numbers

The Japanese use both our Arabic system for writing numbers (1, 2, 3 and so on) and also the kanji system. These kanji are relatively simple – here are the numbers 1–10 followed by some clues to help you recognize them quickly:

一 二 三 四 五 六 七 八 九 十

Clues

一 二 三 are easy – one line, two lines, three lines
四 is a *four*-sided square
五 you can make out the shape of the Arabic number 5 in this – try it!
六 in Japanese, you say **roku** which sounds like 'rocket' – can you see a rocket taking off in this kanji?

七 turn this kanji upside down and you have a continental number 7

八 if you turn Arabic number 8 on its side you have the symbol
for infinity ∞. Think of 八 as a road leading on to infinity!

九 can you see the kanji for 8 and for 1 in this symbol?
8 + 1 = 9!

十 the Roman numeral for 10 is X. Tilt 十 to one side to get
the same.

Reading activity 9.2

How well can you remember the kanji numbers 1–10? Match the
sequences of kanji numbers with the sequences on the right:

1 二 四 六 八 十		**a** 1 2 3 4 5
2 三 六 九 六 三		**b** 2 4 6 8 10
3 一 三 五 七 九		**c** 10 9 8 7 6
4 十 九 八 七 六		**d** 3 6 9 6 3
5 一 二 三 四 五		**e** 1 3 5 7 9

Higher numbers

You have already learned to count from 1–99 in Units 1 and 2.
With this knowledge it is easy to read higher numbers. Here is a
quick reminder of the basic rules:

12 = 10 + 2 = 十二
20 = 2 × 10 = 二十
21 = 2 × 10 + 1 = 二十一
99 = 9 × 10 + 9 = 九十九

Reading activity 9.3

Here are some sequences of numbers. Can you write them down in
Arabic numerals?

1 十一	十二	十三	十四	十五
2 二十	三十	四十	五十	六十
3 九十	九十一	九十二	九十三	九十四

4 三十三　　四十四　　五十五　　六十六　　七十七
5 五十九　　五十八　　五十七　　五十六　　五十五

Reading activity 9.4 dates

Here are some dates using kanji numbers. Can you convert them into English dates?

Example: 八月十二日　（月曜日）→　Monday 12th August

1 十二月二十五日　　　　　（火曜日）
2 六月十七日　　　　　　　（水曜日）
3 九月三日　　　　　　　　（土曜日）
4 ＿＿＿＿＿　四月三十一日　　（金曜日）

100s, 1000s and 10,000s

You learned how to say these in Explanation 3.9. Look back to this now if you need to refresh your memory. Here are the kanji:

百 100 if you turn this kanji on its side you can see the numerals 1 0 0

千 1000 this looks like the kanji 十 (10) but with an extra 'load' on top – two more zeros!

万 10,000 can you see a T and an h in this kanji? T for ten and Th for thousand – ten thousand!

円 **en** this is the kanji for yen, the Japanese currency. Its international symbol is ￥

Reading activity 9.5

Here are some prices. Can you write them in Arabic numerals?

1 cup of coffee = 四百円
2 plate of sushi = 七百円
3 t-shirt = 千九百円
4 underground ticket = 四百九十円

5 kabuki theatre ticket = 五千円
6 bullet train ticket = 二万円
7 designer dress = 七万三千円
8 small new car = 四十万九千九百円

Insight
The Japanese calendar

The kanji for year is 年. It contains the left part of bamboo (竹) and behind that a square shape, which we shall interpret as a house.

In Japan, bamboo decorations are placed in front of houses at new year, hence the link with **year**.

The most common way to write years from the western calendar is like this:

２００８年

You may also see this:

二〇〇八年

However, the Japanese also have their own system of numbering the years based on the length of rule of their Emperor. This is the system of 年号 (**nengō**) – era names. The present Emperor, Akihito, began his reign in 1989 and this era is called 平成 (**Heisei**) which means 'attainment of peace'. To work out the Heisei year from the western calendar year, begin with 1989 as year 1 and count up from there. So 2008 is Heisei 20. This is how 2008 is written using this system:

平成二十年

You can also use Arabic numbers:

平成２０年

Reading activity 9.6

Match the 平成 (**Heisei**) years with their western calendar equivalents. Tip: For Heisei 12 and above, take 12 away from the Heisei year to get the western year (20 – 12 = 8 = 2008):

1 平成十二年		**a** 二〇一〇年	
2 平成十一年		**b** 二〇〇〇年	
3 平成十七年		**c** 一九九〇年	
4 平成二十二年		**d** １９９９年	
5 平成二年		**e** ２００５年	

Reading challenge

Here is the 'learn to say' passage from Unit 3 reproduced in hiragana with kanji words as appropriate. All katakana words are written in rōmaji. As with previous units try reading it with or without the recording to help you:

Post office assistant	いらっしゃいませ！
You	はがき を うっていますか。
Assistant	はい、ここで ございます。
You	この はがきを みせて ください。
Assistant	はい、どうぞ。一まい 百円 でございます。
You	じゃあ、これを 四まい ください。
Assistant	かしこまりました。
You	そして きってを 四まい ください。
Assistant	どこ まで ですか。
You	Amerika まで です
Assistant	一まい 八十円 です。ぜんぶで 七百二十円 でございます。

Final words on reading

You have learned the kanji numbers 1–10, 100, 1000, and 10,000 in this unit as well as the kanji for yen and year. You have also learned to read dates and prices. Review these once more before you move on to the reading section in the next unit.

End-of-unit challenge

In this challenge, you are going to think about how you address family directly in Japanese. Look at the diagram of Takeshi's family. Imagine you are Takeshi and see if you can say out loud the names he would use when speaking to his family.

Finally, how would Takeshi's dad address each member of the family?

10

Kono wain o nomu mae ni, biru demo nomimashō!

Before we drink this wine, let's drink beer or something!

In this unit you will learn:
- *about the plain form*
- *to talk about things you can do and like to do*
- *to state intentions, reasons and justifications*
- *to say what you are interested in*

_____

Getting started

The main purpose of this unit is to introduce you to a verb form known as the plain or dictionary form (it is the form of the verb you will find if you look up a Japanese verb in the dictionary). So far you have learned and used the polite form of verbs known as **masu (tabemasu, tabemashita, tabemasen, tabemasen deshita)**. The plain (dictionary) form is used in more casual (plain) speech and also to make new phrases and structures as you will see.

Opening activity

◀) **CD2, TR 26**

Here is a list of 10 plain verbs for you to listen to and say out loud:

QUICK VOCAB

plain form	English	plain form	English
taberu	eat	kau	buy
miru	watch, see	kaku	write
oshieru	teach	nomu	drink
deru	go out	hanasu	speak
kiku	listen	iku	go

Build-up activity

🔊 **CD2, TR 27**

In this activity, you are going to change short polite sentences into plain ones using the 10 plain verbs you have just said. Follow the example, speak out loud, then listen and practise with the recording:

Example: Asagohan o tabemasu → Asagohan o taberu

1 Terebi o mimasu.
2 Eigo o oshiemasu.
3 Uchi o demasu.
4 Nyūsu o kikimasu.
5 Terebi o kaimasu.

6 E-mēru o kakimasu.
7 Bīru o nomimasu.
8 Nihongo o hanashimasu.
9 Furansu ni ikimasu.

Key sentences

Remember to practise saying the vocabulary first and when you are familiar with it, read through the key sentences and see how much meaning you can work out before you read the translations.

1 Mainichi watashi wa rokuji ni **okiru**.
2 Soshite asagohan o taberu **mae ni shawā o abimasu**.

3 Eri-chan wa mō **oyogu koto ga dekimasu.**
4 Roger-san wa tomodachi to bīru o nomu **koto ga suki desu.**
5 Rainen **minami** Amerika ni iku **tsumori desu.**
6 **Minami** Amerika ni **kyōmi ga aru no de** ikitai desu.
7 Nihongo o naratteimasu **kara** Nihon ni kiteimasu.
8 Dō shita **n** desu ka. Atama ga itai n **desu.**

English translation of the key sentences

1 *Every day I get up at 6.*
2 *And before I eat breakfast I take a shower.*
3 *Eri can already swim.*
4 *Roger likes to drink beer with his friends.*
5 *Next year I intend to go to South America.*
6 *I have an interest in South America so I want to go.*
7 *I am learning Japanese therefore I have come to Japan.*
8 *What's the matter? Well, you see, I've got a headache.*

Language explanations

Here is a list of the grammar points you will learn in Unit 10:

1 introduction to and explanation of the plain/dictionary form

Applications of the plain form:

2 with **mae ni** (*before*)
3 **koto ga dekiru** (*I am able to do/can do*)
4 **koto ga suki** (*I like to do*)
5 **tsumori desu** (*I intend to do*)
6 **kara** and **no de** – giving reasons
7 **no desu/n desu** – justifying or giving a reason, 'you see'
8 **kyōmi ga aru (arimasu)** – saying what you are interested in
9 cultural information: levels of speech in Japanese

You will also be using these new words in the explanations but they will be highlighted as they appear in the text.

demo	*something like, or something*
kinō	*yesterday*
ryōri	*cooking, cuisine*
sukoshi	*a little*
sashimi	*raw fish slices*
tegami	*letter*
dōshite/naze	*why*
takai	*expensive*
kurasu	*class*

Explanation 10.1 Mainichi rokuji ni okiru *I get up every day at 6*

Insight

You have already met the plain (dictionary) form in the opening and build-up activities. One of its uses is as an informal (casual) form of speaking. As an adult and a foreign speaker of Japanese you will mostly use polite forms (**masu** and **desu**) when you speak Japanese but you will hear plain forms being used and you yourself may use them with closer friends and in close relationships. It is also more appropriate to use plain forms with children. Men use plain forms much more than women, women tend to be more polite and use more respectful language.

The plain form is fairly easy to work out from its **masu** form (and vice versa). When you look up a new verb in a dictionary it is always in the dictionary (plain present) form so it is useful for you to know how to convert it into the **masu** form.

Do you remember that there are basically two types of verb, which are called group 1 and group 2 in this book? (See Explanation 8.1.) Here are the rules for changing **masu** into plain for each group.

Group 1 verbs: Drop **masu**, change final **i** to **u**:

kaimasu *buy* → kai → kau

Be careful, though, with **shi** and **chi** endings – these change to **su** and **tsu**:

hanashimasu *speak* → hana*shi* → hana*su*
mochimasu *possess* → mo*chi* → mo*tsu*

Group 2 verbs: Drop **masu**, add **ru**:

nemasu *go to bed* → ne → neru
okimasu *get up* → oki → okiru

Irregular verbs: There are three verbs in Japanese that are called *irregular* (they don't always conform to the rules). These are **ikimasu** (*go*), **kimasu** (*come*) and **shimasu** (*do*). Their plain forms are:

ikimasu → iki → iku (group 1 rule)
kimasu → kuru (irregular)
shimasu → suru (irregular)

You will, in fact, find that **ikimasu** acts like a group 1 verb except for the irregular **te** form (**itte**).

Now you are going to try converting **masu** verbs into plain by completing the following table.

masu form	plain form	English
Group 1		
1 kakimasu		
2 kikimasu		
3 nomimasu		
4 kaimasu		
5 yomimasu		
6 kaerimasu		
7 oyogimasu		
8 asobimasu		
9 hatarakimasu		
10 wakarimasu		
Group 2		
11 tabemasu		
12 mimasu		
13 okimasu		
14 nemasu		
15 dekakemasu		
16 demasu		
Irregular		
17 ikimasu		
18 shimasu		

To convert from plain form to **masu** form you follow the rules in reverse:

Group 1 verbs: Change **u** to **i** and add **masu**:

kaku → kaki → kakimasu

Remember to be careful, though, with **su** and **tsu** endings – they change to **shi** and **chi**:

hanasu → hana*shi* → hanashimasu
mo*tsu* → mo*chi* → mochimasu

Group 2 verbs: Drop **ru** and add **masu:**

taberu → tabe → tabemasu

Insight
How do I know if a verb is group 1 or group 2?

1 *All* group 2 plain form verbs end in **ru** so if the plain verb *doesn't* end in **ru** (e.g. **su, u, ku, bu, mu, nu, gu**) then it must be a group 1 verb

2 Many group 2 verbs have an **e** ending before the **masu** or **ru** (e.g. **tab*e*ru, n*e*ru, dekak*e*masu, d*e*masu**). Group 1 verbs never have this so **e** indicates a group 2 verb

3 There are a number of verbs ending in either **ru** (plain form) or **imasu** (polite form) which could be either group 1 or group 2 (e.g. **wakaru/wakarimasu** (group 1) and **okiru/okimasu** (group 2). If you know both the plain and **masu** forms then you can work out which it is following this rule:

If it is group 1, then **ru** becomes **ri** (and vice versa – **waka*ru*** → **waka*ri*masu**)
If it is group 2, then **ru** is dropped or added *not* changed (**okiru** → **okimasu**)

Some dictionaries aimed at non-Japanese speakers indicate whether a verb is group 1 or group 2.

Explanation 10.2 Asagohan o taberu mae ni . . .
Before eating breakfast . . .

You are going to learn a number of ways of using the plain dictionary form in this unit. The first of these is **mae ni** (*before*). You have already met **mae ni** in Explanation 4.1 – when used with places it means *in front of*. When used with actions it means *before*. The dictionary form is placed *before* **mae ni** to give the meaning *before doing X*. Here are some examples:

neru mae ni	*before going to bed*
nomu mae ni	*before drinking*

You then continue the sentence with the main verb and it is this verb which decides the *tense* (past, present/future) of the whole statement:

Hondō-san wa neru mae ni itsumo hon o yomimasu	*Mr Hondo always reads a book before going to bed*
Ian-san wa bīru o nomu mae ni bangohan o tabemashita	*Ian ate dinner before drinking beer*

And the title of this unit: Kono wain o nomu mae ni, bīru demo nomimashō! *Before we drink this wine, let's drink beer or something!*

By the way, **demo** after a noun means *something like, or something*.

You can also use **mae ni** after nouns to talk about before events:

asagohan no mae ni	*before breakfast*
ryokō no mae ni	*before the trip*

◆) CD2, TR 28

Use the pictures opposite to talk about sequences of actions using **mae ni**. Speak out loud then listen and practise with the recording.

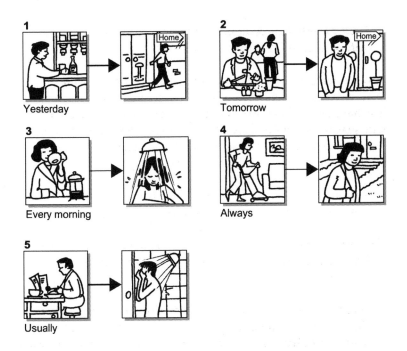

1 Yesterday

2 Tomorrow

3 Every morning

4 Always

5 Usually

Explanation 10.3 Eri-chan wa mō oyogu koto ga dekimasu *Eri can already swim*

Dekimasu means *can, able to*. It is used directly with nouns to talk about things you can do, particularly sports and practical skills, like this:

Rule: *person* **wa** *noun* **ga dekimasu:**
Watashi wa tenisu ga dekimasu	*I can play tennis*
Rie-san wa ryōri ga dekimasu	*Rie can cook*

You can also use it with the dictionary form of verbs to talk about what you can do. To do this you add **koto** to the verb (this effectively changes the verb into a noun):

Rule: *person* **wa** *verb* **koto ga dekimasu:**
Eri-chan wa oyogu koto ga dekimasu	*Eri can swim*
Watashi wa nihongo o kaku koto ga dekimasen	*I can't write Japanese*

Put your learning into practise by working out and saying out loud these statements:

1 Robert can't drink beer.
2 Rie can speak English.
3 Naoe can speak English *a little*. (**sukoshi**)
4 Roger can read a Japanese newspaper.
5 I can't eat raw fish. (**sashimi**)

Explanation 10.4 Bīru o nomu koto ga suki desu
I like drinking beer

You already know **suki desu** and its negative and past tenses (Explanation 7.3). You can use the dictionary form to say what you like (or don't like) doing in this way:

Rule: *person* **wa** *verb* **koto ga suki desu:**

Rie-san wa ryōri o suru koto ga suki desu	*Rie likes cooking*
Katie-san wa ryōri o suru koto ga suki ja arimasen	*Katie doesn't like cooking*

Insight
Did you notice that the structure is very similar to Explanation 10.3 except you use **suki** in place of **dekimasu**? In the same way, you can replace **suki** with any adjective to add a description to what you do.

Here are some examples:

Watashi wa nihongo o hanasu koto ga jōzu desu ga nihongo o yomu koto ga heta desu	*I am good at speaking Japanese but bad at reading Japanese*
Yuki-san wa sūgaku o benkyō suru koto ga tokui desu ga eigo ga nigate desu	*Yuki's strong point is studying maths but her weak point is English*

| Nihonjin to hanasu koto ga omoshiroi desu | *Speaking with Japanese people is interesting* |

To consolidate this, can you make complete sentences from the words given?

Example: Rie, shinbun o yomu, suki → **Rie-san wa shinbun o yomu koto ga suki desu**

1 Katie, tomodachi to, asobu, suki
2 Eri, shukudai o suru, suki ja arimasen
3 Nihonjin to au (*meet*), omoshiroi
4 Naoe, piano o hiku (*playing piano*), jōzu
5 Roger, kanji o kaku, tokui

Explanation 10.5 Saying your plans and intentions using *tsumori desu*

You use the dictionary form plus **tsumori desu** to talk about your plans or intentions or to ask someone else their's. Here are some examples:

Raigetsu atarashii kuruma o kau tsumori desu	*Next month I intend to buy a new car*
Konban uchi de gorogoro suru tsumori desu	*Tonight I intend to chill out at home*
Kurisumasu ni Amerika ni kaeru tsumori desu ka	*Are you planning to go back to America for Christmas?*

◆ **CD2, TR 29**

Can you ask some questions using these verbs: **kaku** (*write*), **nomu** (*drink*), **hataraku** (*work*), **suru** (*do*), **miru** (*watch*)? When you have tried for yourself, listen to the recording, pause and speak out loud:

1 Are you planning to write a letter (**tegami**) to your mother?
2 Do you intend to drink beer tonight?
3 Do you plan to work until late every day?
4 Are you planning to play golf with Naoe on Sunday?
5 Do you intend to watch the football (**sakkā**) tonight?

Explanation 10.6 Giving reasons using *kara* and *no de*

When you give a reason for something in English it often involves words such as 'because', 'since', 'therefore' or 'so'. Look at these examples:

Since I have a headache I am staying at home today
I am staying at home today because I have a headache
I have a headache so I am staying at home today

The reason (or cause) is the headache, the result is I am staying at home.

In Japanese, the sentence order is more rigid. First, you give the reason or cause and then the result. You attach **kara** or **no de** to the end of the reason like this:

Atama ga itai kara kyō wa uchi ni imasu
Atama ga itai no de kyō wa uchi ni imasu

Both these sentences mean *I'm staying at home today because I have a headache.*

Insight

The important thing to remember is that you say the reason first (*headache*), attach **kara** or **no de** then say the result (*staying at home*). It can help to think of **kara** and **no de** as 'therefore' or 'so' rather than 'because' in order to get the order right:

Atama ga itai kara kyō wa   *I have a headache <u>therefore</u>*
  uchi ni imasu   *I'm staying at home today*

You normally use the plain form of the verb with **kara** and **no de** (although you can use **masu** verbs with **kara** in more formal situations). Here are some short examples:

Ōsutoraria ni iku node	*because I will go to Australia*
itsumo kōhī o nomu kara	*because I always drink coffee*
mainichi shinbun o yomu kara	*I read a paper every day therefore*

When using **i** adjectives (including **tai** – *I want to*) you don't need **desu** (but can use it in more formal situations). Here are some examples:

kono hon wa omoshiroi node	*this book is interesting therefore*
rainen Nihon ni ikitai kara	*since I want to go to Japan*

When using **na** adjectives and nouns the rule varies for **kara** and **no de** like this:

- with **no de** use adjective/noun + **na**:

sensei na no de	*because she is a teacher*
kirei na no de	*since she is beautiful*

- with **kara** use adjective or noun with the plain form of **desu** – **da** (you can also use **desu** in more formal situations):

sensei da kara	*because she is a teacher*
kirei desu kara	*since she is beautiful*

You're going to put this into practice now. The table has three columns with a reason, a connector (**kara** or **no de**) and a result. Can you create and say out loud full sentences as in the example? Give the English meaning too.

reason	connector	result
e.g. **byōki desu**	kara	kaisha ni ikimasen
1 Nihon ni ikimasu	no de	mainichi Nihongo o benkyō shimasu
2 sensei ga yasashii desu	kara	eigo ga suki desu
3 Miki-san wa kirei desu	no de	Roger-san wa suki desu
4 mainichi uchi o sōji shimasu	kara	itsumo kirei desu

Example:

Byōki da kara kaisha ni ikimasen   *I'm ill so I'm not going*
                                                    to work

Check your answers then let's take this challenge one step further –
this time you are going to create Japanese sentences from English
prompts as in the example:

reason	connector	result
e.g. *I am working late*	**kara**	*I'm not going to see the film*
5 *I am no good at sports*	**no de**	*I am not a member of the tennis club*
6 *that restaurant is expensive* (**takai**)	**kara**	*let's eat at home*
7 *Katie is a skilful teacher*	**no de**	*her classes* (**kurasu**) *are enjoyable*
8 *my parents are coming to Japan tomorrow*	**kara**	*I want to clean my apartment*

Example:

Osoku made hataraku kara   *Because I'm working late*
  eiga o mimasen   *I'm not going to see the film*

Insight
Is there any difference between kara and no de?

Generally not; they are two words meaning the same thing
(like 'because' and 'since'). However, if you are asking,
suggesting, telling or inviting someone to do something it is
more common to use **kara**.

You can also use **kara** in answer to the question 'why'. In Japanese this is **dōshite** or **naze**. We shall use **dōshite**:

Dōshite heya o sōji shimasu **ka**	*Why are you cleaning your room?*
Ryōshin ga kuru *kara desu*	<u>*Because*</u> *my parents are coming*
Dōshite eiga o mi ni ikimasen ka	*Why aren't you going to see the film?*
Osoku made hataraku *kara desu*	<u>*Because*</u> *I am working until late*

Explanation 10.7 Asking for or giving justification (*you see*)

You use the plain form followed by **no desu** (often shortened to **n desu**) to give an explanation or justification for an action. You use **no desu ka** (**n desu ka**) to ask for an explanation. It is much softer than **kara** and may not always have a specific meaning in English. Here are some concrete examples to help you:

Dōshite machi ni iku no desu ka	*Why are going to town?*
Tomodachi ni au n desu	*'Cos I'm meeting my friend*

You could also say:

Tomodachi ni au kara desu	*Because I'm meeting my friend*
Dōshite osoku okiru n desu ka	*Why do you get up late?*
Maiban osoku made bīru o nomu n desu	*I drink beer until late every night, you see*

In Explanation 5.9 you learned the phrase **dō shita n desu ka** (*what's wrong?*) which uses **n desu ka** because you are asking for an explanation. You can reply with **n desu** – **atama ga itai n desu** (*I have a headache, you see*) – to give an explanation.

Explanation 10.8 Stating your interest using *kyōmi ga aru*

You use this phrase when talking about what you are interested in. Use particle **ni** after the thing you have an interest in:

Nihon no koto ni kyōmi ga arimasu	*I have an interest in Japanese things*
Supōtsu ni zenzen kyōmi ga arimasen	*I have no interest in sport*
Minami Amerika ni kyōmi ga aru no de ikitai desu	*I have an interest in South America so I want to go*

Explanation 10.9 Levels of speech in Japanese: an introduction

Every country and culture uses different types of language depending on the situation ('hi' to a friend, 'hello' to be more polite, 'pleased to meet you' on first acquaintance). You have learned about the plain form in this unit and in doing this have also been introduced to one of the layers of formal and informal language in Japanese.

In Japanese, as well as using different words and phrases for particular situations, you also use different verbs or forms of verb depending on the formality or informality of the situation or on the status of the person you are speaking with. Japanese people use *respectful language* (**sonkeigo**) when speaking to higher status people and *humble language* (**kenjōgo**) when referring to themselves and family in formal situations. Neutral polite language or **teineigo** (**masu/desu**) is used when there is no need to show specific respect to someone and is safe for non-Japanese people to use in most situations.

Another interesting point is that there is a gender divide in language use (and this is certainly not exclusive to Japan – women in general tend to use more polite, 'softer' language). Therefore, plain forms are used much more by men and if women do use them they tend to make them sound less abrupt by using **wa** and **no** at the end of the sentence. **Wa** has the effect of making the statement either softly assertive or friendly and can be used with plain and polite forms. Here are some examples:

Watashi mo Amerika ni iku wa　　*I'm also going to America*
Miki-san wa hazukashigari　　　*Miki isn't shy*
　ja nai wa

No is used by women (and children and sometimes men too) to ask for or give explanations (like **no desu**) or for emphasis:

Kono eiga wa omoshiroi no　　　*This film is interesting*

Why are you going home?

('cos) I've got a headache

Main dialogue

🔊 **CD2, TR 30**

Roger phones Miki to propose a second date. As with the previous unit, familiarize yourself with the new vocabulary first then close the book and listen to the recording at least three times, each time for a different purpose: listen out for the new words, listen out for the new structures, listen out for general meaning then try pausing and repeating section by section. Once you have done this, open the book and see if you can answer the questions.

Miki	Moshi moshi.
Roger	Moshi moshi, Miki-san desu ka. Roger desu ga . . .
Miki	Roger-san! Konnichiwa.
Roger	Konnichiwa. **Ano ne**, konban **hima** desu ka.
Miki	Konban desu ka. Konban wa chotto . . . Rie-san to eiga o mimasu. Miru mae ni resutoran de taberu tsumori desu.
Roger	Sō desu ka. Jā, doyōbi no ban wa dō desu ka.
Miki	Doyōbi wa ii desu yo. Nani o shimashō ka.
Roger	Tenisu o shimashō ka.
Miki	Tenisu desu ka. Tenisu wa amari dekimasen.
Roger	**Jā, badominton** wa dō desu ka.
Miki	**Nē**, Roger-san, sumimasen ga supōtsu o suru koto ga amari suki ja nai desu.
Roger	[*Sounding disappointed*] **Ā, sō desu ka**.
Miki	**Demo** supōtsu o miru koto wa suki desu **yo**! Doyōbi no ban **yakyūjō** de **yakyū** o mi ni ikimashū ka.
Roger	[*Brightening up*] Sō shimashō!
Miki	**Yakyūjō** no chikaku ni **iroirona** resutoran ga arimasu. **Yakyū** o miru mae ni **shabu-shabu** demo tabemashō!
Roger	[*Sounding doubtful*] **Shabu shabu** wa **niku** desu ne. Boku wa **bejitarian** na no de **niku** o taberu koto ga dekimasen.
Miki	**Sakana** wa dō desu ka.
Roger	**Sakana** wa daijōbu desu. Taberu koto ga dekiru n desu.
Miki	**Jā, yakyū** no mae ni **sushiya-san** de tabemashō!

QV

ano ne	*hey, erm (friendly)*
hima (na)	*free*
jā	*ok, right, in that case*
badominton	*badminton*

True or false?

Write either **O** (**maru** = true) or **X** (**batsu** = false) next to these statements:

1 Miki-san wa Roger-san ni denwa shimashita.
2 Miki-san wa konban hima ja arimasen.
3 Roger-san wa tenisu ya badominton o shitai desu.
4 Miki-san wa yakyū ga suki ja arimasen.
5 Roger-san wa sakana o taberu koto ga dekimasen.

Japanese questions

Write your answers in Japanese (there isn't one right way of writing these answers, by the way, but the answers in the back model one correct version):

6 Miki-san wa konban nani o suru tsumori desu ka.
7 Miki-san wa dōshite yakyū o mitai desu ka.
8 Roger-san wa shabu shabu o taberu koto ga dekimasu ka.
9 Dōshite desu ka.
10 Doko de taberu tsumori desu ka.

English questions

11 Why doesn't Miki want to play tennis or badminton?
12 What does she suggest doing instead and why?
13 What does she suggest doing before that?
14 What does Miki say there is near the stadium?
15 What new piece of information have you learned about a) Miki and b) Roger?

Learn to say: My plans

◀) **CD2, TR 31**

On their second date, Miki and Roger get on much better and Miki tells him about her plans for next year. Listen to the recording, pausing and copying (or read the script in 'chunks').

Insight

Focus particularly on pronunciation and see if you can say the speech out loud from memory or with just a few prompts. This is a good activity to do on a long journey!

Miki	Rainen Minami Amerika ni ikitai no de ima Supeingo o naratteimasu. Supeingo o hanasu koto ga mada amari jōzu ja arimasen ga Minami Amerikajin to hanasu koto wa totemo omoshiroi to omoimasu. Soshite Supein no ryōri mo totemo suki desu ga tsukuru koto wa dekimasen. Konban machi de tomodachi to atte, oishii resutoran de Supein no ryōri o taberu tsumori desu.
Miki	*Next year I want to go to South America and so I am learning Spanish at the moment. I am not very good at speaking Spanish yet but I think that speaking with South American people will be very interesting. Also I really like Spanish food but I can't make it. Tonight I plan to meet a friend in town and eat Spanish food in a nice restaurant.*

Activities

Activity 10.1

You are going to rewrite the 'learn to say' passage so that you can say something different! The passage that follows has various parts underlined. Change these to include the following information:

1 You want to go to Japan next year so you are learning Japanese.
2 You're not very good at Japanese yet but you are interested in Japanese things.
3 You like Japanese food as well but can't make it.
4 You plan to meet a friend in town tomorrow and eat Japanese food at an famous restaurant.

When you have done this and checked your answers, practise saying this out loud – can you do it without looking at the book?

Rainen <u>Minami Amerika</u> (1) ni ikitai no de ima <u>Supeingo</u> (1) o naratteimasu. <u>Supeingo</u> (2) o hanasu koto ga mada amari jōzu ja arimasen ga <u>Minami Amerikajin to hanasu koto wa totemo omoshiroi to omoimasu</u> (2). Soshite <u>Supein</u> (3) no ryōri mo totemo suki desu ga tsukuru koto wa dekimasen. <u>Konban</u> (4) machi de tomodachi to atte, ocshii (4) resutoran de <u>Supein</u> (4) no ryōri o taberu tsumori desu.

Activity 10.2

◀) CD2, TR 32

Miki and Roger separately report back to 'matchmaker' Rie about their second date. Listen to one at a time and select the pictures in order that they happened to match:

| A | Miki's version of events |
| B | Roger's version |

Activity 10.3

Can you supply the correct verb and ending to give sense to these sentences. Use the endings **koto ga dekimasu, tsumori desu, koto ga suki desu, koto ga jōzu desu.**

1 Eri-san wa _____. (*Eri can swim*)
2 Miki-san wa supōtsu o _____. (*Miki likes watching sports*)
3 Ian-san wa konban Indo ryōri o _____. (*Ian plans to make Indian food tonight*)

4 Katie-san wa Indo ryōri o _____. (*Katie enjoys/likes eating Indian food*)

5 Roger-san wa tenisu ya bōringu o _____.
(*Roger is good at playing tennis and bowling*)

6 Hondō-san wa konban osoku made _____.
(*Mr Hondo can't work late tonight*)

Activity 10.4

Using **kara** or **no de** can you give reasons for the following situations as in the example:

Example: You're off work because you have a bad throat

Nodo ga itai no de shigoto o yasundeimasu (**shigoto ni itteimasen**)

1 You're off work because you are sick.
2 You plan to make Indian food because Katie likes it.
3 Roger is good at playing tennis because he practises every day.
4 You came to Japan because you want to study Japanese.
5 Miki is drinking coffee now because she has a headache.

Introduction to kanji 漢字 (4)

In this section you will learn:

- 15 verb kanji
- more about kanji radicals
- more kanji compound words

Start reading

The kanji you will learn in this section are used with the verbs you have learned in Units 2 and 8. Here are five kanji broken down into components with stories to link them to their meaning. Can you match each story and meaning with the correct kanji?

1 言   **4** 聞

2 食   **5** 見

3 売

Story 1   can you see a pile of earth (土) on top of a table (兀)? At the table-top sale one person was *selling* earth. Meaning: *to sell*

Story 2   can you see gates (門) and an ear (耳)? The nosey neighbour keeps her ear at the gate (door) to *listen* out for any gossip. Meaning: *to listen, hear*

Story 3   can you see mouth (口) with four horizontal lines rising from it? Those are the words that the mouth is *saying*. Meaning: *to say*

Story 4   this kanji has a roof (人) on top, white (白) in the middle and a 'squashed' fire (火) below. White symbolizes rice which is being cooked in the home to *eat*. Meaning: *to eat*

Story 5   an eye (目) running around on human legs (儿) is a *looking* machine! Meaning: *to look, see, watch*

Here are the new kanji again with their meanings:

言 *to say*   聞 *to listen*

食 *to eat*   見 *to see, watch, look*

売 *to sell*

Kanji radicals

Remember that these are components of a kanji that can give a very general meaning to the whole kanji? Here are a selection with their meanings:

儿   *human legs*

人   *person*, also 'squashed' into a roof on top (食) and a 'leaning T' on the left side (休)

口　*mouth/opening*

土　*earth*

士　*samurai warrior.* Looks like earth but has longer 'arms'

女　*woman*

彳　*to go,* the '*going person*' (see *person* earlier in the list)

水　*water.* Looks like this on left side 氵 – three splashes

心　*heart.* (Can you see two sides of heart?). Used in 'emotion' and 'thought' words

日　*sun/day/time*

月　*moon* or *flesh* (from 肉　niku meaning meat)

木　*tree* or *wood* (material)

火　*fire.* Looks like this when written at bottom 灬 (e.g. 黒 black)

牛　*cow*

貝　*shellfish.* This is an eye on small animal legs

言　*to say, words*

Reading activity 10.1

Here are some new kanji. Can you identify their radical? They will either be on the left or at the bottom:

1 休 *rest*　　　　　**6** 海 *sea*

2 物 *thing*　　　　**7** 畑 *cultivated field*

3 買 *buy*　　　　　**8** 時 *time*

4 吹 *blow*　　　　**9** 行 *go*

5 思 *think*　　　　**10** 背 *back, height*

Complex kanji: More verbs

Here are a further 10 verbs which are made up of simpler kanji components:

行 *to go.* This has the 'going person' radical on the left

読 *to read.* You can see *words* on the left (radical) and *to sell* on the right. Words for sale are books for *reading*

話 *to speak, talk.* Words (radical) on the left, *mouth with forked tongue* on right – the tongue is *speaking* words

買 *to buy.* A horizontal *eye* looks carefully at the *shellfish* to decide which to *buy*

休 *to rest, holiday.* A *person resting* under a *tree*

出 *to exit, go out.* Two sets of *mountains* – find the mountain pass to *exit*

入 *to enter.* This is a simple kanji and a radical in its own right. Be careful not to confuse it with person 人

飲 *to drink.* *Eat* is on the left and can you see a person raising a glass up to *drink* on the right?

書 *to write.* The lower part looks like sun but in fact is from this kanji 曰 meaning to utter (say). Think of it as a condensed form of 言 with the words about to come out. The upper part was developed from the picture of a brush! Here is a drawing to help you. So *spoken words* are *written* with a *brush*:

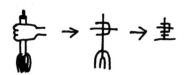

分 *to understand* (also *minute, divide*). This consists of the number 8 (八) and the kanji for sword (刀). The *sword divides* up time into *minutes*. You might *divide* up a difficult kanji into parts to make it easier *to understand*!

Reading activity 10.2

You have now been exposed to 15 kanji for verbs. How well can you recall them? Here they are – what do they mean in English?

1 食	**2** 飲	**3** 書	**4** 出	**5** 入
6 言	**7** 話	**8** 売	**9** 読	**10** 見
11 買	**12** 分	**13** 聞	**14** 行	**15** 休

Kanji compounds

There are lots of new words that can be created by combining two or three of these new kanji words. A useful new kanji for creating more words is 'thing' – 物. This kanji basically turns verbs into nouns. Here are two examples:

食 *eat* → 食べ物 tabemono = food
飲 *drink* → 飲み物 nomimono = a drink

Now try Reading activity 10.3, which identifies lots more compound words.

Reading activity 10.3

Here are some more compound kanji words (1–10) using kanji from this and the previous unit. Can you match them with their English meaning(a-j)? Some have hiragana elements but simply focus on the kanji meanings:

1 入口　　　　　　**a** reading

2 出口　　　　　　**b** buyer

3 買い物　　　　　**c** entrance

4 見物　　　　　　**d** exit

5 売り物　　　　　**e** drinking water

6 読書　　　　　　**f** shopping

7 休日　　　　　　**g** sightseeing

8 売買　　　　　　**h** items for sale

9 飲水　　　　　　**i** holiday

10 買手　　　　　**j** buying and selling

Insight

Be careful not to confuse 入口 (*entrance*) with 人口 (*population*).

Reading activity 10.4

You are now going to try to read simple sentences which use some of the kanji from this and previous units. Read them out loud and work out the meanings. The reading of the kanji is written in **furigana** over the top.

1 あさごはん を 食(た)べます。

2 ときどき しん聞(ぶん) を 読(よ)みます。

3 まい日(にち) nyūsu を 聞(き)きます。

4 ちちと terebi を 見(み)ます。

5 明日(あした) 日本(にほん)に 行(い)きます。

6 日本(にほん)ご を 話(はな)しました。

しろ　　ほん　　か

7 おも白い 本 を 買いました。

8 土曜日に 買い物を します。
<small>どようび</small>　　<small>か</small>　<small>もの</small>

9 日曜日に くるまを 売りました。
<small>にちようび</small>　　　　　　<small>う</small>

10 まい日 かんじを 書いてみます。
<small>にち</small>　　　　　<small>か</small>

Reading challenge

Here is the main dialogue from Unit 2 rewritten in hiragana with kanji words as appropriate. All katakana words are written in rōmaji. As with the previous units try reading it with or without the recording to help you:

Robert is interviewing Mr Hondo about his daily routine as part of his article on work/home balance.

Mr Hondo	まい日 六じに おきます。あさご はん に 大てい tōsuto を 食べま す。そして kōhī を 飲みます。でん しゃで じむしょに 行きます。い つも 八じに つきます。おそく まで はたらきます。そして たび たび じむしょの 人と resutoran で ばんごはんを 食べます。
Robert	なんじに かえりますか。

Mr Hondo	十じ、十一じ ごろ です。つまと terebi を 見ます。そして ねます
Robert	日曜日に なにを しますか。
Mr Hondo	ときどき じむしょの 人と gorufu をします が 大ていかぞくと うちで ごろごろ します。

Final words on reading

You have learned 16 single kanji in this unit as well as 12 kanji compound words and 16 radicals. Review these before you move on to the reading section in the next unit.

End-of-unit challenge

Here is a table of dictionary form verbs. Your challenge is to convert them into their **masu** form. The group is given only when there is no other way of working it out. Many are new verbs – you don't need to remember them, the purpose of the challenge is to practise forming **masu** from verbs you might look up in a dictionary. Look back to Explanation 10.1 if you need to review the rules.

dictionary form	English	masu form
tsutaeru	*report, tell*	1
ireru	*put in*	2
dasu	*take out*	3
okureru	*be late*	4
gambaru (group 1)	*try hard*	5
hashiru (group 1)	*run*	6
aruku	*walk*	7
tsukau	*use*	8
oku	*put*	9
arau	*wash*	10
kariru (group 2)	*borrow*	11

11

Gaikoku ni sundeita koto ga arimasu
I have lived abroad

In this unit you will learn
- *more about talking in the past (plain form)*
- *how to talk about your experiences*
- *how to give advice*
- *more about describing routines and actions*
- *how to make comparisons*
- *how to quantify your actions*

Getting started

The main purpose of this unit is to explain to you the past plain form of verbs and adjectives (actually you know the adjective plain form already but more of this later). The plain form, like the polite **masu** form has past and negative tenses (*I do*, *I did*, *I don't do*, *I didn't do*) all of which are used in plain or informal language as well as having other uses too.

Opening activity

Let's start with how to make the past plain form. You'll be pleased to know that you already have the tools with which to do this. Do you remember learning the **te** form (Unit 8)? All you need to do to make the plain past form is change the **te** ending to ta (and the **de** ending to **da**):

tabete → tabeta *I ate*
katte → katta *I bought*
itte → itta *I went*
asonde → asonda *I socialized*

Now you try. Put these **te** forms into the plain past and give the English meaning too.

te form	plain past	English
1 mite		
2 okite		
3 nete		
4 kaite		
5 kiite		
6 nonde		
7 yonde		
8 hanashite		
9 ryōri shite		
10 kaette		

Build-up activity

◀) CD2, TR 33

Now let's put these plain past verbs into sentences. Complete the sentences, speak out loud then listen to and repeat the recording:

Example: kinō, Ōsaka (yesterday I went to Osaka) → kinō Ōsaka ni itta

1 senshū, eiga (*last week I saw a film*)
2 kesa, 7 ji (*this morning I got up at 7*)
3 yūbe, 12 ji (*last night I went to bed at about 12*)
4 tomodachi, tegami (*I wrote a letter to a friend*)
5 tomodachi, ongaku (*I listened to music with a friend*)
6 yūbe, bīru, ippai (*last night I drank lots of beer*)
7 Nihongo, manga (*I read a Japanese comic book*)
8 atarashii, sensei (*I talked to the new teacher*)

9 heya, Indo ryōri (*I made Indian food in my room/lodgings*)
10 kinō, ryōshin, Igirisu (*yesterday my parents went back to England*)

Key sentences

Go over the vocabulary and try and work out the meanings of the sentence for yourself first.

··
Insight
From now on the dictionary form of all new verbs will also be given in the vocabulary.
··

1 Yūbe sushiya-san de sushi o **ippai** tabeta.
2 **Gaikoku** e itta **koto ga arimasen.**
3 Mainichi bangohan o tabeta **ato de** terebi o mimasu.
4 Kono **kusuri** o nonda **hō ga ii desu yo.**
5 Pātī de wain o **nondari** tomodachi to **hanashitari** shimashita.
6 Tōkyō **no hō ga** Rondon **yori** ōkii desu.
7 Amerika ni sundeita **toki** mainichi eigo o hanashita.
8 Kanji o **zembu wasurete shimatta.**

ippai	*lots*
gaikoku	*abroad, foreign country*
koto ga arimasen	*I have never*
ato de	*after*
kusuri	*medicine*
hō ga ii desu	*you ought to, should, you'd better*
yo	*you know, hadn't you!* (assertion)
pātī	*party*
nondari . . . hanashitari	*drank and talked*
a **no hō ga** *b* **yori**	*A is … er* (comparison) *than B*
toki	*when*
zembu	*all*
wasurete (wasureru)	*forget*
shimatta (shimau)	*gone and …, completely*

QUICK VOCAB

English translation of the key sentences

1 *Last night I ate lots of sushi at the sushi bar.*
2 *I have never been abroad.*
3 *Every day after eating dinner I watch TV.*
4 *You'd better take this medicine, hadn't you!*
5 *At the party I drank wine and talked to friends.*
6 *Tokyo is bigger than London.*
7 *When I lived in America I spoke English every day.*
8 *I have completely forgotten all my kanji.*

Language explanations

Here is a list of the grammar points you will learn in Unit 11:

1 introduction to the plain past form

Applications of the past plain form:

2 **ta** form + **koto ga arimasu/arimasen** – talking about your experiences
3 **ta** form + **ato de** – after doing something (review **mae** and **te kara** too)
4 **ta** form + **hō ga ii desu**: you ought to/should – giving advice
5 listing actions in random order or giving examples

Also:

6 making comparaisons using **yori** and **hō ga**
7 using **toki** to say when
8 **te** form + **shimau** – to have completed something
9 'amount' words with verbs (**ippai, takusan, sukoshi, yoku, daibu, zembu**)
10 past time expressions

You will also use the following new words in the explanations but they will be provided in the text when you need them.

Fujisan	*Mount Fuji*
konsāto	*concert*
sugu	*straightaway*
yasai	*vegetables*
mizu	*water*
kurisumasu	*Christmas*
kōcha	*black tea*
kowashite (kowasu)	*to break*
otosu (otoshite)	*lose, drop*
tsukareru (tsukarete)	*tired*

Explanation 11.1 Introduction to the past plain form

You have already learned how to form the plain past form in the opening activity (change **te** to **ta**). You can also make past and present plain forms from the **teimasu** (*doing* – Unit 9). You change **imasu** to its plain dictionary form **iru** and its plain past form ita:

tabeteimasu	→ tabeteiru	*am eating*
	→ tabeteita	*was eating*

You try. Change these **teimasu** verbs into their plain present and past forms:

Example: hanashiteimasu → hanashiteiru (talking) → hanashiteita (was talking)

1 nondeimasu
2 kaiteimasu
3 sundeimasu
4 itteimasu
5 shiteimasu

Explanation 11.2 Gaikoku ni sundeita koto ga arimasu
I have lived abroad

You use the past plain form with **koto ga arimasu** to talk about experiences you have had (or not had – **arimasen**). It translates into English as 'I have' or 'I haven't (I have never)'. Look at how it differs from the simple past:

Gaikoku ni ikimashita	*I went abroad*
Gaikoku ni itta koto ga arimasu	*I have been abroad*
Nihon ni ikimasen deshita	*I didn't go to Japan*
Nihon ni itta koto ga arimasen	*I haven't been to Japan*

◄) CD2, TR 34

Put your learning into practice now by putting these sentences into Japanese. Say out loud then listen to the recording to check and practise speaking:

1 I have eaten raw fish.
2 I have never seen Mount Fuji.
3 I have written letters in Japanese.
4 I have never read a Japanese newspaper.
5 I haven't been to South America.

Explanation 11.3 Bangohan o tabeta ato de
After eating dinner

Ato de means *after* and is placed after the past plain form of the verb:

kōhī o nonda ato de	*after drinking coffee*
uchi ni kaetta ato de	*after returning home*

It can also be used after nouns, especially events, and then you need to place **no** in between:

konsāto no ato de	*after the concert*
pātī no ato de	*after the party*

286

Insight

Do you remember learning te form with **kara** to mean 'after'? (Explanation 8.3). There is a slight difference in meaning although in most situations they mean pretty much the same thing. However, **te kara** carries the nuance of 'from, since' and is often used in situations where you have been doing 'B' since 'A' happened:

Nihon ni kite kara,   *Since coming to Japan (A) I have*
  Nihongo o benkyō shiteimasu   *been learning Japanese (B)*

Ato de, by way of contrast, is a definite 'after one action finishes the next begins':

Nihon ni tsuita ato de haha   *After I arrived in Japan I wrote a*
  ni tegami o kakimashita   *letter to my Mum*

However, in most cases you can use either so don't worry too much about this. Now can you link each of these pairs of clauses with **ato de** to make full sentences:

Example: took a shower, had breakfast → **shawā o abita ato de asagohan o tabemashita**

1 drank beer, slept straightaway
2 did homework, went to a party
3 went home, phoned (to) a friend
4 after the concert, went to a bar

Explanation 11.4 Giving advice using *hō ga ii desu*

You use the plain past with **hō ga ii desu** to say 'you should, you ought to, you'd better'. Here are some examples:

Kono kusuri o nonda hō ga ii desu yo	*You ought to take (drink) this medicine*
Konban shukudai o shita hō ga ii desu yo	*You'd be better off doing your homework tonight*

Insight

Yo adds even more assertion to the advice (*you know, I tell you*) but doesn't always need to be translated into English.

You can 'soften' the advice to make it more friendly or tentative by changing desu to **deshō**, which has the meaning *probably*:

Denwa shita hō ga ii deshō	*You'd probably better phone*
Kono kusuri o nonda hō ga ii deshō	*You probably ought to take this medicine*

Can you give assertive (use **yo**) advice in the following situations:

1 Eri won't eat her vegetables.
2 Roger is ill, needs sleep.
3 Katie is thirsty, beer or water?
4 Mr Hondo still in office, should go home.
5 Miki needs to contact a friend; email is best.
Now can you give the same advice in a friendlier manner (use **deshō**)?

Explanation 11.5 Bīru o nondari sushi o tabetari shimashita *I drank beer and ate sushi*

You use what is known as the **tari tari** form when you list actions in random order or when you give examples of actions. To form this structure you add **ri** to the **ta** form and end the sequence with **shimasu** (present) or **shimashita** (past). Here are some more examples:

Doyōbi ni kaimono o shitari, eiga o mitari, resutoran de tabetari shimasu	*On Saturdays I (do things like) go shopping, watch films and eat at restaurants*
Yūbe terebi o mitari, denwa o shitari, sōji o shitari shimashita	*Last night I watched TV, made phone calls and did some cleaning*
Pātī de bīru o nondari, wain o nondari shimashita	*At the party I drank drinks such as beer and wine*

Insight

You may have noticed that sometimes the ending is **dari** not **tari**. This happens when the verb ends in **da**, such as **nonda** (*drank*) and **yonda** (*read*). These verbs become **non<u>dari</u>**, **yon<u>dari</u>** and so on.

In some situations the **tari tari** form has the meaning 'sometimes . . . sometimes':

Niku o tabetari, sakana o tabetari shimasu	*I sometimes eat meat and I sometimes eat fish*

What is the difference between the te ... te and the tari ... tari sequence?

You learned to use the **te** form (Explanation 8.1) when saying a sequence of actions. The difference is that this form of sequence has a rigid order – 'first I did this, then this, then this' – whereas **tari ... tari** has no order and the actions given are just examples. Look at this example for clarity:

Yūbe bangohan o tabete, terebi o mite, soshite uchi o sōji shimashita	*Last night I ate dinner, then watched TV and then cleaned the house*

Yūbe bangohan o tabetari,	*Last night I (did things like)*
terebi o mitari, uchi o	*eat dinner, watch TV and*
sōji shitari shimashita	*clean the house*

Can you give examples of what you do in random sequence using **tari ... tari**? Here are the situations:

1 On Sundays you chill out, read the paper and send (**dasu**) emails.
2 At Christmas (**kurisumasu**) you eat a lot, watch TV, meet up with friends.
3 Last week you studied Japanese, did some shopping and went to Osaka.
4 For breakfast, you sometimes drink coffee and sometimes tea (**kōcha**).

Explanation 11.6 Tōkyō no hō ga Rondon yori ōkii desu
Tokyo is bigger than London

When you make comparisons between two things in English, it is the adjective (describing word) that changes, usually by adding 'er': *bigger, smaller, older, happier.*

In Japanese, the adjective does not change. Instead the 'item' that 'wins' the comparison (it is bigger, smaller ...) has **hō ga** attached to it and the 'item' that 'loses' has **yori** (*than*) attached to it. It is important to remember that these are placed *after* the item they belong to. The structure is:

A **no hō ga** *B* **yori** *adjective* **desu**   (*A is ____er than B*)

(You will also come across this order: *B* **yori** *A* **no hō ga** *adjective* **desu**, but the meaning is the same.)

Look at these examples:

Densha no hō ga basu	*The train is quicker than*
yori hayai desu	*the bus*

Kono jaketto no hō ga sono	*This jacket is more expensive*
jaketto yori takai desu	*than that jacket*
Eiga yori hon no hō ga	*The book was more*
omoshirokatta desu	*interesting than the film*

You can also use verbs in the plain form to make comparisons like this:

| **Densha de iku hō ga basu** | *It is quicker to go by train* |
| **de iku yori hayai desu** | *than by bus* |

Insight

Notice that, with verbs, you don't need **no** after **hō ga**.

If you have established the two comparisons, you can miss out the **yori** part and simply say:

Hon no hō ga omoshirokatta	*The book was more*
desu	*interesting*
Densha de iku hō ga hayai desu	*It is quicker to go by train*

Now can you use this information to make comparisons. You can use **to omoimasu** instead of **desu** if you feel it is a matter of opinion. You are given the adjective to use as in the example:

Example: Tōkyō, Ōsaka, omoshiroi (interesting) → Tōkyō no hō ga Ōsaka yori omoshiroi to omoimasu

1 Roger, Miki, majime (serious)
2 Roger, Miki, supōtsu ga jōzu (good at sports)
3 Yuki, Eri, se ga takai (taller)
4 watching sport, playing sport, tanoshii (enjoyable)
5 drinking beer, drinking water, ii (good/better)

Explanation 11.7 Amerika ni sundeita toki *When I lived in America*

Toki after a plain verb (past or present) means *when* as in these examples:

Amerika ni ita toki Eigo o naraimashita	*When I was in America I learned English*
Nihon ni itta toki Fujisan o mimashita	*When I went to Japan I saw Mount Fuji*
Asagohan o taberu toki itsumo terebi o mimasu	*When I eat breakfast I always watch TV*

You can also use **toki** with nouns – you need **no** in between:

Gakusei no toki Supeingo o benkyō shimashita	*When I was a university student I studied Spanish*

Explanation 11.8 Wasurete shimatta *I've completely forgotten*

The **te** form with **shimau** is used when you have either finished something or done something that you can't undo. So it can sometimes have negative undertones or a sense of regret such as 'I have gone and ...', 'I've totally ...'. Here are some examples:

Takeshi-san wa nete shimatta	*Takeshi fell fast asleep*
Kamera o kowashite shimatta	*I've gone and broken my camera*
Yasai o zembu tabete shimaimashita ka	*Have you eaten up all your vegetables?*
Asagohan o tabeta ato de tegami o kaite shimaimasu	*I will finish the letter after I've had my breakfast*

Here are some situations for you to say in Japanese using the plain form **shimatta**:

1 You've gone and forgotten about your homework.
2 You've gone and lost (**otoshite**) your camera.
3 You've drunk up all your beer.
4 You've finished reading that book.
5 You're totally exhausted (**tsukarete**).

Explanation 11.9 Using quantity words with verbs

You've already used the words **amari** (*not very*), **zenzen** (*not at all, never*) and **sukoshi** (*a little*) to add more information to a verb (these words are called adverbs – they add information to a verb). Here are some examples:

Kōhī o zenzen nomimasen	*I don't drink coffee at all*
Kōhī o amari nomimasen	*I rarely drink coffee (not very much)*
Kōhī o sukoshi nomimasu	*I drink coffee a little*

Notice in these examples that the quantity word is placed between the particle and the verb. You can, however, also place it before the object:

Zenzen kōhī o nomimasen	*I never drink coffee*

Insight

There isn't much difference in meaning between the two examples but whereas in English we use intonation to emphasize something, in Japanese you use sentence order to achieve this with the more important or emphasized information normally coming towards the end of the sentence.

Here is a short list of useful quantity words for you to use and refer to. You have heard or read some of these in this and previous units.

zenzen (+ negative)	*(not) at all, never*
amari (+ negative)	*not very, hardly*
sukoshi	*a little*
tokidoki	*sometimes*
yoku	*often, well*
daibu(n)	*greatly, quite a lot*
takusan	*a lot*
ippai	*loads, full amount*
zembu	*all*

QUICK VOCAB

Look at the difference between **takusan** and **ippai** in these examples:

Sushi o takusan tabemashita	*I ate a lot of sushi*
Sushi o ippai tabemashita	*I ate my fill of sushi*
	(implying I was full up)

> ### Insight
> You can use **ippai** to say you are full up or you don't want any more:
>
> Sumimasen, mō ippai desu   *Thank you (sorry) but I'm full*

Now you try saying sentences with quantity words. Say them out loud and place the quantity word between the particle and the verb:

1 I read quite a lot of the Japanese newspaper.
2 I sent loads of emails.
3 I often go to Osaka.
4 I ate up (use **shimatta**) all the rice.
5 I watched a little of the baseball.

Explanation 11.10 Past time expressions

In Explanation 2.6, you learned time expressions for week, month and year. Let's now add past time expressions to these (you know some already). Read through this chart and refer to it when necessary.

kinō	*yesterday*
kesa	*this morning*
yūbe	*last night*
senshū	*last week*
sengetsu	*last month*
kyonen	*last year*

> ### Insight
> If you want to say *yesterday morning*, *last Saturday* and so on, insert **no** between the two words like this: kinō no asa, senshū no doyōbi.

Main dialogue

◄) CD2, TR 35

Miki goes to a party held by a university student friend and meets Takeshi. Listen to their conversation and see if you can answer the questions.

Insight

Remember to read through the vocabulary then to listen several times, giving yourself different targets each time (e.g. listen for specific vocabulary, listen for new structures, listen for general meaning, listen for information relating to the questions).

Takeshi	Miki-san wa **daigakusei** ja nai desu ne.
Miki	Ē. **Sannen** mae ni **sotsugyō** shiteimashita kara. Soshite **ninen kan** Amerika de nihongo o oshietari, ryokō shitari shimashita.
Takeshi	Amerika desu ka. Boku mo Amerika ni itta koto ga ari masu. Kyonen no **natsu** boku no **bando** to **rokku tsuā** o shiteimashita. Totemo subarashikatta desu.
Miki	Doko de **ensō** shimashita ka.
Takeshi	Ē to, Minneapolis, Milwaukee, Chicago …
Miki	Chicago desu ka. Bando no **namae** wa nan desu ka.
Takeshi	**Rabu rabu bōizu** desu.
Miki	**Are!** Mita koto ga arimasu yo! Chicago ni sundeita toki iroirona konsāto ni ikimashita. **Rabu rabu bōizu** wa **hontō ni** subarashikatta wa!
Takeshi	Mita n desu ka. Shinjirarenai!
Miki	Nē, ano, **jazu** to **rokku** no **mikkusu** desu ne. Watashi wa totemo suki deshita.
Takeshi	Arigatō. **Jazu** ga suki desu ka.
Miki	Hai, **poppusu** yori **jazu** no hō ga suki desu.

Unit 11 **I have lived abroad** 295

Takeshi	Boku mo suki desu. Ano, **roppongi** ni totemo ii **jazu** kurabu ga arimasu. Kono **pātī** no ato de issho ni ikimashō ka.
Miki	**Pātī** no ato desu ka. Chotto osoi wa.
Takeshi	Jā, wain o nonde shimaimashō ka. Sorekara ikimashō.
Miki	Ii desu ne!

daigakusei	*university student*
sannen	*3 years*
sotsugyō shimasu	*to graduate*
ninen kan	*2-year period*
natsu	*summer*
bando	*band*
rokku tsuā	*rock tour*
ensō shimasu	*perform*
ē to	*er, erm*
namae	*name*
rabu rabu bōizu	*Love Love Boys* (name of Takeshi's band)
are!	*hey!, what!*
hontō ni	*really*
jazu	*jazz*
mikkusu	*mix*
poppusu	*pop music*
Roppongi	trendy area of Tokyo
pātī	*party*

True or false?

Write either **O** (**maru** = true) or **X** (**batsu** = false) next to these statements:

1 Miki-san wa daigakusei desu.
2 Takeshi-san wa kyonen Amerika de ensō shimashita.
3 Miki-san wa sannen kan Amerika ni sundeimashita.
4 Miki-san wa jazu yori poppusu no hō ga suki desu.
5 Miki-san wa jazu kurabu ni ikitakunai desu.

Japanese questions

Write your answers in Japanese:

6 Miki-san wa doko de Takeshi-san ni aimashita ka.
7 Takeshi-san no bando no namae wa nan desu ka.
8 Miki-san wa Amerika de nani o shimashita ka.
9 Takeshi-san wa itsu Amerika no rokku tsuā o shimashita ka.
10 Takeshi-san wa dōshite Roppongi ni ikitai desu ka.

English questions

11 When did Miki graduate from university?
12 When did Miki see Takeshi's band and what did she think of them?
13 What type of music do they play?
14 What music does Miki prefer over pop music?
15 When does Takeshi suggest they go to the jazz club?

Learn to say: Plain speech

◀) **CD2, TR 36**

Here is your chance to listen to and say a short piece in plain speech. Listen to the recording as Takeshi tells his friend Robert about his night out with Miki then pause it sentence by sentence and practise saying it out loud.

Yūbe totemo sutekina hito ni atta. Namae wa Miki desu. Miki-san wa jazu ga suki dakara issho ni boku no sukina jazu kurabu ni itta. Sono kurabu de bīru o nondari, hanashitari, ii ongaku o kiitari shita. Totemo tanoshikatta. Osoku made kurabu ni ite soshite niji goro uchi ni kaetta. Mata Miki-san ni aitai!

Last night I met a really nice person. Her name is Miki. Miki likes jazz so together we went to my favourite jazz club. At that jazz club we drank beer, chatted and listened to good music. It was really enjoyable. We stayed at the club until late then at about 2 o'clock went home. I want to meet with Miki again!

Activities

Activity 11.1

◄) CD2, TR 37

Listen to the recording as people are given advice about various matters then match the advice 1–6 on the recording with the pictures a–f. (The script is in the key.)

Activity 11.2

Katie describes her busy day today in the passage that follows. Can you, first, match the sequence of events as they appear in the passage with the English summaries a–h and write this out as a sequence of letters? Then, second, can you fill in the gaps 1–8 with the missing quantity words so that they match the English meanings (see Explanation 11.9)?

Kyō e-mēru o (1) _____ dashitari, denwa o (2) _____ shitari, tegami o (3) _____ kaitari shimashita. Soshite kinjo no hito to (4) _____ hanashimashita ga sōji o (5) _____ shimasen deshita. Isogashikatta no de hirugohan o (6) _____ tabemasen deshita. Gogo nihongo no shukudai ga (7) _____ dekimashita kara konban terebi o (8) _____ mitari, gorogoro shitari suru tsumori desu.

English summary: write this out in sequence (e.g. c, a, and so on):

a watch lots of TV and relax this evening
b sent huge amounts of email
c pm, was able to do all Japanese homework
d spoke with neighbour a little
e made lots of phone calls
f hardly ate any lunch because busy
g didn't do any cleaning
h wrote quite a lot of letters

Activity 11.3

Can you change these plain form verbs back into their polite versions?

example: **ryōri shita**	**ryōri shimashita**
kaita	
tabeta	
yonda	
itta	
tsukutta	
katta	
oyoida	

Introduction to kanji 漢字 (5)

In this section you will learn:

• some kanji for weather and seasons
• some kanji for members of the family
• kanji used for the names of countries

Start reading

You learned about weather and seasons in Explanations 6.6 and 6.7. Look back at these now if you need to refresh your memory. Here are five kanji broken down into components with stories to link them to their meaning. Can you match each story and meaning with the correct kanji?

1 雨   **2** 雪   **3** 晴
4 天   **5** 秋

Story 1   autumn is the time when the rice stubble (禾) is burnt (火). Meaning: *autumn*
Story 2   sun (日) and blue (青) mean fine weather. Meaning: *fine, sunny*
Story 3   drops of rain at the window. Meaning: *rain*
Story 4   rain falling over a sideways mountain (山) freezes to snow. Meaning: *snow*
Story 5   the number one (一) and big (大) add up to the biggest/greatest. Meaning: *sky, heaven, celestial, weather*

Here are the new kanji again with their meanings.

雨 rain   雪 snow   晴 fine weather
天 heaven   秋 autumn

The seasons

Here are the other three seasons with stories to help you:

春   *spring* (haru) can you see the components *three* (三) *person* (人) and *sun* (日)? Spring arrives in the *third* month (March) and seeing the *sun* again puts a *spring* in a *person's* step!

冬   *winter* (fuyu) This radical 夂 means *winter*. The two drops of ice create a chilly feel

夏   *summer* (natsu) The winter radical 夂 is here again but this time it is smothered by one (一) and eye (目) – the eye of the hot sun!

Reading activity 11.1

Here are the seasons and weather terms with some compound words which include them. Can you match each word to its English meaning?

1	夏休み	**a**	clear skies
2	冬休み	**b**	the Milky Way (*heavenly river*)
3	春休み	**c**	snowy mountain
4	天気	**d**	summer holidays
5	天の川	**e**	winter holiday
6	雨水	**f**	spring holiday
7	雨天	**g**	Snow Woman (Japanese legend)
8	雪山	**h**	weather
9	雪女	**i**	rainy weather
10	雪明	**j**	snow light
11	秋分	**k**	fall (autumn) equinox
12	晴天	**l**	rain water

The family

Here are the kanji for members of the family:

母 *mother* (haha)   a mother is drawn as two breasts, showing her role in rearing children

父 *father* (chichi)   he has dimples in his cheeks and a long moustache!

兄 *older brother* (ani)   easy to remember – a mouth on legs!

姉 *older sister* (ane)   woman (女) on the left and on the right the kanji for city 市 – can you see someone carrying bags on both arms after shopping in the city? The older sister works in the city!

弟 *younger brother* (otōto)   a snake-like shape with horns – like a little brother up to mischief?

妹 *younger sister* (imōto)　woman on the left and a tree that has not fully grown (shorter upper branch – 未) – a younger sister is not yet a woman

Reading activity 11.2

Here are the six family kanji again, this time written with hiragana to make them into the 'other family' terms. What do they mean in English?

1 お父さん (otōsan)
2 お母さん (okāsan)
3 妹さん (imōtosan)
4 弟さん (otōtosan)
5 お姉さん (onēsan)
6 お兄さん (onīsan)

Insight

Kanji compounds: countries

The names for countries that you have learned are borrowed words such as **Amerika** (*America*), **Doitsu** (*Germany*) and **Igirisu** (*England*). However, there is also a Japanese word using kanji for most countries of the world. For example: China is 中国 meaning *middle country* because it is in the centre of Asia.

The kanji for *country* is 国 made up of 囗 which is a surround showing *boundaries* and 玉 meaning *jewel* or *king*. Therefore a king rules to the *boundaries* of his *country*.

Here is a selection of country names in kanji. Generally the kanji were chosen not for their meaning but because their pronunciation is close to the sounds (syllables) of a country's name but the meaning is given, anyway. These kanji words are often used in newspaper articles:

英国　　　England ('excellent' country)
米国　　　America ('rice' country)

独国	Germany ('independent' country)
韓国	Korea (kanji means 'Korea')
豪州	Australia ('outstanding province')
新西蘭	New Zealand ('new west Holland')
仏国	France (means 'France' and also 'the Buddha')
西国	Spain (west country)

Reading activity 11.3

You have learned 15 single kanji in this unit. Here they are in random order – give their English meaning:

1 弟	2 妹	3 雨	4 雪	5 晴
6 春	7 秋	8 母	9 父	10 天
11 夏	12 冬	13 兄	14 姉	15 国

Reading challenge

Here is the 'learn to say' speech from Unit 6 rewritten in hiragana with kanji words as appropriate. All katakana words are written in rōmaji. As with the previous units try reading it with or without the recording to help you.

Ian explains briefly about the weather and seasons in New Zealand.

Nyū Jīrando は きせつが 四つ あります。春は
九月から 十一月 まで です。天気は 晴れ
ときどき 雨 です。だんだん あたたかく
なります。夏は 十二月から 二月まで です。
だんだん あつくなります。秋は 三月から

です。天気は 晴れ、かぜ、雨 … 冬は
六月から です。とても さむい です。雪が
いっぱい ふります。

Final words on reading

You have learned 15 single kanji in this unit as well as 12 kanji compound words and some words for countries. Review these before you move on to the reading section in the next unit.

End-of-unit challenge

Here are 10 English sentences using structures that you have learned in Unit 11. Can you say them out loud and write them down in Japanese?

1 I have been to South America.
2 I haven't heard the Love Love Boys' music.
3 I prefer rock music to jazz.
4 When I was a student I went to lots of concerts.
5 When I lived in Australia I spoke English well.
6 I went to bed late last night so I am completely exhausted.
7 I have finished all the cooking.
8 I think that this camera is better than that camera.
9 After talking to Takeshi, Miki phoned (to) Roger.
10 At the weekend I sometimes go shopping and sometimes watch a film.

12

··

Rainen Amerika ni kaerō to omoimasu

I'm thinking of going to America next year

In this unit you will learn:
- *more about the plain form (let's)*
- *to talk about plans and decisions*
- *to talk about possibilities and probabilities*
- *to talk about things you've tried to do*
- *more about hours, weeks, months and years*

Getting started

Opening activity

You have already learned the polite way to make suggestions using **mashō** and **mashō ka** (*let's, shall we?*). There is also a plain, more casual form – the **yō/ō** form. The rules are straightforward:

Group 1 verbs: Change dictionary form **u** ending to **ō**:

kau → kaō
nomu → nomō
motsu → motō
wakaru → wakarō

Group 2 verbs: Replace **ru** ending with **yō**:

taberu → tabeyō
okiru → okiyō

◆) CD2, TR 38

Now it's your turn. Convert these verbs into their **yō/ō** form then listen and repeat with the recording. The group is given when you need it.

English	dictionary form	yō/ō form (let's)
see	**miru** (2)	1
hear	**kiku**	2
write	**kaku**	3
meet	**au**	4
go	**iku**	5
rest	**yasumu**	6
talk	**hanasu**	7
swim	**oyogu**	8
show	**miseru**	9
wait	**matsu**	10

Build-up activity

◆) CD2, TR 39

Using the verbs from the opening activity, you are now going to make plain speech suggestions using English prompts as in the example. Then listen to the recording and practise saying the suggestions:

Example: Shall we watch a film? → Eiga o miyō ka

1 Shall we listen to the news?
2 Shall we write an email?
3 Shall we meet in front of the cinema?
4 Shall we go to the party now?
5 Shall we have a rest?

6 Shall we talk in Japanese?
7 Shall we swim in the sea (**umi**)?
8 Shall we show it (to) the teacher?
9 Shall we wait for Miki?

Key sentences

Go over the vocabulary and try and work out the meanings of the sentences for yourself first:

1 Boku wa raishū Kyōto ni ikō.
2 Rainen **Yōroppa** ni ikō to omoimasu.
3 Supeingo o naraō **to shimashita** ga amari jōzu ja arimasen deshita.
4 Ashita wa **ame ga furu darō**.
5 Kyō wa hare desu ga ashita wa **ame ga furu kamo shiremasen**.
6 Hondō-san wa pātī ni kuru **n ja nai deshō ka**
7 Konban indo ryōri o suru **koto ni shimashita**.
8 Mainichi **pūru de ichi jikan gurai** oyogu **koto ni shiteiru**.
9 Ashita Hondō-san ni au **koto ni narimashita**.
10 Nihon de wa ofuro ni hairu mae ni **arau koto ni natte imasu**.

Yōroppa	*Europe*
to shiteimasu (to suru)	*attempt to, try to*
ame ga furu	*rain falls, it will rain*
darō (plain form of deshō)	*will probably*
kamo shiremasen	*might, may* (not certain)
n ja nai deshō ka	*probably* (polite)
koto ni shimashita (koto ni suru)	*I've decided* (decide on)
pūru	*swimming pool*
ichi jikan	*one hour*
gurai	*about*
koto ni shiteiru	*make it a rule, be in the habit of*
koto ni narimashita	*has been arranged that*
arau	*wash*
koto ni natte imasu	*supposed to, the custom is*

QUICK VOCAB

English translation of the key sentences

1 *I will go to Kyoto next week.*
2 *I think I will go to Europe next year.*
3 *I tried to learn Spanish but I wasn't very good.*
4 *It will probably rain tomorrow.*
5 *Today is fine but tomorrow it might rain.*
6 *Is it not probable that Mr Hondo will come to the party?*
   (Mr Hondo will probably come to the party.)
7 *This evening I have decided to cook Indian food.*
8 *Every day I make it a rule to swim in the pool for about one hour.*
9 *Tomorrow it has been arranged (for me) to meet Mr Hondo.*
10 *In Japan, before you get in the bath you are supposed to wash (yourself).*

Language explanations

Here is a list of the grammar points you will learn in Unit 12:

1 the plain 'let's' form – **yō/ō form**
2 the **yō/ō** form + **to omoimasu** – *I think I will*
3 he **yō/ō** form + **to suru** – *to try* (but not succeed)
4 degrees of certainty – **deshō, ka mo shiremasen** and **n ja nai deshō ka**
5 plain form + **koto ni suru** – *to decide, to make it a rule*
6 plain form + **koto ni naru** – *to be decided, arranged, supposed to*
7 quantities of time using **kan**

You will also use these new words in the explanations but they will be provided in the text when you need them. They are here for reference.

atarashii	*new*
sanpo suru	*take a walk*
yameru	*give up*
repōto	*report*
teishoku	*set meal*

Explanation 12.1 Eiga o miyō ka *Shall we watch a film?*

You have learned how to form the plain 'shall we/let's' structure in the opening activity.

As well as being used among friends and in casual speech to say *shall we?* and *let's* it is also used to say *I will* (when you are being decisive) or *shall I?*, when talking to or about yourself:

Watashi wa eiga o miyō	*I will watch the film*
Neyō ka	*Shall I go to bed?*

As well as these two uses (casual speech, talking to self) it is also used to make other structures as you will see in Explanations 12.2 and 12.3.

Explanation 12.2 Yōroppa ni ikō to omoimasu *I think I will go to Europe*

You use the **yō/ō** form with **to omoimasu** to say *I think I will* – and you use it with **to omotteimasu (omotteiru)** to say *I think someone else will* or *I am thinking of doing . . .*

Here are some examples:

Indo ryōri o shiyō to omou	*I think I will make Indian food*
Miki-san wa Minami Amerika ni ikō to omotteimasu	*Miki is thinking she will go to South America*

You have learned two similar structures – **tai to omoimasu** (Explanation 5.6) and **tsumori desu** (Explanation 10.5). Look at the difference in meaning:

Minami Amerika ni ikitai to omou	*I hope to go to South America*
Minami Amerika ni ikō to omou	*I think I will go to South America*
Minami Amerika ni iku tsumori desu	*I plan to go to South America*

The examples are in order of certainty with **tsumori desu** being the most definite, a concrete plan, **yō to omoimasu** a statement of intent (but not sure it will happen) and **tai to omoimasu** a wish or hope that may or may not happen.

Now you practise using **yō/ō to omou** by saying these sentences out loud. Use either polite **masu** form or plain:

1 I think I will go to Japan next year.
2 My mother thinks she will go to Europe next year.
3 I think I will buy a new car.
4 I think I will send that email.
5 Takeshi thinks he will meet with Miki again.

Explanation 12.3 Supeingo o naraō to shimashita
I tried to learn Spanish

You have already learned how to say *give something a try* using the **te** form plus **miru** (Explanation 9.6) but when you use **yō/ō** plus **suru** it implies that you have tried and failed or that something is a struggle. Look at the difference:

| Supeingo o naraō to shimashita | *I tried to learn Spanish (but failed)* |
| Supeingo o naratte mimashita | *I had a go at learning Spanish* |

Insight

You can also use **to suru** in the continuous (**teiru**) form if you are about to do something:

| Asagohan o tabeyō to shiteimasu | *I'm about to eat breakfast* |

Can you say these sentences out loud in Japanese using the English prompts?

1 You're trying to learn the piano. (or you're about to)
2 You've tried (and failed) to write that report (**repōto**).
3 Your father tried (and failed) to buy a new jacket.
4 You tried to go to Japan last year. (but didn't)

Explanation 12.4 Degrees of probability using *deshō* and *kamo shiremasen*

When you use **deshō** (or its plain form **darō**) preceded by a plain form verb, you are saying something will probably happen whereas when you use **kamo shiremasen** (plain form **kamo shirenai**) preceded by the plain verb, you are saying that something will possibly happen but it is not certain. Here are some examples:

| Ame ga furu deshō | *It will probably rain* |
| Ame ga furu kamo shiremasen | *It will possibly rain* |

| Zembu tabeta darō | *He probably ate it all* |
| Zembu tabeta kamo shirenai | *He might have eaten it all* |

If you add the word **kitto** to a **deshō** phrase then you are even more definite – *I bet that* . . .:

| Kitto pātī ni iku deshō | *I bet that he goes to the party* |

When you need to be especially polite or show particular respect to someone, for example your boss, then you can express **deshō** in a negative phrase: plain verb form **+ n ja nai deshō ka**:

Hondō-san wa pātī ni iku	*Is it not probable that*
n ja nai deshō ka	*Mr Hondo will go to the*
	party? (Mr Hondo will
	probably go to the party)

Insight

You will find that the negative is used a lot in Japanese to add uncertainly and therefore respect (as it sometimes is in English – *wouldn't you like another cup of coffee? Shouldn't you phone your mother?*).

Look at the following sentences and decide whether you should complete them with: (a) **kitto . . . deshō**, (b) **deshō**, (c) **n ja nai deshō ka** or (d) **kamo shiremasen**:

1 Ashita kaisha o yasumu _____. (*I will probably have a day off work tomorrow*)
2 Ian-san wa kibun ga warui kara kyō uchi ni iru _____. (*Ian isn't well so he might stay at home today*)
3 Kyō wa hare dakara ashita mo _____ hare _____. (*Today it is fine so I bet it'll be fine tomorrow*)
4 Miki-san wa mata Takeshi-san to au _____. (*Miki might meet Takeshi again*)
5 Shachō wa Hondō-san ni denwa suru _____ (*Won't the director probably phone Mr Hondo?*)

Explanation 12.5 Talking about decisions and rules using *koto ni suru*

You use the plain dictionary form or nouns with **koto ni suru** to say *I will decide* and **koto ni shita** to say *I've decided*. If you use **suru** in the continuous form (**shiteiru**) it means 'decisions' you make routinely, in other words, things you do as a rule or habit. Here are some examples:

Kōhī ni shimasu	*I've decided on (I will have) a coffee* (e.g. when ordering from a menu)
Ashita kaisha o yasumu koto ni shimashita	*I decided to take a day off work tomorrow*
Yōroppa o ryokō suru koto ni shimashō	*Let's (decide to) travel through Europe*
Maiasa sanpo suru koto ni shiteiru	*As a rule I take a walk every morning*

Insight

Notice in the third example that it is not always necessary or natural to include the word 'decide' in English although by implication a decision has been or will be made.

Have a go using these scenarios to talk about decisions or rules in Japanese:

1 You've decided to order sushi off the menu.
2 You decided to go home at 10 o'clock.
3 You decided to give up (**yameru**) beer.
4 Suggest going to Kyoto by bullet train. (**shinkansen**)
5 You make it a rule to drink plenty of (**takusan**) water every day.

Explanation 12.6 Talking about decisions, arrangements and rules using *koto ni naru*

You use **koto ni naru/natta** rather than **koto ni suru** when you are not in control of the decision – *it has been (will be) decided*. You can also translate it as *it has been (will be) arranged.* You can also use **koto ni natta** even when you have made a decision if you wish to appear more humble and not 'boasting' or being over-assertive about your decisions. The Japanese use language in this kind of indirect way to be more polite, more tentative. **Koto ni natteiru** takes on the meaning of how things are supposed to be done or how they work so is often used with rules and customs. Look at these examples:

Raishū Ōsaka ni shutchō suru koto ni narimashita	*It has been decided that I will go on a business trip to Osaka next week*
Ashita Hondō-san ni au koto ni narimashita	*It has been arranged (for me) to meet Mr Hondo tomorrow*
Kazoku to Igirisu ni ryokō suru koto ni natta	*The decision has been made to travel to England with my family* (maybe this is a family decision – no one is 'taking credit' for or 'boasting' about this decision)
Nihon de wa ofuro ni hairu mae ni arau koto ni natte imasu	*In Japan, before you get in the bath you are supposed to wash* (custom)

Explanation 12.7 Giving lengths of time using *kan*

Kan means 'period of time' and when you attach it to words such as **ji** (o'clock), **shū** (week) and **nen** (year) it changes these words into lengths of time as shown in the table opposite.

When you want to ask how long it takes you can say:

Nan jikan kakarimasu ka	*How many hours does it take?*
Dono gurai kakarimasu ka	*How long does it take?*
Dono gurai desu ka	*How long (far) is it?*

time word	length of time	example	how many?
ji *o'clock*	jikan *hour*	ni jikan 2 *hours*	nan jikan?
shū *week*	shūkan *week*	ni shūkan 2 *weeks*	nan shūkan?
getsu *month*	kagetsu *month*	ni kagetsu 2 *months*	nan kagetsu?
nen *year*	nenkan *year*	ni nenkan 2 *years*	nan nen (kan)?

Insight

Notice that for months you do something slightly different – you add **ka** and don't need to use **kan**. You can also use **nen** (*years*) without **kan**.

Main dialogue

◄» **CD2, TR 40**

Katie meets up with Rie to tell her that she and Ian will shortly be leaving Japan. As with previous units, read through the vocabulary then listen to the recording several times, giving yourself different targets each time (listen for specific vocabulary, listen for new structures, listen for general meaning, listen for information relating to the questions).

Katie	**Zannen** desu ga Ian wa **mōsugu Chūgoku** ni **tenkin suru** koto ni narimashita.
Rie	**Chūgoku** desu ka. Ii **chansu** desu ne.
Katie	Tokyo de **hoka no** shigoto o **mitsukeyō** to shimashita ga shigoto wa zenzen **arimasen** deshita.

Rie	Katie-san wa **dō** shimashita ka.
Katie	Sō desu ne. Mada Nihon de hatarakitai desu ga watashi mo **Chūgoku** ni ikō to omoimasu.
Rie	**Zannen** desu ne. Nan nenkan Nihon ni sundeimashita ka.
Katie	Ian wa ni nenkan desu. Watashi wa sannen **kurai** da to omoimasu.
Rie	Itsu **tenkin shimasu** ka.
Katie	Ian wa raigetsu Chūgoku ni iku kamo shiremasen ga mada **hakkiri** wakarimasen. Soshite watashi wa hachigatsu ni ikō to omoimasu.
Rie	Chūgoku de nani o suru tsumori desu ka.
Katie	Mada wakarimasen ga **watashitachi** wa kekkon suru koto ni shimashita.
Rie	**Hontō** desu ka. **Omedetō gozaimasu**. Jā, Chūgoku ni iku mae ni pātī o shimashō ne! Nihon de wa **tenkin suru** mae ni 'sayōnara pātī' o **okonau** koto ni natte imasu yo!
Katie	Ii desu ne. Sayōnara to kekkon no pātī o shimashō!

QUICK VOCAB

zannen desu	*it's a shame, pity*
mōsugu	*shortly, soon*
Chūgoku	*China*
tenkin suru	*transfer*
chansu	*chance*
hoka no	*other*
mitsukeyō (mitsukeru)	*find*
dō	*how, what*
kurai	*about*
hakkiri	*clearly*
watashitachi	*we*
hontō	*really, real*
omedetō gozaimasu	*congratulations*
okonau	*hold (an event)*

True or false?

Write either O (**maru** = true) or X (**batsu** = false) next to these statements:

1 Ian-san wa mōsugu Amerika ni tenkin shimasu.
2 Katie-san wa Chūgoku ni iku tsumori wa arimasen.
3 Ian-san wa ni nenkan Nihon ni sundeimasu.
4 Ian-san to Katie-san wa raigetsu ni kekkon suru koto ni shimashita.
5 Rie-san wa sayōnara pātī o okonau koto ni shimashita.

Japanese questions

Write your answers in Japanese:

6 Katie-san wa itsu Chūgoku ni iku tsumori desu ka.
7 Ian-san wa dōshite Chūgoku ni ikimasu ka.
8 Rie-san wa Ian-san ga Chūgoku ni iku koto ni tsuite dō omoimasu ka.
9 Ian-san to Katie-san wa nani o suru koto ni shimashita ka.
10 Chūgoku ni iku mae ni nani o suru tsumori desu ka.

English questions

11 What did Ian try to do when he found out he was going to be transferred to China?
12 What was Katie's reaction to Ian's transfer?
13 When exactly will Ian go to China?
14 To what 'custom' does Rie refer?
15 What does Katie think of this?

Learn to say: Making excuses

🔊 **CD2, TR 41**

Eri hasn't done her piano practice. But she *is* practising the excuses she will give to her teacher. Listen to the recording, check your understanding then pause it sentence by sentence and practise saying it out loud.

Sumimasen ga konshū piano no renshū jikan wa amari arimasen deshita. Renshū o shiyō to shiteimashita ga iroirona **mondai** ga arimashita. Getsuyōbi ni kazoku to yakyū gēmu ni iku koto ni narimashita. Soshite kayōbi mo suiyōbi mo shukudai ga takusan arimashita. Mokuyōbi ni **totsuzen** watashi wa jūdō no shiai ni sanka suru koto ni narimashita. Raishū wa isshūkan kitto hima da to omoimasu. Dakara mainichi ichi jikan gurai wa renshū o shiyō to omoimasu.

I'm sorry but this week I haven't had much time for piano practice. I tried to practise but I had various problems. On Monday it was decided that I would go to a baseball game with my family. Then on Tuesday and Wednesday I had a lot of homework. On Thursday it was unexpectedly arranged for me to take part in a judo contest. Next week I will almost definitely be free all week. Therefore, I think I will practise every day for about one hour.

mondai (ga aru)	*problem (have a)*
totsuzen	*unexpectedly*

Activities

Activity 12.1

🔊 **CD2, TR 42**

Listen to the recording about journey times and note down the mode of transport and the length of time:

1 Tokyo to Hiroshima
2 London to Edinburgh
3 Seattle to New York
4 Tokyo to Sapporo
5 Melbourne to Sydney

Activity 12.2

◀) CD2, TR 43

Here is the 'learn to say' passage once more, this time with parts underlined. Your task is to replace the underlined parts with the information that follows to make a new set of excuses then check your answer with the recording and practise saying it out loud:

Sumimasen ga konshū <u>piano no renshū jikan wa amari arimasen</u> deshita. <u>Renshū</u> o shiyō to shiteimashita ga <u>iroirona mondai ga arimashita</u>. Getsuyōbi ni <u>kazoku</u> to <u>yakyū gēmu ni iku</u> koto ni narimashita. Soshite kayōbi mo suiyōbi mo <u>shukudai ga takusan arimashita</u>. Mokuyōbi ni totsuzen watashi wa <u>jūdō no shiai ni sanka suru</u> koto ni narimashita. Raishū wa isshūkan kitto hima da to omoimasu. Dakara mainichi <u>ichi</u> jikan gurai wa <u>renshū</u> o shiyō to omoimasu.

You didn't do much Japanese study this week. You meant to but you were very busy (**isogashii**). On Monday it was arranged that you have a meal with the sales manager (**eigyō buchō**). Then on Tuesday and Wednesday you worked at the company until late. On Thursday it was unexpectedly decided that you go on a business trip to Nagoya. Next week you're bound to be free so you'll do two hours' study every day!

Activity 12.3

The sentences that follow require either **koto ni suru** or **koto ni naru** (in their various forms) – you decide!

1 Nihon de wa hashi de gohan o taberu _____ _____. (*in Japan, you are supposed to eat rice with chopsticks*)
2 Miki-san ni denwa suru _____. (*I decided to call Miki*)
3 Kono repōto o Hondō-san ni dasu _____. (*it has been arranged for me to send this report to Mr Hondo*)
4 Sashimi teishoku _____. (*I'm going for the raw fish set meal*)

5 Shokuji o taberu mae ni te o arau _____. (*before eating a meal you're supposed to wash your hands*)

6 Mainichi kanji o sukoshi narau _____. (*I make it a rule to learn a few kanji every day*)

Introduction to katakana

In this section you will learn:

- to recognize all 46 basic katakana symbols
- ideas to help you remember the symbols
- how to read some simple words

Introduction

In Unit 1, you had a brief introduction to katakana. This section will look at this script in more detail. Katakana is used primarily to write non-Japanese words. There are many borrowed words in the Japanese language such as food items, drinks, clothes and electrical goods so katakana is very useful and it is very rewarding to be able to read a word and understand its meaning straightaway.

The first 15 katakana symbols (a–so)

The katakana script has 46 basic symbols and follows all the same rules as hiragana. The only difference is that the symbols are different although some look very similar to their hiragana counterparts. In the same way, we have upper and lower case letters which also represent the same sound. Here are the first 15 katakana symbols with their pronunciation. Look back to the introduction to this book and listen again to the recording if you need to remind yourself how to pronounce each sound:

ア	イ	ウ	エ	オ
a	i	u	e	o

カ	キ	ク	ケ	コ
ka	ki	ku	ke	ko

サ	シ	ス	セ	ソ
sa	shi	su	se	so

Hints for remembering katakana symbols

This aim of this book is to give you an overall feel for katakana. At the end of the book there are also suggestions for ways to take your learning further. As suggested with hiragana, it is useful to use mnemonics to visually link the symbol with its sound. There are also a number of katakana that look similar to their hiragana and counterpart and you may find these similarities a useful way to remember them. Here they are. The katakana symbol is listed first:

ウ う = u	hiragana is more curvy
エ え = e	not immediately similar but closer on examination
オ お = o	partially similar when you look closely
カ か = ka	hiragana is more curvy and extra dash
キ き = ki	hiragana is more curvy and extra dash/curve
ケ け = ke	hiragana is separated out into two sides
コ こ = ko	katakana has joined up into three sides
セ せ = se	hiragana has extra dash

Try thinking of some mnemonics too – perhaps you can visualize an antelope in ア (**a**), a cupola in ク (**ku**) or a superwoman in ス (**su**)!

Similar looking katakana

The following katakana symbols look quite similar and you may find that this is confusing at times. Here are some clues to help you tell them apart:

ク ケ (ku, ke) the horizontal line in **ke** is longer
サ セ (sa, se) **se** faces the same way as roman alphabet e

Reading activity 12.1

You are going to try reading some katakana words that use the first 15 symbols.

Can you match each word to one of the English words in the box?

1 アイス
2 ケーキ
3 ウイスキー
4 ココア
5 スキー

6 クイズ
7 キウイ
8 キス
9 アジア
10 ガス

| **a** kiwi | **b** cake | **c** cocoa | **d** quiz | **e** ski (skiing) |
| **f** gas | **g** whisky | **h** kiss | **i** Asia | **j** ice |

The middle 15 katakana symbols (ta–ho)

Here are the middle 15 katakana. Use the recording in the book introduction to practise reading them as you listen to the pronunciation:

タ	チ	ツ	テ	ト
ta	chi	tsu	te	to
ナ	ニ	ヌ	ネ	ノ
na	ni	nu	ne	no
ハ	ヒ	フ	ヘ	ホ
ha	hi	fu	he	ho

Similarities with hiragana

Katakana symbols are listed first:

テ	て	both have a 'table top' – katakana has a 'plate' on the table!
ナ	な	katakana is the left half of the hiragana
ニ	に	hiragana has an additional vertical line
フ	ふ	katakana is created from the middle section of hiragana
ヘ	へ	very similar, katakana version is shorter

Ideas for mnemonics

Can you see a *che*erleader in チ (**chi**), a plant on *top* of the ground ト (**to**), the kanji for number two – *ni* 二 (**ni**), a *ne*st in a tree ネ (**ne**), the bridge of a *no*se ノ (**no**), kanji number eight – *ha*chi ハ (**ha**) and a jolly father Christmas face – **ho**, ho, ho ホ (**ho**)?

Similar looking katakana

チ テ	(**chi, te**)	the vertical line cuts through in **chi**
シ ツ	(**shi, tsu**)	the long stroke in **tsu** has a steeper angle

タ ヌ (ta, nu) think of **nu** as a continental number 7 (with a line through)

ウ フ (u, fu) **u** has two extra dashes

Reading activity 12.2

As with Reading activity 12.1 try matching the katakana words with their English meaning. Numbers 1–8 use the middle 15 katakana only, 9–16 use the first 30.

> ## Insight
> When working out the meaning, remember that there is no sound for 'ti' or 'tu' in Japanese, **chi** and **tsu** are used instead.

1 ヒーター		9 タバコ	
2 ツナ		10 タクシー	
3 ノート		11 チーム	
4 データ		12 バス	
5 タヒチ		13 ドイツ	
6 パート		14 チーズケーキ	
7 ドーナツ		15 ハイテク	
8 バー		16 ネクタイ	

a tuna	**b** data	**c** team	**d** taxi
e necktie	**f** Germany	**g** Tahiti	**h** high tech
i bus	**j** doughnut	**k** bar	**l** heater
m cheesecake	**n** cigarette (tobacco)	**o** note (book)	**p** part (time)

The final 16 katakana symbols (ma–n)

Here are the final 16 katakana. Read the symbols out loud, use the recording to help you if you wish:

マ	ミ	ム	メ	モ
ma	mi	mu	me	mo
ヤ		ユ		ヨ
ya		yu		yo
ラ	リ	ル	レ	ロ
ra	ri	ru	re	ro
ワ				ヲ
wa				(w)o
ン				
(n)				

Insight

Notice that there is a symbol for (**w**)**o** although this has only a grammatical function, normally written in hiragana. It used to be used for writing telegrams – telegram messages were traditionally written only in katakana – so it is rarely used nowadays.

Similarities with hiragana

Katakana symbols are listed first:

モ	も	hiragana is more curvy and vertical cuts through
ヤ	や	hiragana is more curvy with extra dash
リ	り	hiragana is more curvy

Ideas for mnemonics

Can you see drops of rain in the *mist* ミ (**mi**), a *moo*se ム (**mu**), a number 1 – *you* are no. 1 ユ (**yu**), a *ra*zor レ (**re**), a *ru*ined razor ル (**ru**) and a *ro*tation ロ (**ro**)?

Similar looking katakana

ウ フ ワ (u, fu, wa)   we've discussed **u** and **fu**. **Wa** has one additional dash

ア マ (a, ma)   **ma** is shorter and squatter

ナ メ (na, me)   **me** tips to one side and is slimmer

ル レ (ru, re)   **ru** has an additional line (the *ru*ined part!)

ソ ン (so, n)   the angle on **so** is steeper

Reading activity 12.3

Once again, match the katakana words with the English meanings.

> ## Insight
> *Reading tips:*
>
> - Remember there is no distinction between 'l' and 'r' in Japanese so if an 'l' sound won't work, try 'r'. For example, *hotel* is pronounced **hoteru**. You will find it really helps to change **ru** into 'l' as a general rule
> - Also, there is no 'th' sound in Japanese – **s** sounds are used instead

The first eight words use only the final 15 sounds, the others use all 45 sounds (not including ヲ **wo**):

1	レモン	9	アイスクリーム
2	メモ	10	レンタカー
3	メロン	11	ロンドン
4	ルール	12	マラソン
5	ローマ	13	ミルク
6	ローン	14	マイカー
7	リレー	15	ラジオ
8	メモリー	16	チキン

Contracted sounds

In Unit 5 you learned about contracted sounds for hiragana symbols. Exactly the same rules apply to katakana. For example:

キ (ki)	キャ (kya)	キュ (kyu)	キ (kyo)
ギ (gi)	ギャ (gya)	ギュ (gyu)	ギ (gyo)
シ (shi)	シャ (sha)	シュ (shu)	シ (sho)
ジ (ji)	ジャ (ja)	ジュ (ju)	ジ (jo)

Look back to Unit 5 to remind yourself of these rules.

Taking your katakana study further

This book has given you a comprehensive introduction to katakana but 'practice makes perfect' and finding the opportunity to read more katakana words will really help you to build your skills and confidence. There are many online programmes (see end of book for selection) and you can also find reading material such as menus online. If you want further practice and would like to learn how to write katakana correctly (and this is also a good way to help you remember the symbols), this is covered in *Read and write Japanese Scripts* (Helen Gilhooly, Hodder & Stoughton, 2010).

Reading challenge

You have learned many borrowed words throughout this course. There follows a selection grouped by theme. Can you read them and match them with the English words in the box?

Sport	1 スポーツ 2 ボーリング 3 テニス 4 プール
Food and drink	5 コーヒー 6 トースト 7 メニュー
Countries	8 アメリカ 9 イギリス 10 イタリア 11 オーストラリア 12 ニュージーランド
Technology	13 テレビ 14 ニュース 15 カメラ 16 コンピューター
Places	17 レストラン 18 ユースホステル 19 スーパー 20 デパート

Sport	a tennis b sport c bowling d swimming pool
Food and drink	e toast f menu g coffee
Countries	h Italy i England j America k New Zealand l Australia
Technology	m TV n computer o camera p news
Places	q department store r supermarket s youth hostel t restaurant

---

End-of-unit challenge

The following 10 sentences are incomplete. Using the structures you have learned in this unit, can you complete them (the verb is given in **masu** form)?

1 Atarashii kamera o (kaimasu). (*I hope to buy a new camera*)
2 Rainen Chūgoku ni (ikimasu). (*I think I will go to China next year*)
3 Ashita tomodachi ni (aimasu). (*I intend to meet my friend tomorrow*)
4 Kinō tomodachi to (aimasu). (*I tried to meet up with my friend yesterday*)

5 Itariago o (naraimasu). (*I have decided to learn Italian*)

6 Kono eiga wa omoshirokunai no de uchi e (kaerimasu).
(*this film isn't interesting so he might go home*)

7 Kitto ashita no yakyū no shiai o (mi ni ikimasu). (*I bet he goes to see the baseball match tomorrow*)

8 Kyō asobi ni (kimasu). (*I think I will come and visit today*)

9 Mainichi mizu o takusan (nomimasu). (*as a rule I drink lots of water every day*)

10 Raishū shigoto o (yasumimasu). (*I don't plan to be off work next week*)

13

Ano kaigishitsu ni hairanai de kudasai

Please don't go into that meeting room

In this unit you will learn
- *the negative* (**don't, didn't**) *plain forms*
- *more about polite and plain forms*
- *how to say* you must, you don't have to, you shouldn't
- *how to say* if *and* when *(the conditional)*
- *different ways to say* while

Getting started

You have learned to make and use the plain present and past verb forms (Units 10 and 11). In this unit, you will add the final pieces to the jigsaw by learning how to make the plain negative (present and past) forms.

Opening activity

Here are the rules for making the plain present negative ('I don't'):
Group 1 verbs: Change final **u** (or **i** in **masu**/stem form) to **a** + **nai**:

kak*u* → kak*a* → kak*anai*
(kak*imasu* → kak*i* → kak*a* → kak*anai*)

There is one exception to this rule. You replace **u** with **wa** (not **a**) when the verb ends in **au** (or **ai** in **masu** form). Look at these examples to clarify this: **kau** (*buy*), **au** (*meet*) and **okonau** (*hold an event*) all end with **au**.

In their **masu** form they all have **ai** before **masu**:

*kai*masu, *ai*masu, okon*ai*masu

For these verbs, you change **u** to **wa** to form the negative:

a*u* → a*wa*nai
(aimasu → ai → awanai)

Insight

The reason you do this is because double **aa** would sound awkward and be difficult to say → **aanai**.

Group 2 verbs: As usual, very straightforward – drop **ru** (or **masu**), add **nai**:

tabe*ru* → tabe*nai* (tabe*masu* → tabe*nai*)

For this activity, you are going to practise changing plain (dictionary) form verbs into their negative (**nai**) form. The group is given in brackets so that you can just focus on making the **nai** form. Complete the table, check your answers at the back then say the words out loud.

English	plain form	nai form
speak	**hanasu** (1)	1
read	**yomu** (1)	2
listen	**kiku** (1)	3
make	**tsukuru** (1)	4
use	**tsuk*au*** (1)	5
play, socialize	**asobu** (1)	6

English	plain form	nai form
enter	**hairu** (1)	7
swim	**oyogu** (1)	8
look, see, watch	**miru** (2)	9
show	**miseru** (2)	10

Build-up activity

In Unit 8 (opening activity), you learned to give polite commands using **te** form + **kudasai: tabete kudasai** (*please eat*). Using the **nai** form + **de kudasai** you can say 'please don't':

tabenai de kudasai   *please don't eat*

◀ᴗ CD2, TR 44

You are going to use the verbs 1–10 from the opening activity to say 'please don't'. The following table lists the 'please do' commands, listen to the recording, pause after each 'please do', say the 'please don't' command, then play the recording to check you were correct. The first one is done for you.

te kudasai (*please do*)	nai de kudasai (*please don't*)	English
hanashite kudasai	1 hanasanai de kudasai	*please don't speak*
yonde kudasai	2	*please don't read*
kiite kudasai	3	*please don't listen*
tsukutte kudasai	4	*please don't make* (*it*)
tsukatte kudasai	5	*please don't use* (*it*)
asonde kudasai	6	*please don't play*
haitte kudasai	7	*please don't enter*
oyoide kudasai	8	*please don't swim*

| mite kudasai | 9 | *please don't look* |
| misete kudasai | 10 | *please don't show (me)* |

Key sentences

Go over the vocabulary and try and work out the meanings of the sentences for yourself first.

Insight

Translation tips:

- The ending **nai de** means don't do and can also mean without *doing*
- The ending **kunakatta** is the past negative of adjectives (*it wasn't*)
- Check the vocabulary for the meanings of words and structures in bold
- Your translation will often move 'backwards' to the English order, so find your subject (if there is one) then go to the verb at the end and move backwards
- In sentence 9, there are two people – Katie and Ian – doing actions at the same time, so work out what each person is doing

1 Ano **kaigishitsu** ni hairanai de kudasai.
2 Sono eiga wa omoshirokunakatta to omoimasu.
3 Asagohan o **tabenai de** kaisha ni ikimashita.
4 Sono repōto o kakanai de **hoshii** desu.
5 Hondō-san ni denwa **shinakereba narimasen**.
6 **Kaigi** ni **shusseki shinakutemo ii desu**.
7 **Tabako o suwanai hō ga ii desu**.
8 Ame ga fura**nai uchi ni** gorufu o shimashita.
9 Ian-san ga ryōri o shiteiru **aida** Katie-san wa hon o yondeimashita.
10 **Moshi** Chūgoku ni **kitara, renraku** shite kudasai.

kaigishitsu	meeting room
tabenai de	without eating
kakanai de hoshii	I want you not to write
shinakereba narimasen	(you) must do
kaigi	meeting
shusseki (suru)	attend
shinakutemo ii desu	you don't have to
tabako o suu	smoke cigarettes
suwanai hō ga ii desu	it's better not to smoke, you shouldn't smoke
-nai uchi ni	while not (before)
aida (ni)	while, during
moshi	if
ittara	if I go
renraku (shimasu)	(make) contact

English translation of the key sentences

1 *Please don't go into that meeting room.*
2 *I think that that film wasn't interesting.*
3 *I went to work (to the company) without eating breakfast.*
4 *I want you not to write that report.*
5 *I must ring Mr Hondo.*
6 *You don't have to attend the meeting.*
7 *You shouldn't smoke cigarettes.*
8 *I played golf while it wasn't raining (before it rained).*
9 *While Ian was cooking Katie was reading a book.*
10 *If you come to China, please make contact.*

Language explanations

Here is a list of the grammar points you will learn in Unit 13:

1 plain negative (present and past forms)
2 plain forms of adjectives and **desu**

Applications of plain negative:

3 **nai de** – without doing
4 **nai de hoshii** – I want you not to
5 **nakereba narimasen** – must, need to
6 **nakutemo ii desu** – don't have to
7 **nai hō ga ii desu** – you shouldn't, you'd better not

In addition:

8 summary of the phrases: *you may, you don't have to, you should, you shouldn't, you must, you are not allowed to*
9 saying *while* using **nagara, aida n**i and **uchi ni**
10 saying *if* and *when* (the conditional tense)

You will also use the following new words, which will be explained as they appear.

keitai (denwa)	*mobile* (*phone*)
hiku	*play* (instrument)
furui	*old* (things)
sagasu	*look for*
atatakai	*warm*

Explanation 13.1 Kōhī wa nomanai yo! *I don't drink coffee, you know!*

In the opening activity, you were introduced to the rules for making the plain negative form of verbs. You can use this form in plain, casual speech and it can be 'softened' by adding **desu**:

Kōhī wa nomanai desu yo!

You also need to be aware that as well as using **wa** instead of **a** for **au** ending verbs there are some other adjustments as follows:

* verbs ending in **tsu** (**chi** in **masu** form) change to **ta**:

matsu (*wait*) → ma*t*anai
motsu (*hold*) → mo*t*anai
(ma*chi*masu → ma*t*anai)
(mo*chi*masu → mo*t*anai)

- verbs ending in **su** → **sa** as expected but if you are converting from the **masu** form you must remember to change **shi** → **sa**:

hanasu (*speak*) → hana*s*anai
hana*shi*masu → hana*s*anai

- irregular verbs change like this:

iku → ikanai
suru → shinai
kuru → konai

This is how you make the past plain negative of verbs: change **nai** → **nakatta** (add **desu** to be more polite):

tabenai → tabe*nakatta*
kawanai → kawa*nakatta*

You are already familiar with this structure. You used it to make the past negative of i adjectives in Explanation 6.2:

omoshiroi → omoshiroku*nai* → omoshiroku*nakatta*

Notice, though, that the i adjectives also have a **ku** in their negative form.

Can you convert these **masu** form verbs into first their **nai** form (*I don't*) and then their past negative form (*I didn't*)? Watch out for **i**, **shi** and **chi** (in italics in the table). Group 2 verbs are indicated.

masu form	I don't do	I didn't do
Example: tabemasu (2)	tabenai	tabenakatta
1 hana*shi*masu		
2 mimasu (2)		
3 yomimasu		
4 a*i*masu		
5 nara*i*masu		
6 ta*chi*masu *stand*		
7 nemasu (2)		
8 ikimasu		
9 benkyō shimasu		
10 kimasu		

Explanation 13.2 Sono eiga wa omoshirokunakatta
That film wasn't interesting

It is not only verbs that have polite and plain forms. Adjectives and
desu also have them and, in fact, you already know them. They are
summarized in the following chart.

	i adjective	na adjective	desu
present polite (is)	ōkii desu	jōzu desu	desu
present plain	ōkii	jōzu da	da
past polite (was)	ōkikatta desu	jōzu deshita	deshita
past plain	ōkikatta	jōzu datta	datta
negative polite (isn't)	ōkikunai desu	jōzu dewa (ja) arimasen	dewa/ja arimasen
negative plain	ōkikunai	jōzu ja nai (desu)	ja nai (desu)
negative past polite (wasn't)	ōkikunakatta desu	jōzu dewa (ja) arimasen deshita	dewa (ja) arimasen deshita
negative past plain	ōkikunakatta	jōzu ja nakatta (desu)	ja nakatta (desu)

Points to notice:

- You make the plain forms of i adjectives by dropping **desu**
- You make the plain form of **na** adjectives by using plain forms of **desu**
- The negative **desu** forms have layers of politeness, not a simple choice of two

Here are the negative **desu** forms in order of politeness.

	negative (isn't)	past negative (wasn't)
most polite	dewa arimasen	dewa arimasen deshita
most polite	ja arimasen	ja arimasen deshita
middle polite	dewa nai desu	dewa nakatta desu
polite	ja nai desu	ja nakatta desu
plain	ja nai	ja nakatta

Let's practise with this last table by saying simple sentences with different levels of politeness. You'll use the nouns **kamera** (*camera*), **keitai** (*mobile phone*) and **shinbun** (*newspaper*):

1 It is a newspaper. (polite)
2 It was a camera. (polite)
3 It isn't a mobile. (most polite)
4 It isn't a camera. (middle polite)
5 It wasn't a newspaper. (polite)
6 It isn't a mobile. (polite)
7 It isn't a mobile. (plain)
8 It wasn't a camera. (plain)

Insight

You will find it safer when speaking Japanese to use either the most polite or the polite forms of the negative.

Explanation 13.3 Asagohan o tabenai de kaisha ni ikimashita *I went to work without eating breakfast*

In the build-up activity, you learned to say **nai de kudasai** to mean *please don't*. You can use **nai de** part-way through a sentence to mean 'without doing':

Repōto o yomanai de dashimashita	*I submitted the report without reading it*
Kuruma o minai de kaimashita	*I bought the car without seeing it*

Say the following out loud in Japanese using the English prompts:

1 went home without drinking beer
2 went to restaurant without phoning Miki
3 played baseball without eating lunch
4 played (**hiku**) piano without practising

Explanation 13.4 Sono repōto o kakanai de hoshii desu *I want you not to write that report*

You've learned to give a simple negative command: **kakanai de kudasai** – *don't write it*. You can turn a polite negative command into a request by replacing **kudasai** with **hoshii** (you learned to say 'I want you to do' in Explanation 9.7 using **te** form with **hoshii**):

Terebi o minai de hoshii desu	*I want you not to watch the TV* *I don't want you to watch the TV*

Here are some things you don't want someone to do. Say them out loud. You don't want them to:

1 smoke cigarettes
2 play the piano now
3 go into the meeting room
4 socialize with Takeshi
5 drink up (use *shimau*) all the beer

Explanation 13.5 Saying *I must*

🔊 **CD2, TR 45**

To say *must, have to, need to* in Japanese sounds initially long and complicated but once you know it as a phrase it is not difficult and there are some sentences recorded for you to listen to and practise. The basic rule is that you take off **nai** of the **nai** verb form and add the phrase **nakereba narimasen**. Look at, listen to and repeat these examples. What do the 'must' sentences mean in English?

1 Benkyō shi*nai* → Benkyō shinakereba narimasen
2 Kaisha ni ika*nai* → Kaisha ni ikanakereba narimasen
3 Kusuri o noma*nai* → Kusuri o nomanakereba narimasen
4 Tabako o yame*nai* → Tabako o yamenakereba narimasen
5 Repōto o kaka*nai* → Repōto o kakanakereba narimasen

You can say this phrase in the plain form by changing **narimasen** to **naranai**:

Denwa shinakereba naranai   *I must phone*

Explanation 13.6 Saying *you don't have to*

To say *you don't have to* you take off **nai** and add **nakutemo ii desu**. (Or, if you like, think of it as taking off the final **i** and adding **kutemo ii desu**.) This phrase literally means 'even if you don't, it's alright' so has the English meanings of *you don't have to*, *it's alright if you don't*:

Piano o renshū shinakutemo   *It's all right if you don't practise*
 ii desu   *the piano*
Kusuri o nomanakutemo   *You don't have to take*
 ii desu   *the medicine*

🔊 **CD2, TR 46**

Listen to the recording, practise saying the phrases and work out their English meanings:

1 Konshū Nihongo o benkyō shinakutemo ii desu.
2 Sono repōto o kakanakutemo ii desu yo.
3 Nihongo o hanasanakutemo ii desu yo.
4 Sono takai kamera o kawanakutemo ii desu.
5 Kibun ga warui kara kaisha ni ikanakutemo ii desu ka.

Explanation 13.7 Saying *you shouldn't, it's better not to*

You have already learned how to give positive advice (*you should*)
using the plain past with **hō ga ii desu** (Explanation 11.4):

Kono kusuri o nonda hō ga ii desu yo	*You ought to take (drink) this medicine*

To advise someone *not* to do something you use the **nai** form with
hō ga ii desu:

Sono bīru o nomanai hō ga ii desu yo	*You'd better not drink that beer*
Sono kamera o kawanai hō ga ii desu yo	*You shouldn't buy that camera*
Osoku uchi ni kaeranai hō ga ii desu	*It's better if you don't go home late*

Can you give advice to someone using the prompts? It's better not to:

1 meet Roger tonight
2 take a day off work today
3 send an email to the boss (**shachō**)
4 phone Mr Hondo late
5 eat old (**furui**) sushi

Explanation 13.8 Summary of the phrases: *you may, you don't have to, you should, you shouldn't, you must, you are not allowed to, please do, please don't*

You've now learned a number of these phrases, some using **te** form,
some using **ta** form and some using **nai**. You may find it useful

to look at these altogether in a chart and have them here as a reference point.

meaning	verb form	connecting phrase/rule	example
you may, it's all right to	te	mo ii desu (ka)	tabetemo ii desu (ka) *you may eat (may I?)*
you are not allowed to	te	wa ikemasen (ikenai)	tabete wa ikemasen *you're not allowed to eat*
please do	te	kudasai	tabete kudasai *please eat*
I want you to do	te	hoshii desu	tabete hoshii desu *want you to eat*
you should, you'd better	ta	hō ga ii desu	tabeta hō ga ii desu *you should eat*
you shouldn't, it's better not to	nai	hō ga ii desu	tabenai hō ga ii desu *you shouldn't eat*
please don't	nai	de kudasai	tabenai de kudasai *please don't eat*
I want you not to do	nai	de hoshii desu	tabenai de hoshii desu *I want you not to eat*
you must	nai	nakereba narimasen (drop **nai**)	tabenakereba narimasen *you must eat*
you don't have to	nai	nakutemo ii desu (drop **nai**)	tabenakutemo ii desu *you don't have to eat*

Explanation 13.9 Nagara, uchi ni, aida ni *while*

You learned how to say *while* using **nagara** in Explanation 7.4:

Maiasa Naoe-san wa kōhī
o nominagara shinbun
o yomimasu

*Every morning Naoe reads
the paper while drinking
coffee*

You can only use this structure when the same person is doing both actions. If you want to talk about two different people you can use **aida (ni)**:

Ian-san ga ryōri o shiteiru
aida Katie-san wa hon
o yondeimashita

*While Ian was cooking Katie
was reading a book*

Ian-san ga Chūgoku ni iru
aida ni Katie-san wa shigoto
o sagashimasu

*During the time that Ian is in
China Katie will be looking
for a job*

Insight

Points to notice:

- The plain verb form before **aida** is either **teiru** (present continuous) or **iru** (*to be*)
- The verb form is always plain present tense
- **Aida** means *throughout the whole time* whereas **aida ni** means *at some point(s) during that time*
- The person/subject of the **aida** part of the sentence takes particle **ga** not **wa**
- The same person can do both actions with **aida** in which case the particle is **wa**:

Miki-san wa Amerika ni
iru aida ni ryokō o
shiteimashita

*During the time Miki was
in America she did some
travelling*

- **aida** can also be used with two nouns to mean *between*:

Tokyo to Ōsaka no aida ni   *between Tokyo and Osaka*

Uchi ni is used with the **nai** verb form to mean *while it is not* or *before*:

| Ame ga furanai uchi ni | *I played golf while it wasn't raining* |
| gorufu o shimashita | *(I played golf before it rained)* |

You can also use **uchi ni** with **teiru** to mean *while* – it tends to be used instead of **aida ni** (or **nagara**) when there isn't a specific time period:

| Kōcha ga atatakai uchi | *Drink the tea while it's warm* |
| ni nonde kudasai | |

Insight

So remember these basic rules:

- **Nagara** for the same person
- **Aida** for two different people/throughout the time
- **Aida** ni for two different people and during the time
- **Uchi** ni with the negative

Explanation 13.10 The conditional *if/when*

There are several ways to say *if* in Japanese but we shall focus on the most wide-ranging one (which also happens to be the easiest). You simply add **ra** to the past plain (positive or negative) of the verb or adjective as shown in the following table.

plain past form	if/when I do	if/when I don't
tabeta/tabenakatta	tabetara *if/when I eat*	tabenakattara *if/when I don't eat*
omoshirokatta/ omoshirokunakatta	omoshirokattara *if it is/were interesting*	omoshirokunakattara *if it isn't/wasn't interesting*

kirei datta/kirei ja nakatta	kirei dattara *if she is/were beautiful*	kirei ja nakattara *if she isn't/wasn't beautiful*
datta/ja nakattara	dattara *if it is/were*	ja nakattara *if it isn't/wasn't*

You can usually tell if the meaning is *if* or *when* from the context of the sentence. When **moshi** (*if*) is added to the beginning of the sentence, then it is clearly an *if* sentence. The tense of the sentence (present or past) is decided by the phrase that follows **ra**. Look at these examples:

Nihon ni ittara, sushi o tabete mite kudasai	*If you go to Japan, please try the sushi*
Nihon ni ittara, Miki-san ni aimasu	*When I go to Japan, I will meet Miki*
Sake o nondara, atama ga itaku narimashita	*When I drank the sake, I got a headache*
Omoshirokunakattara, yomitakunai yo!	*If it's not interesting, I don't want to read it!*

Insight

The first two sentences could mean either *if* or *when*, it isn't always clear without context. You can use **moshi** to make if sentences crystal clear.

Now you try. Select a verb or adjective from the box and try saying the following sentences:

1 If I go to Japan, I want to see Mount Fuji.
2 When I listened to the teacher's explanation, I understood quickly.
3 When Ian goes to China, he will work in Shanghai.
4 If I study well, I will be able to speak Japanese.
5 If she is not beautiful, I don't want to *date her*. (**dēto o shimasu**)
6 If you don't eat it, *it won't do*. (**yokunai desu**)
7 If you like sumo, please watch tonight's tournament.
8 If that film had been interesting, I would have watched it *all*. (**zembu**)

Main dialogue

🔊 **CD2, TR 47**

Robert and Rie are holding a farewell and pre-wedding party for Katie and Ian before they go to China. All the characters from this book are there. Listen to the different conversations then see if you can answer the questions.

Conversation 1: Katie is talking with Tatsuya-san and Eri-chan.

Eri	Nē, Katie-san, chansu ga attara, Chūgoku **e asobi ni itte**mo ii desu ka.
Tatsuya	Eri-chan! Dame desu yo. **Sonna koto o itte wa** ikenai desu yo.
Katie	**Daijbu** desu. Moshi chansu ga attara, **zehi** go-kazoku de Chūgoku e **asobi ni** kite kudasai.

Eri	Arigatō! **Tanoshimi ni shiteimasu.**
Tatsuya	Nē, Eri, Chūgoku ni ikitakattara, sono mae ni mainichi piano no renshū o shinakereba narimasen yo!
Eri	[*In a resigned voice*] Hai.

Conversation 2: Ian is talking with Naoe.

Naoe	Itsu kekkon o suru tsumori desu ka.
Ian	Mada hakkiri wakarimasen ga, dekitara Chūgoku ni iku mae ni kekkon shitai to omoimasu.
Naoe	Sō desu ka. Tenki ga atsukunai uchi ni kekkon shita hō ga ii desu ne.
Ian	Shikashi **kyū ni** shitara yokunai to omoimasu.
Naoe	Ian-san, **iiwake** shinai de kudasai!

Conversation 3: Robert and Rie realize that Miki is dating both of their friends.

(Notice that this conversation is in plain speech because they are all are of a similar age and know each other well.)

Robert	Nē, Miki-san, Takeshi-san wa **anata no koto** o totemo suki da to omou yo.
Rie	Takeshi-san? Rabu rabu bōizu no Takeshi-san? Roger-san to dō shita no?
Robert	Roger-san? Roger-san to **mo** dēto o shita no?
Miki	Sō nē Takeshi-san mo Roger-san mo totemo ii hito da to omou. Itsumo tanoshiku sugoshiteiru wa.
Rie	Demo Roger-san wa anata ga hontō ni suki yo. **Takeshi-san no koto** o iwanakereba naranai to omou wa.
Miki	**Daijōbu** yo. Yūbe sannin de asonda kara. Eiga o mitari, oishii resutoran de tabetari, iroirona bā de nondari shita no. Totemo tanoshikatta.
Robert	Miki-san! **Futari** no hito to dēto o shinai hō ga ii yo.

Miki	Heiki yo. **Shinpai** shinai de. Ā, **futari** ga kita.
	[*Roger and Takeshi enter the room together*]
	Roger-san, Takeshi-san, konban wa! Yūbe hontō
	ni arigatō!
Rie and Robert	Shinjirarenai!

asobi ni itte (iku)	*go and visit*
asobi ni kite (kuru)	*come and visit*
sonna koto o itte (iu)	*say those sorts of thing*
daijōbu	*fine*
zehi	*be sure to*
tanoshimi ni shiteimasu	*I'm looking forward to it*
kyūni	*suddenly*
iiwake	*excuse*
anata no koto	*you* (lit. *your things*)
takeshi-san no koto	*Takeshi, about Takeshi*
mo	*also, as well*
futari	*two* (*people*)
heiki	*it's cool, ok*
shinpai (suru)	*worry*

True or false?

Write either **O** (**maru** = true) or **X** (**batsu** = false) next to these statements:

1 Eri-chan wa Chūgoku ni ikitai desu
2 Ian-san to Katie-san wa Chūgoku de kekkon suru tsumori desu
3 Miki-san wa Takeshi-san no koto ga amari suki ja arimasen
4 Robāto-san wa futari no hito to dēto o suru koto ga ii to omotteimasu
5 Miki-san to Takeshi-san to Roger-san to san nin ga ii tomodachi deshō

Japanese questions

Write your answers in Japanese:

6 Eri-chan wa dōshite mainichi piano no renshū o shinakereba narimasen ka

7 Ian-san to Katie-san wa itsu kekkon shitai desu ka

8 Ian-san wa nani ga yokunai to omotteimasu ka

9 Miki-san wa yūbe nani o shimashita ka

10 Dōshite Robōto-san to Rie-san wa 'shinjirarenai' to iimashita ka

English questions

11 What is Mr Hondo's reaction when Eri asks if she can visit Katie in China?

12 What is Naoe's advice about the best time to get married?

13 What is Naoe's reaction when Ian says it won't do to rush the wedding?

14 What does Rie advise Miki to tell Roger?

15 Does Miki prefer one over the other?

Learn to say: Farewell speech

◀) **CD2, TR 48**

Ian makes a speech during the party to thank everyone. He uses polite Japanese with a number of specific respectful expressions (these are underlined). The speech is written first in Japanese script and then in rōmaji so, if you have been learning how to read Japanese, take this chance to practise! Listen to the recording in chunks and try to learn the speech off by heart – you may find it very useful if you go to Japan!

きょうは ケーティ と わたしたち の ために
こんな に せいだいな そうべつかい と

けっこん **ぜんやさり** を <u>ひらいて くださって</u> ありがとう ございます。とても **かんしゃ** しています。日本に いる あいだ、たくさん の **人たち** に あい、たくさん の こと を べんきょう しました。日本 の **みなさん** は とても **しんせつ** で たいへん <u>おせわ に なり ました</u>。らい月 中 国 へ 行くこと に なりました が まだ したい こと や 見た い ところ が あった ので、すこし ざんねん です。でも、また **いつか** 日本に きて、 **みなさん** と あいたい です。いろいろ と ありがとう ございました。もし 中国に くる チャンス が あったら、ぜひ **れんらく** して ください。ありがとう ございました。

Kyō wa Katie to watashi**tachi** no **tame ni konna ni seidai na** sōbetsukai to kekkon **zenyasai** o <u>hiraite kudasatte</u> arigatō gozaimasu. Totemo **kansha** shiteimasu. Nihon ni iru aida, takusan no hito**tachi** ni ai, takusan no koto o benkyō shimashita. Nihon no **minasan** wa totemo **shinsetsu** de taihen <u>osewa ni narimashita</u>. Raigetsu Chūgoku e iku koto ni narimashita ga, mada shitai koto ya mitai tokoro ga atta node, sukoshi zannen desu. Demo, mata **itsuka** Nihon ni kite, **minasan** to aitai desu. Iroiro to arigatō gozaimashita. Moshi Chūgoku ni kuru chansu ga attara, zehi **renraku** shite kudasai. Arigatō gozaimashita.

Thank you for having/organizing such a splendid farewell and pre-wedding party for me and Katie today. We really appreciate it. While we were in Japan, we met many people and learned many things. People in Japan were very kind and you have really looked after us. We will go to China next month but we still had lots of things we want to do and places we want to see, so it is a bit of a shame. But we want to come to Japan again one day and we want to see you all. Thank you for everything. If you have a chance to come to China, be sure to contact us. Thank you.

tachi	makes certain words plural
tame ni	*for*
konna ni	*such*
seidai na	*splendid*
sōbetsukai	*farewell party*
kekkon zenyasai	*pre-wedding party*
hiraite kudasatte (kudasaru)	*organize (hold) for us*
kansha (suru)	*appreciate*
ai = au	*meet*
minasan	*everyone*
shinsetsu (na)	*kind*
osewa ni narimashita	*you have helped us/looked after us*
itsuka	*sometime, one day*
renraku (suru)	*contact*

End-of-unit challenge

You are now going to personalize Ian's speech ('learn to say' section). Change it to include the following information:

1 Say thank you for a farewell party organized for you.
2 Say you will go back (return) to your own country next month.
3 Invite people to contact you if they come to your country.

All other information remains the same. When you have done this you will have your own farewell speech!

Taking it further

Omedetō gozaimasu! Congratulations! You have completed the full *Complete Japanese* course. The aim of this course has been to give you a thorough grounding in practical Japanese structures and vocabulary and a solid foundation on which to build your knowledge and skills in Japanese. You can look up the rules for all the verb and adjective structures you have learned in the grammar and structures index at the back. You might find it useful to compile a chart with columns for each of these structures and add to it all the verbs and adjectives you know (use the verb table at the back of this book) with all their different endings to help you make this learning your own.

There are many intermediate and advanced Japanese language books on the market and many courses now available online. A selection follows.

Books and journals

Basic kanji I, II and *III* (Bonjinsha)
A Dictionary of Japanese Grammar: Basic, Intermediate (Japan Times)
Japanese for Busy People II and *III* (Kodansha)
Japanese for Everyone (Gakken)
Oxford Starter Japanese Dictionary (Oxford University Press)
Read and Write Japanese Scripts (Teach Yourself, Hodder & Stoughton)
Speak Japanese with Confidence – CD-only course, 3 CDs including 1 CD of listening challenges (Teach Yourself, Hodder & Stoughton)
Michel Thomas Method Japanese – Introduction, Foundation and Advanced Sets – CD course focusing on building up speaking skills from everyday structures (Hodder & Stoughton)

Hiragana Times (monthly newspaper), www.hiraganatimes.com/
  Nihongo Journal, www.alc.co.jp/nj/

Online courses and websites

These change and are added to all the time. The Teach Yourself website relates expressly to this current volume, of course: www.teachyourself.co.uk

Here is a current selection of others that you may find useful:

- Japan Information Network: www.jinjapan.org/menu.html. Follow links via *Japan Web Navigator – Education*
- Japanese Writing Tutor. Shows you how to write hiragana and katakana – www.members.aol.com/writejapan/
- Jim Breen's Japanese Page: www.csse.monash.edu.au/~jwb/ japanese.html
- Kanji tutor: www.kanjicards.com
- Top 20 Japanese language and cultural activities: www.quia. com/dir/japanese
- Web resources for the teaching and learning of Japanese: www.essex.ac.uk/centres/japan/resources/menu.html

Key to the exercises

U = unit, OA = opening activity, BA = build-up activity,
OD = opening dialogue, E = explanation, MD = main dialogue,
LS = learn to say; A = activity, SR = start reading; RA = reading activity,
RC = reading challenge, EUC = end-of-unit challenge

Unit 1

E1.1 Watashi wa jānarisuto desu. Kore wa Tōkyō Ginkō desu. Kazoku wa rokunin desu. Watashi wa Amerikajin desu. Watashi wa jussai dewa arimasen

E1.3 **1** England **2** Italy **3** New Zealand **4** Spain **5** Portugal **6** Mexico **7** Brazil **8** Germany **9** Argentina **10** Australia

E1.8 **1** Kono meishi wa watashi no desu **2** Sore wa Robāto-san no desu **3** Sono wain wa itaria no desu **4** Are wa Supein no desu

A1.1 **1** Hajimemashite, name desu. (Dōzo) yoroshiku (onegaishimasu). **2** Arigatō gozaimasu. Watashi no (meishi) desu. (Dōzo) **3** Ā, Suzukisan wa tōkyō ginkō no eigyō buchō desu ne. **4** Oisogashi deshō ne

A1.2 Pictures L→R: ohayō gozaimasu; konnichi wa; sumimasen; Baibai; sayōnara; konbanwa; oyasumi nasai

A1.3 **1** Amerika no **2** Furansugo no **3** Nihon no **4** Eigo no **5** Chūgokujin no **6** Kankokujin no/kankokugo no (could be either)

A1.4 (Hondō Naoe-san no) go-kazoku wa yonin desu. Go-shujin no Hondō Tatsuya to musume-san no Yuki-chan (or san – she is older) to Eri-chan desu. Yuki-chan (or san) wa jū roku sai desu. Soshite Eri-chan wa jussai desu. Go-shujin wa eigyō buchō desu. (Okusan no) Naoe-san wa shufu desu)

A1.5 **1** Kono **2** Ano **3** Sono **4** Kocchi **5** kochira **6** Are

A1.6 **1** desu **2** dewa arimasen **3** dewa arimasen **4** desu **5** dewa arimasen **6** desu **7** desu

RA1.1 **1** = hiragana, **2** = kanji, **3** = katakana

Key sentences **1** Kazoku to asagohan o tabemasu **2** Tokidoki terebi o mimasu **3** Itsumo kōhī o nomimasu **4** Kinjo no hito to Nihongo o hanashimasu **5** Asa sōji o shimasu

E2.1 **1** Hirugohan o tabemasu **2** Tokidoki shinbun o yomimasu **3** Itsumo nyūsu o kikimasu **4** Chichi to hatarakimasu **5** Ashita Nihon ni ikimasu **6** E o kakimasu **7** Hirugohan o tsukurimasu **8** Hayaku nemasu **9** Terebi o kaimasu **10** Haha wa asa sōji o shimasu

E2.2 **1** Kanojo wa ashita kankoku ni ikimasu **2** Anatatachi wa hayaku okimasu ne! **3** Watashitachi wa itsumo issho ni bangohan o tabemasu **4** Kare wa otōsan to hatarakimasu **5** Anata wa kazoku to resutoran ni ikimasu ka

E2.3 **1** Asa itsumo shinbun to kōhī o kaimasu **2** Tokidoki kyōdai to terebi o mimasu **3** Itsumo haha to shujin to bangohan o tsukurimasu

E2.5 **1** Ashita jimusho ni (e) ikimasu **2** Musuko to sūpā ni (e) ikimasu **3** Tokidoki hayaku uchi ni kaerimasu **4** Chichi wa asa koreji ni (e) kimasu **5** Ashita Nihon ni kaerimasu

E2.7 **1** Mainichi jimusho de kōhī o nomimasu **2** Tama ni sūpā de shinbun o kaimasu **3** Musuko wa raishū koreji de sakkā o shimasu **4** Ashita kazoku to resutoran de tabemasu *or* ashita resutoran de kazoku to tabemasu

E2.8 **1** Ano depāto ni ikimashō **2** Kono sūpā de sushi o kaimashō **3** (Watashi no) uchi ni kaerimashō ka

E2.9 **1** kōhī o/wa nomimasen **2** (Kare wa) shigoto o/wa shimasen (*or* kare wa hatarakimasen) **3** Tsuma wa uchi o sōji shimasen (*or* Tsuma wa sōji o shimasen) (can also use Kanai for wife)

MD **1** 6 o'clock **2** toast, coffee **3** 8 o'clock **4** has dinner at restaurant with people from office **5** around 10 or 11 o'clock **6** watches TV with wife **7** plays golf with colleagues sometimes, usually relaxes with family at home

A2.1 **1** hirugohan ni tamago to tōsuto o tabemasu. Soshite kōhī o nomimasu **2** Mainichi rokuji ni okimasu. Sorekara asagohan o tsukurimasu **3** Ashita kinjo no hito to gorufu o shimasu **4** Gogo taitei shinbun o yomimasu. Tokidoki nyūsu o mimasu **5** Itsumo osoku uchi ni kaerimasu. Tama ni kazoku to bangohan o tabemasu

A2.2 **1** Kazoku to shokuji o shimasen **2** Kinjo no hito to hanashimasen **3** Asagohan ni kōhī o nomimasen **4** Uchi o sōji shimasen **5** Hayaku shigoto (or kaisha/jimusho) ni ikimasen

A2.3 **a** 2 **b** 5 **c** 3 **d** 1 **e** 4

A2.3 Answers to questions: **1** Jūji, jūichiji goro kaerimasu **2** Mainichi rokuji ni okimasu **3** Osoku made hatarakimasu **4** Tokidoki jimusho no hito to gorufu o shimasu ga taitei kazoku to uchi de gorogoro shimasu **5** Asagohan ni taitei tōsuto o tabemasu

A2.4 **1** de, to, o **2** de, to (or wa), o **3** ni, to (or wa), ni **4** ni, ni, ka **5** de, to (or wa), o

RA2.1 **1** f **2** h **3** i **4** b **5** c **6** a **7** d **8** j **9** g **10** e

RA2.2 **1** e **2** ai **3** au **4** ue **5** kao **6** aoi **7** akai **8** aki **9** eki **10** kusa **11** kesa **12** koe **13** sushi **14** seki **15** soko **16** suki **17** sekai **18** seiki **19** ookii **20** oishii

RA2.3

あ		け	く			う	え
	う	あ	さ			え	
	す	き		せ	か	い	
	し			い		そ	こ
お				き			え
	お	せ			あ	い	
	え	き			か	お	
お	い	し	い		い		い

RC ka shi u ku sa; ki so a o ke; e su i ko se

Unit 3

BA **1** kādo yon-mai **2** terebi nana-dai **3** kuruma go-dai **4** kami kyū-mai **5** kompyūta ni-dai **6** tōsuto ichi-mai

E3.2 **1** Sumimasen, yukata ga arimasu ka **2** Hagaki ga arimasu ka **3** Sumimasen, kitte o utteimasu ka **4** Kamera no denchi o utteimasu ka **5** Kono sensu wa ikura desu ka **6** Sono o-hashi o misete kudasai **7** Ano ningyō o misete kudasai **8** Kono o-sake o kudasai **9** Kono tokei to kono kaban o kudasai

E3.3 (System A): **1** kutsu hassoku **2** ringo rokko **3** sake gohon **4** bīru yonhon **5** yukata sanmai **6** terebi ichidai **7** hon jussatsu; (System B): **8** kōhī mittsu **9** keitai denwa futatsu **10** kēki hitotsu **11** kaban tō **12** tokei yottsu

E3.4 **1** kaban o futatsu kudasai **2** tokei o itsutsu kudasai **3** kōhī o yottsu kudasai **4** sake o nihon kudasai **5** bīru o roppon kudasai **6** ringo o sanko kudasai **7** kitte o gomai kudasai **8** nōto o sansatsu kudasai

E3.5 **1** imasu **2** arimasu **3** arimasu **4** imasu **5** arimasu **6** hon ga arimasu **7** ringo ga arimasu **8** kinjo no hito ga imasu **9** Amerikajin ga imasu **10** Amerikajin to Nihonjin ga imasu

E3.6 **1** Jimusho ni chichi ga imasu **2** Uchi ni kazoku ga imasu **3** Ikkai ni kaban ya tokei ga arimasu **4** Sankai ni sūpā ga arimasu **5** Ano jimusho ni Furansujin to Igirisujin no jānarisuto ga imasu

E3.7 **1** Yonkai ni nani ga arimasu ka **2** Rokkai ni nani ga arimasu ka **3** Kono jimusho ni nani ga arimasu ka **4** Jimusho ni dare ga imasu ka **5** Uchi ni dare ga imasu ka **6** Sankai ni dare ga imasu ka

E3.8 **1** Kono jimusho ni dare ka imasu ka **2** Ikkai ni nani ka arimasu ka **3** Uchi ni dare ka imasu ka **4** Kono jimusho ni dare mo imasen **5** Ikkai ni nani mo arimasen **6** Uchi ni dare mo imasen

E3.9 **1** O-hashi wa gohyaku-en desu **2** Shinbun wa sambyaku gojū-en desu **3** Yukata wa yonsen yonhyaku-en desu **4** Ningyō wa rokusen happyaku en desu **5** Kono kamera wa kyūsen kyūhyaku kyūjū kyū-en desu **6** sanman gosen, roppyaku-en **7** sanjū goman, rokusen roppyaku-en **8** sanjū goman rokusen roppyaku rokujū roku-en

E3.10 **1** ya, nado **2** to **3** mo, mo

MD + dialogue: 1st dialogue: buying 3 postcards and 3 stamps. Stamps = 100 yen each, postcards = 75 yen each, total = 525 yen; 2nd dialogue:

buying one kilo of apples and two kilos of bananas, apples = 400 yen per kilo, bananas = 600, total = 1600 yen; 3rd dialogue: buying one yukata and three folding fans, 4500 yen and 1500 yen, total = 9000 yen; 4th dialogue: buying camera, camera at sale price = 24650 yen

Script for main dialogue: SA = shop assistant, C = customer: <u>Dialogue 1</u>: SA Irasshaimase   C Sumimasen, hagaki o utteimasu ka   SA Hai, asoko desu   C Ā, sō desu ka. Ikura desu ka   SA Ichi-mai, hyaku-en desu   C Jā, kono hagaki o san-mai to nanajū go-en no kitte mo san-mai kudasai   SA kashikomarimashita. Zembu de gohyaku nijū go-en desu; <u>Dialogue 2</u>:   SA Irasshai, irasshaimase   C Sumimasen, ano ringo wa ichi-kiro ikura desu ka   SA Ringo desu ka. Ichi-kiro yonhyaku-en desu   C Jā, ichi-kiro onegaishimasu. Soshite banana wa ikura desu ka   SA Sore wa ichi kiro roppyaku-en desu   C Ē to, ni kiro kudasai   SA Hai, zembu de sen roppyaku-en desu   C Dōzo; <u>Dialogue 3</u>: C Sumimasen, ano yukata o misete kudasai   SA Kore desu ka. Dōzo. Kore wa rokusen-en de gozaimasu   C Chotto takai desu ne. . .   SA Kore wa yonsen gohyaku-en de gozaimasu   C Ā, sō desu ka. Jā, kore o kudasai; Soshite sensu ga arimasu ka   SA Hai, kore wa sen gohyaku-en de gozaimasu   C Jā, kore o sanbon kudasai   SA Kashikomarimashita. Zembu de kyūsen-en de gozaimasu; <u>Dialogue 4</u>:   SA Irasshaimase   C Sumimasen, kono kamera wa ikura desu ka   SA Sore wa sanman-en desu   C Sō desu ka. Ano sony F × 10 o utteimasu ka   SA Sony F×10 . . . hai, kochira ni arimasu. Kore mo sanman-en desu ga kyō no sēru de niman yonsen roppyaku gojū-en desu yo   C Niman yonsen roppyaku gojū-en desu ne. Sore wa ii desu ne. Jā, sono sony no kamera o kudasai

A3.1   **1** b   **2** a   **3** b   **4** a   **5** c   A3.1 Script: **1** A Sumimasen, ima nanji desu ka B Shichiji desu; **2** A Okāsan, piano no ressun wa nanji kara desu ka B yoji kara desu yo. Hayaku!; **3** A Irasshaimase! B Sumimasen, kono ningyō wa ikura desu ka A Sore wa nisen-en desu; **4** A Ano ne . . . kono apāto no yachin wa ikura desu ka B Ikkagetsu sanman issen-en desu B Sanman issen-en desu ka. Takai desu ne! **5** A O-tanjōbi wa nangatsu desu ka B Atashi desu ka. Rokugatsu desu

A3.2   **1** g   **2** i   **3** h   **4** d   **5** a   **6** k   **7** b   **8** e   **9** l   **10** c   **11** f **12** j

A3.3   All end in 'kudasai'   **1** yukata o nimai   **2** bīru o sanbon   **3** ningyō o yottsu   **4** kitte o hachimai   **5** ringo o goko

A3.4   **1** ni, ga, arimasu   **2** ni, ga, imasu   **3** ni, ga, arimasen   **4** ni, imasen   **5** ni, ga, imasu

A3.5 **1** dare ka imasu **2** dare mo imasen **3** nani ka arimasu
4 nani mo arimasen **5** dare ka imasu **6** dare ka imasu

RA3.1 **1** tate **2** nani **3** fune **4** chichi **5** hitotsu **6** futatsu
7 nanatsu **8** haha **9** heta **10** nuno **11** hone **12** te **13** natsu
14 hana **15** hito

RA3.2 **1** tokei **2** heso **3** kata **4** saifu **5** ani **6** ane **7** otōto
(otouto) **8** uchi **9** kanai **10** ashita **11** ohashi **12** osake **13** hōhō
(houhou) **14** senaka **15** taitei **16** futsū (futsuu) **17** itsutsu
18 kokonotsu **19** tō (tou) **20** ikutsu

RA3.3 Odd one out is **1** し **2** け **3** あ **4** さ **5** ね
6 こ **7** さ Correct symbol is **1** さ **2** は **3** お **4** き
5 ぬ **6** い **7** ち

RC ta nu ka hi shi tsu u ho ku na sa chi ki he
so te a fu o to ke e ni su ha i no ko ne se

EUC **1** f **2** h **3** d **4** g **5** j **6** i **7** a **8** b **9** e **10** c

Unit 4

OA Say the name of the 10 places followed by wa doko ni
arimasu ka

BA **1** Resutoran wa soko ni arimasu **2** kaisha wa koko ni arimasu
3 gakkō wa kono chikaku ni arimasu **4** yūbinkyoku wa asoko ni arimasu **5** bijutsukan wa soko ni arimasu

E4.1 **1** hoteru no mae **2** depāto no ushiro **3** ginkō no mae
4 bijutsukan no ushiro **5** resutoran no ushiro **6** resutoran no
tonari **7** ginkō no yoko **8** gakkō no soba **9** haukubutsukan no
ue **10** depāto no shita **11** gekijō no naka **12** yūbinkyoku no
mukaigawa **13** The hotel is opposite the post office **14** The restaurant
is above the museum **15** my camera is in that bag **16** Katie is by
me **17** Yūbinkyoku wa ginkō no mukaigawa ni arimasu **18** ginkō wa
sūpā no tonari ni arimasu **19** sūpā wa gakkō no ushiro ni arimasu
20 Gakkō wa hakubutsukan no chikaku ni arimasu **21** Sensei wa
gakkō (no naka) ni imasu **22** (Watashi no) meishi wa kaban no naka ni
arimasu

E4.2 **1** Ni-kai ni dare ga imasu ka **2** Ginkō no ushiro ni nani ga
arimasu ka **3** Gakkō no soba ni nani ga arimasu ka **4** yūbinkyoku no
mukaigawa ni nani ga arimasu ka **5** sūpā wa doko ni arimasu ka (doko
desu ka)

E4.3 **1** Massugu itte kudasai **2** Kōsaten o hidari ni magatte kudasai **3** Ōdan hodō o watatte kudasai **4** Hitotsu-me no shingō o migi ni magatte kudasai **5** Hodōkyō o watatte, kado o hidari ni magatte kudasai

E4.5 M Tomorrow shall we go somewhere together? **R** Yes, where shall we go? **M** How about the cinema? **R** Yes, let's go to the cinema? **M** What time shall we meet? **R** How about 7 o'clock? **M** That'll be great. See you tomorrow

E4.6 **1** Asagohan o tabemashita **2** Kōhī o nomimasen deshita **3** Nyūsu o kikimashita **4** Terebi o mimasen deshita **5** Shichiji ni resutoran de aimashita

E4.7 **1** Raishū Furansu ni ikitai desu **2** Uchi de nyūsu o kikitai desu **3** O-hashi de gohan o tabetai desu **4** Nihon no kamera o kaitai desu **5** Kinjo no hito to o-sake o nomitai desu

E4.10 **1** ichiji jū gofun **2** ichiji nijuppun **3** ichiji nijū gofun **4** ichiji sanjuppun

MD **1** have coffee and cake at a coffee shop **2** Roger isn't keen – he suggests bowling instead **3** He suggests tomorrow/Wednesday **4** Thursday at 7.30 **5** The first landmark given is the New Tokyo Theatre. There are traffic lights in front of this. Turn right at the traffic lights and go straight ahead. On the left is a cinema. Behind this is the bowling alley

LS Main sentences (changes only): **Miki** gekijō ni ikimashō ka **Roger** gekijō wa chotto . . . Tenisu wa dō desu ka **Miki** watashi wa tenisu ga heta desu ga tenisu o shimashō **Miki** Ashita wa kinyōbi desu ne. Kinyō bi wa chotto . . . doyōbi wa dō desu ka **Roger** Rokuji han ni Roppongi tenisu jō no mae de aimashō **Roger** Tōkyō hakubutsukan o gozonji desu ka; hakubutsukan no mae ni basu tei ga arimasu. Sono basutei o hidari ni magatte, massugu itte kudasai. Migigawa ni Mitsukoshi depāto ga arimasu. Depāto no mukaigawa ni Roppongi tenisu jō ga arimasu

A4.1 **1** Question: Sumimasen, *name of place* wa doko ni arimasu ka/desu ka **2** Hitotsu-me no shingō o migi ni magatte, massugu itte kudasai. Sūpā wa eigakan no mukaigawa ni arimasu **3** Futatsu-me no shingō o hidari ni magatte kudasai. Depāto wa hidarigawa ni arimasu. Gekijō no tonari desu **4** Tsugi no shingō o hidari ni magatte, massugu itte kudasai. Hakubutsukan wa gakkō no mukaigawa desu **5** Tsugi no shingō o migi ni magatte kudasai. Eigakan wa sūpā no mukaigawa desu

A4.2 **1** (11), (3) **2** (2), (9) **3** (15), (16) **4** (13), (18) **5** (1), (17) **6** (14), (5) **7** (12) **8** (4), (6) **9** (7) **10** (8), (10)
Translations: **1** The restaurant is there **2** Turn right at those traffic

lights and go straight on   **3** My house is alongside the school
4 My business cards is in my bag   **5** What is there opposite the post
office?   **6** Cross over the footbridge and turn left at the corner
7 Would you like to go to the cinema?   **8** We met at the restaurant at
7 o'clock   **9** I didn't drink coffee   **10** I want to drink sake with my
neighbour

A4.3   **1** mashita   **2** tai desu   **3** masu   **4** masen   **5** masen deshita
6 masen   **7** tai desu   **8** tai desu

A4.4   **1** = e   **2** = b   **3** = a   **4** = f   **5** = c   **6** = d

A4.5   **1** (3), (a)   **2** (6), (g)   **3** (1), (e)   **4** (5), (d)   **5** (2), (b)   **6** (7),
(f)   **7** (4), (c)

RA4.1   **1** mura   **2** yoru   **3** yume   **4** yuri   **5** yama   **6** momo
7 mori   **8** mimi   **9** mon   **10** wareware   **11** wan   **12** maru

RA4.2   **1** hon   **2** kaimono   **3** watashi   **4** namae   **5** ohayō
(ohayou)   **6** sumimasen   **7** oyasumi nasai   **8** nomimasu
9 shimasu   **10** kakimasu   **11** kaimasu   **12** kikimasu
13 kaerimasu   **14** okimasu   **15** nemasu   **16** mimasu
17 yomimasu   **18** hanashimasu   **19** tsukurimasu
20 hatarakimasu

RA4.3   **1** tokei o kaimashita – I bought a watch   **2** hanashi o
kikimashita – I listened to the talk/story   **3** hayaku okimashita – I got up
early   **4** osoku nemashita – I went to bed late   **5** hon o yomimashita – I
read the book   **6** mainichi hatarakimasu – I work every day   **7** osoku
uchi ni kaerimashita – I went home late   **8** ashita haha to kaimono o
shimasu – I am doing the shopping with my mum tomorrow   **9** watashi
no namae o kakimashita – I wrote my name   **10** yoru taitei osake o
nomimasu – in the evenings generally I drink rice wine

RC   **1** na n ri hi a ki ru so mo wa ni fu   **2** nu he u ko ma ro shi (w)o o
ho to yu   **3** ya ta re ne tsu sa mi ha su i ka   **4** no te ra ku mu yo ke e me
se chi

Unit 5

OA   All start with Ano hito wa   **1** utsukushii desu   **2** akarui
desu   **3** yasashii desu   **4** otonashii desu   **5** hazukashii desu   **6** ii desu

BA   All begin with Ano hito wa   **1** akarukute yasashii desu
2 otonashikute hazukashii desu   **3** yasashikute utsukushii desu
4 otonashikute ii desu   **5** yasashikute ii desu

OD **1** A bit shy and quiet but beautiful **2** She doesn't think Miki is especially shy **3** He hopes to play tennis **4** He is very cheerful and kind and he is very good at bowling **5** Miki says they are going to see a movie whereas Roger told Rie he's hoping to play tennis

E5.1 na is needed in 1, 4, 5 and 6 Meanings: **1** Miki is a beautiful person, isn't she? **2** Roger is good at bowling isn't he? **3** Tokyo is lively isn't it? **4** This is a lively place isn't it? **5** I think Tatsuya Hondo is a serious person **6** This is a clean room isn't it?

E5.2 **1** Kono tokoro wa nigiyakana tokoro desu **2** Tōkyō wa totemo nigiyaka desu ne **3** Kore wa hirokute kireina heya desu **4** Haha wa me ga ōkii desu **5** (Watashi wa) me ga itai desu **6** Roger-san wa se ga takakute me ga ōkii desu **7** Naoe-san wa origami ga jōzu desu **8** Miki-san wa bōringu ga heta desu

E5.3 **1**–3 start with watashi wa then **1** se ga takai desu **2** se ga takakute me ga aoi desu **3** se ga takakute, me ga aokute, kami ga kinpatsu desu; 4–6 begin with haha wa then **4** kao ga marui desu **5** kao ga marukute, hana ga takai desu **6** kao ga marukute, hana ga takakute, me ga chairo desu **7** Kami ga nagakute, kuroi desu

E5.4 **1** (Kare wa) majime de otonashii hito desu **2** Tōkyō wa nigiyaka de hiroi desu

E5.5 **1** Yūmei da to omoimasu **2** Hiroi tokoro da to omoimasu **3** Hazukashigari da to omoimasu

E5.6 **1** Rainen Nihon ni ikitai to omoimasu **2** Nihon de sushi o tabetai to omoimasu **3** Soshite Fujisan o mitai to omoimasu

MD **1** feels bad; headache, stomach ache, sore throat, shoulder ache **2** It's a cold **3** He's hungover!

A5.2 **1**, 4, 5, 7 and 8 are i adjectives so drop final i and add correct ending; 2, 3 and 6 are na adjectives so add correct ending

A5.3 **1** C **2** G **3** E **4** F **5** D **6** A **7** B Picture (Clockwise from shoulders): 1, 5, 3, 7, 2

RA5.1 **1** ga za da ba pa **2** ga gi gu ge go **3** go zo do bo po **4** za ji zu ze zo **5** ge ze de be pe **6** bi bu pi pu

RA5.3 **1** kazoku – family **2** shinbun – newspaper **3** ginkō – bank **4** go – five **5** Nihongo – Japanese **6** asagohan – breakfast **7** bangohan – dinner **8** tamago – egg **9** denwa – phone **10** shigoto

– work **11** tokidoki – sometimes **12** zenzen – not at all **13** ichi-gatsu – January **14** gozen – am/morning **15** gogo – pm/afternoon **16** eigakan – cinema **17** hakubutsukan – museum **18** ohayō gozai-masu – good morning **19** arigatō gozaimasu – thank you very much

RA5.4 **1** shachō (shachou) – company director **2** kaisha – company **3** jimusho – office **4** shufu – housewife **5** shokuji – meal **6** kyōdai (kyoudai) – siblings **7** ryokō – travel **8** Chūgoku – China **9** tōkyō **10** kyōto **11** densha – train **12** yūbinkyoku – post office **13** benkyō – study **14** hyaku – 100 **15** raishū – next week

RC **1** ga kya gya **2** ji sha ja cha **3** hyo byo pyo **4** de gi za bu pe **5** gyu ju byu pyu **6** cho nyo hyo myo ryo **7** rya myu hyu pyu **8** gyo jo byo pyo **9** zu gu bu ryu **10** pa pi pu pe po

EUC **1** Rainen Nihon ni ikitai to omoimasu **2** Sonna ni hazukashi-gari ja nai to omoimasu **3** Tōkyō wa nigiyaka de hiroi desu **4** Kono depāto wa totemo nigiyaka desu ne **5** Watashi wa se ga takakute, me ga aokute, kami ga kinpatsu desu **6** Haha wa se ga takakute me ga ōkii desu **7** Totemo akarukute yasashii hito da to omoimasu **8** Ano hito wa majime desu ga yasashii desu **9** Supōtsu ga heta desu ga origami wa jōzu desu **10** Miki-san wa kireina (utsukushii) hito desu ne

Unit 6

BA **1** omoshirokute tanoshikatta desu **2** omoshirokute yokatta desu **3** subarashikute tanonshikatta desu **4** yokute tanoshikatta desu

E6.1 **1** Yokatta desu **2** tanoshikatta **3** fuyukai deshita **4** yūmei deshita

E6.2 **1** tanoshikunakatta desu – it wasn't enjoyable **2** yokunakatta desu – it wasn't good **3** subarashikunakatta desu – it wasn't wonderful **4** tsumaranakunakatta desu – it wasn't boring 5–7 all end in dewa (or ja) arimasen deshita **5** kirei **6** majime **7** fuyukai

E6.4 **1** Miki writes kanji skilfully **2** Robert speaks Japanese well (or often) **3** Mr Hondo does his work seriously/ conscientiously **4** Naoe cleans beautifully/neatly **5** Katie speaks English kindly/softly/ sympathetically

E6.6 All end in deshō **1** Ame nochi hare **2** kumori tokidoki yuki **3** ichinichi hare **4** kumori tokidoki kiri

E6.7 All start with 'Soon it will be' **1** summer. Gradually it will get hot **2** winter. Gradually it will get cold **3** fall. Gradually it will get cooler

E6.8 **1** basu de ikimashita **2** machi ni basu de (or basu de machi ni) ikimashita **3** haha no uchi ni kuruma de ikimashita (or reverse order) **4** nyū yōku ni densha de (or reverse) ikimashita

MD **1** He thinks it's a great place (just the business trip that was not interesting!) **2** He went by bullet train (he bought a single ticket) and returned in a colleague's car (not enjoyable and too far!) **3** It was not especially warm and it snowed all day Thursday **4** Tomorrow it will get cold. Rain later snow **5** Iie, omoshirokunakatta desu **6** Iie, katamichi no kippu o kaimashita **7** Ichinichi yuki deshita (fuyukai deshita) **8** Iie samuku narimasu

A6.1 **1** windy sometimes snow, 0 degrees, very cold **2** cloudy later fine, 5 degrees **3** cloudy later rain, 10 degrees **4** rainy all day, 12 degrees **5** fine sometimes cloudy, 15 degrees **6** Sunny/fine all day, 22 degrees warm

Script for weather report: Ashita no tenki yohō desu. Mazu hokkaidō no tenki desu. Sapporo wa kaze ga tsuyokute tokidoki yuki deshō. Rei do deshō. Totemo samui deshō. Sendai wa kumori nochi hare desu. Go do deshō. Tōkyō wa kumori nochi ame deshō. Jū do deshō. Ōsaka wa ichinichi ame deshō. Kion wa jūni do deshō. Tsugi wa kyūshū no tenki yō hō desu. Fukuoka wa hare tokidoki kumori deshō. Kion wa jūgo do deshō. Okinawa wa ichinichi hare deshō. Kion wa nijū-ni do deshō. Atatakai desu

A6.2 **1** desu. This film was interesting and good **2** deshita. Last week's business trip was boring and disagreeable **3** deshō. Tomorrow's weather will be cloudy later rain **4** masu. Tomorrow I will be 32 **5** mashita. This room has become clean **6** masen. I don't read a newspaper very much **7** kute, kunai desu. The neighbour has big eyes and isn't tall **8** kunakatta desu. The trip wasn't at all enjoyable **9** dewa arimasen/ja nai desu. Your room is not clean **10** katta desu; masen deshita. Last night I had a headache. I didn't eat anything

A6.4 **1** wa o **2** wa ga **3** wa no de ni **4** ni de **5** wa to ni **6** wa kara made o **7** wa mo mo **8** wa ga ga **9** wa no ni **10** wa ga wa

SR **1** kyōdai **2** benkyō **3** yūbinkyoku **4** ginkō **5** kyūshū **6** tōkyō **7** raishū **8** ryokō **9** ōkii **10** onēsan **11** oniisan/onī san **12** okāsan

EUC Food and drink: **1** hh **2** jj **3** q **4** l **5** s **6** e; Time: **1** m **2** ee **3** X **4** k **5** n **6** d; People: **1** j **2** o **3** a **4** bb **5** w **6** c; Places: **1** ii **2** gg **3** p **4** y **5** cc **6** f;

Directions: **1** h **2** u **3** i **4** z **5** ff **6** r Verbs: **1** t **2** v
3 aa **4** dd **5** g **6** b

Unit 7

E7.1 **1** tabetai desu **2** banana o/ga tabetai desu **3** tōsuto wa
tabetakunai desu **4** Kōhī wa nomitakunai desu **5** O-sake wa
nomitakunakatta desu **6** Yūbe bīru wa nomitakunakatta desu

E7.3 **1** Miki-san wa supōtsu ga amari suki ja arimasen **2** Roger-san
wa tenisu ga totemo suki desu **3** Rie-san wa kaimono ga suki desu
4 Miki-san wa eiga ga totemo suki desu **5** Ian-san wa ame ga kirai desu

E7.4 **1** kai **2** kaki **3** kiki **4** yomi **5** nomi **6** mi **7** iki
8 hataraki **9** shi **10** hanashi **11** Katie-san wa nyūsu o kikinagara
ocha o nomimasu **12** Naoe-san wa shokuji o tsukurinagara yuki-san to
(ni) hanashimasu **13** Robāto-san wa ongaku o kikinagara kanji o
kakimasu **14** Ian-san wa asagohan o tabenagara hon o yomimasu
15 Hondō-san wa hatarakinagara hirugohan o tabemasu

E7.5 **1** sushi no tabekata **2** sushi no tsukurikata **3** kanji no kakikata
4 Nihongo no yomikata **5** Eigo no hanashikata. Full sentences: all end
in o oshiemashita

E7.6 **1** tabe ni ikimasu **2** resutoran e tabe ni ikimasu **3** resutoran e
washoku o tabe ni ikimasu **4** Watashi wa resutoran e washoku o tabe
ni ikimashita **5** Watashi wa Katie-san to resutoran e washoku o tabe ni
ikimashita

E7.7 **1** Yūmeisō desu **2** Kono eiga wa tsumaranasō desu **3** Atama
ga itasō desu **4** Totemo utsukushisō desu ne (or kireisō desu ne)
5 Nihongo o hanashisō desu

E7.8 **1** Miki-san wa eiga ga ichiban suki desu **2** Bijutsu ga ichiban jō
zu desu **3** Supōtsu ga ichiban heta desu **4** Tenisu ga ichiban kirai desu
ga . . . **5** yakyū ga wa ichiban tsumaranai desu

MD **1** Robert says he's not very good at golf but he'll give it a try
2 He offers to teach him how to play golf and to pick him up at his
apartment **3** This Sunday at 12 **4** batsu/false **5** maru/true
6 batsu **7** 12-ji ni mukae ni ikimasu **8** Iie, kuruma de ikimasu
9 Iie, amari jōzu dewa arimasen

A7.1 **1** kata. Mr H taught Robert how to play golf **2** nagara. Naoe
watches TV while eating her breakfast **3** ni ikimasu. Tomorrow I

will go with Katie to town to watch a film **4** sō. A filmstar's lifestyle looks unpleasant, doesn't it? **5** tai desu. Next year I want to go to Japan **6** kata. I don't know how to make cakes **7** sō: Miki looks like she will eat that sushi doesn't she (technically tai also fits but isn't usually used in situations when you don't know for certain what another person wants)

A7.2 All begin with Katie-san wa: **1** eiga ga suki desu **2** terebi ga totemo suki desu **3** hon ga suki ja arimasen (ja nai desu) **4** kaimono ga totemo suki desu **5** gorufu ga amari suki ja arimasen **6** tenisu ga jōzu desu **7** gorufu ga heta desu **8** yakyū ga jōzu desu **9** ryōri ga nigate desu **10** sūgaku ga tokui desu

A7.3 **1** X **2** O **3** X **4** O **5** O

SR **a** 3 **b** 7 **c** 8 **d** 9 **e** 1 **f** 15 **g** 6 **h** 10 **i** 13 **j** 11 **k** 14 **l** 4 **m** 12 **n** 5 **o** 2

RA7.1 **1** mountain **2** river **3** bamboo **4** woman **5** child **6** forest **7** stone **8** root **9** sun **10** moon **11** wood **12** fire **13** rice field **14** power **15** earth/ground **16** water **17** tree **18** gold

RA7.2 **1** c **2** e **3** d **4** b **5** a

RA7.3 Sunday 3 **a** Monday 6 **d** Tuesday 5 **b** Wednesday 1 **g** Thursday = 2 **f** Friday 7 **e** Saturday 4 **c**

Unit 8

E8.1 From top to bottom: nete; okite; oshiete; hataraite; wakatte; atte; yonde; benkyō shite

E8.2 **1** Every day I get up at 6, eat breakfast then go to work **2** On Saturdays I get up at about 9, I drink coffee then I shop in town **3** Yesterday I worked until late, then I went to a restaurant with a colleague **4** In the evening I eat dinner, watch TV then go to bed late **5** Tomorrow I will go shopping with a neighbour, return home then chill out **6** Mainichi shichiji ni okite, asagohan o tabete, (uchi o) sōji shimasu **7** Mainichi jūniji ni hirugohan o tabete, shigoto ni ikimasu **8** Kinō osoku okite, kōhī o nonde, machi ni ikimashita **9** Ashita rokuji ni uchi ni kaette, bangohan o tabete, terebi o mimasu **10** Getsuyōbi ni Nihongo o. benkyō shite, resutoran e hirugohan o tabe ni ikimasu

E8.3 **1** Terebi o mite kara, nemashita **2** hirugohan o tabete kara, itsumo nyūsu o kikmasu **3** Nihongo o benkyō shite kara, taitei gorogoro shimasu **4** Ryōshin ni denwa shite kara, tomodachi no uchi ni ikimashita **5** Shinbun o yonde kara, uchi o sōji shimashita

E8.5 All begin with Koko de then: **1** netemo ii desu **2** yondemo ii desu **3** benkyō shitemo ii desu **4** terebi o mitemo ii desu **5** Nihongo o hanashitemo ii desu **6** ongaku o kiitemo ii desu **7** asondemo ii desu **8** Koko de tabetemo ii desu ka **9** Kono shinbun o yondemo ii desu ka **10** Koko de ongaku o kiitemo ii desu ka **11** Mado o aketemo ii desu ka **12** Mado o shimetemo ii desu ka **13** Kono heya o haittemo ii desu ka **14** Ofuro ni haittemo ii desu ka

E8.6 **1** Koko de nonde wa ikemasen **2** Mado o akete wa ikemasen **3** Sono doa o akete wa ikemasen **4** Kono heya ni haitte wa ikemasen **5** Ofuro ni haitte wa ikemasen

E8.7 **1** Kono ginkō wa jūji kara niji made desu **2** Yūbinkyoku wa kuji kara goji made desu **3** Eiga wa shichiji han kara jūji han made desu **4** Tōkyō kara Kyōto made ikimashita **5** Tōkyō kara Kyōto made shinkansen de ikimashita

MD **1** X **2** O **3** O **4** X **5** X **6** Jūji made aiteimasu **7** Nikai ni arimasu **8** Goji kara shichiji made desu **9** Iie, haite wa ikemasen **10** Shokudō de tabetemo ii desu **11** It closes at 10am and opens at 4pm **12** Men can take a bath from 5–7, women from 7 – 9 **13** until 9 **14** The film tonight finishes at 10.30 but the TV room closes at 10 (and there appears to be no flexibility) **15** He is surprised by the sleeping time rule of 10.30 and he didn't know that men and women have separate rooms!

A8.1 Script: Korekara gakkō no kisoku o setsumei shimasu.
1 akusesarī ya iyaringu nado o shitewa ikemasen **2** Kyōshitsu de hirugohan o tabetemo ii desu **3** Gakkō no naka de wa kutsu o haite wa ikemasen **4** Jugyō no aida toire ni itte wa ikemasen **5** Sensei to hanashitai baai wa shokuinshitsu ni haittemo ii desu. Answers to questions: **A** 3 **B** 1 **C** 4 **D** 2 **E** 5

A8.2 Script: Hajimemashite, Ishibashi Takeshi desu. Korekara boku no ichinichi ni tsuite hanashimasu. Mainichi osoku made neteimasu. Jūichiji goro okite, kōhī o nonde kara daigaku ni ikimasu. Daigaku de tomodachi ni atte, shokudō de hirugohan o tabemasu. Soshite tama ni daigaku no sensei to atte, benkyō ni tsuite hanashimasu. Maiban bando no membā to issho ni bando no renshū shimasu. Boku wa rīdo gitā o yatteite, poppu no ongaku o tsukutteimasu. Bando no renshū ga owatte kara bando membā to pabu ni itte, osoku made bīru o nondari poteto chippusu nado o tabetari shimasu. Yoru ichiji ka niji goro heya ni kaette sugu nemasu Sequence answers: **A** 5 **B** 4 **C** 2 **D** 1 **E** 6 **F** 7 **G** 3

A8.3 **1** motte **2** keshite **3** utatte **4** erande **5** hiite **6** yasunde **7** nuide **8** kimete **9** dete **10** tsukete

A8.4 **1** Kono kamera o motte kudasai **2** Denki o tsuketemo ii desu ka **3** Denki o keshite kudasai **4** Koko de utatte wa ikemasen **5** Hitotsu erande kudasai **6** Kono heya de gitā o hiitemo ii desu **7** Yasundemo ii desu ka **8** Kutsu o nuide kudasai **9** Hayaku kimete kudasai **10** Yoru dete wa ikemasen

A8.5 **1** either i or b **2** either b or i **3** g **4** e **5** d **6** h **7** a **8** j **9** f **10** c

SR **1** eye **2** ear **3** foot **4** hand **5** mouth/opening **6** person **7** big **8** small **9** above **10** below **11** middle

RA8.1 **1** big **2** ear **3** small **4** below **5** middle **6** above **7** mouth **8** eye **9** person **10** foot **11** hand

RA8.2 **1** d **2** e **3** g **4** h **5** a **6** b **7** c **8** f

RA8.3 **1** above, below, middle **2** mouth, ear, eye, foot, hand **3** person, woman, man, child, power **4** small, big, few, blue, black, white, bright, like **5** mountain, river, tree, forest, wood, bamboo, rice field, sun, moon, root **6** water, fire, gold, earth, stone

Unit 9

OA **1** Ima ongaku o kiiteimasu **2** Ima nyūsu o kiiteimasu **3** Terebi o miteimasu **4** Nihongo no shinbun o yondeimasu **5** Kazoku to shokuji o shiteimasu **6** Ima uchi o sōji shiteimasu **7** Tomodachi ni tegami o kaiteimasu **8** Tomodachi to hanashiteimasu **9** Depāto de kamera o katteimasu **10** Ima yasundeimasu

BA All sentences end in masahita and ima (now/at the moment) is left out

E9.5 **1** Ima nani o shiteimasu ka **2** Dejikame o katteimasu **3** Hondō-san wa nani o shiteimashita ka **4** Denwa o shiteimashita **5** Ima ikebana o naratteimasu **6** Maishū no nichiyōbi ni gorufu o shiteimasu **7** Katie-san mo Ian-san mo Nihon de Eigo o oshieteimasu **8** Haha wa Shidonī ni sundeimashita **9** Katie-san

wa Amerika ni kaetteimasu   **10** Ryōshin wa Amerika ni
kaerimashita   **11** Robāto-san wa Igirisu kara Nihon ni kiteimasu

E9.6 **1** sutekina jaketto o kitemimashita   **2** Nihon no bīru o
nondemitai desu   **3** Hondō-san ni denwa o shitemitemo ii desu
ka   **4** Nihongo de kaitemite kudasai   **5** Gorufu o shitemimashō

E9.7 **1** Nihongo de kaite hoshii desu   **2** Roger-san ni Eigo o
oshiete hoshii desu   **3** Amerika no shinbun o katte hoshii desu
4 Rie-san ni watashi no uchi ni kite hoshii desu   **5** ōkii kuruma ga
hoshii desu

E9.8 **1** Mada nyūsu o kiiteimasu   **2** Rie-san wa mō piano o
naratteimasen   **3** Mō Hondō-san ni denwa o shimashita ka. Iie
mada desu   **4** Mada dejikame o katteimasen ga mō atarashii terebi
o kaimashita   **5** Eri-san wa mada shukudai o shitteimasen ga
Yuki-san wa mada shitteimasu

E9.9 **1** a okāsan 1 b otōsan c Eri-chan d ojīchan   **2** a okāchan b
otōchan c onēchan d obāchan

MD **1** X   **2** X   **3** O   **4** X   **5** O   **6** Tenisu kurabu ni sanka
shimasu   **7** Nikai juku ni ikimasu   **8** Doyōbi ni tokidoki sampo
shimasu   **9** Taitei uchi ni kaette, haha to issho ni bangohan o
tsukurimasu . . .   **10** Gakkō de shimasu   **11** Yuki does club at
school on Saturday mornings then she generally goes into town with
friends and does some shopping. Sometimes she goes to see a film.
On Sundays she often goes for a drive with the family and sometimes
goes with Grandad for a walk   **12** Eri often goes to town with her
mum and granddad on Saturdays to do some shopping. Sometimes
she takes part in judo tournaments at school. She always spends
time with the family on Sundays   **13** Yuki does her homework until late at night   **14** Eri does a little each day but hasn't done any
yet this week. Yuki says that Eri doesn't like homework much and
Eri says she wants Yuki to do her homework for her to which Yuki
says: 'No way, do it yourself!'   **15** She studies maths and English

A9.1 **1** c   **2** j   **3** e   **4** f   **5** i   **6** a   **7** d   **8** b   **9** g   **10** h

A9.2 **1** mada   **2** mō   **3** mō or mada   **4** mada   **5** mō   **6** mada
or mō   **7** mada   **8** mō. Meanings: **1** Roger hasn't played tennis
with Miki yet   **2** Miki has already had a date with Roger
3 Mr Hondo isn't at home now. He is already (mō) at work; or he
is still (mada) at work   **4** Eri hasn't done her homework yet this
week   **5** Yuki has already done her homework this week

6 Katie's parents are still (mada) in Japan; or they are already (mō) in Japan **7** Takeshi doesn't work yet **8** Naoe's father no longer works. He is at home every day

A9.3 **1** g **2** c **3** a **4** h **5** e **6** b **7** d **8** f

RA9.1 **1** g **2** i **3** j **4** h **5** c **6** f **7** b **8** d **9** e **10** a

RA9.2 **1** b **2** d **3** e **4** c **5** a

RA9.3 **1** 11, 12, 13, 14, 15 **2** 20, 30, 40, 50, 60 **3** 90, 91, 92, 93, 94 **4** 33, 44, 55, 66, 77 **5** 59, 58, 57, 56, 55

RA9.4 **1** Tues 25th Dec **2** Wed 17th June **3** Sat 3rd Sept **4** Fri 21st April

RA9.5 **1** ¥400 **2** ¥700 **3** ¥1900 **4** ¥490 **5** ¥5000 **6** ¥20,0 00 **7** ¥73,000 **8** ¥409,900

RA9.6 **1** b **2** d **3** e **4** a **5** c

EUC **1** otōsan **2** okāsan **3** onīsan **4** Mari(ko)chan **5** ojīsan/ ojīchan **6** obāsan/obāchan. Takeshi's father would most probably call his wife okāsan in front of children, anata in private and first name with friends; he would call his children by their first names with or without chan and call the grandparents ojīsan and obāsan.

Unit 10

BA **1** terebi o miru **2** Eigo o oshieru **3** uchi o deru **4** nyūsu o kiku **5** terebi o kau **6** e-mēru o kaku **7** bīru o nomu **8** Nihongo o hanasu **9** Furansu ni iku

E10.1 **1** kaku (write) **2** kiku (listen) **3** nomu (drink) **4** kau (buy) **5** yomu (read) **6** kaeru (return, go back) **7** oyogu (swim) **8** asobu (socialize) **9** hataraku (work) **10** wakaru (understand) **11** taberu (eat) **12** miru (look) **13** okiru (get up) **14** neru (go to bed) **15** dekakeru (set off) **16** deru (go out) **17** iku (go) **18** suru (do)

E10.2 **1** Kinō uchi ni kaeru mae ni bā ni ikimashita **2** Ashita uchi ni kaeru mae ni resutoran de tabemasu **3** Maiasa shawā o abiru mae ni kōhī o nomimasu **4** Itsumo deru (dekakeru) mae ni uchi o sōji shimasu **5** Shawā o abiru mae ni taitei asagohan o tabemasu

E10.3 **1** Robāto-san wa bīru o nomu koto ga dekimasen **2** Rie-san wa Eigo o hanasu koto ga dekimasu **3** Naoe-san wa

sukoshi Eigo o hanasu koto ga dekimasu **4** Roger-san wa
Nihongo no shinbun o yomu koto ga dekimasu **5** Watashi (boku)
wa sashimi o taberu koto ga dekimasen

E10.4 1 Katie-san wa tomodachi to asobu koto ga suki desu
2 Eri-chan wa shukudai o suru koto ga suki ja arimasen **3** Nihonjin
to au koto ga omoshiroi desu **4** Naoe-san wa piano o hiku koto ga
jōzu desu **5** Roger-san wa kanji o kaku koto ga tokui desu

E10.5 1 Okāsan ni tegami o kaku tsumori desu ka **2** Konban
bīru o nomu tsumori desu ka **3** Mainichi osoku made hataraku
tsumori desu ka **4** Nichiyōbi ni Naoe-san to gorufu o suru
tsumori desu ka **5** Konban sakkā o miru tsumori desu ka

E10.6 1 Nihon ni iku no de mainichi Nihongo o benkyō shimasu
– I am going to Japan so I am studying Japanese every day
2 Sensei ga yasashii (desu) kara Eigo ga suki desu – because
the teacher is kind I like English **3** Miki-san wa kirei na no de
Roger-san wa suki desu – because Miki is beautiful Roger fancies
her **4** Mainichi uchi o sōji suru (shimasu) kara itsumo kirei desu
– because I clean the house every day it is always clean **5** Supōtsu
ga heta na no de tenisu kurabu o sanka shimasen **6** Ano (sono)
resutoran wa takai kara uchi de tabemashō **7** Katie-san wa jōzuna
sensei na no de kurasu ga tanoshii desu **8** Ryōshin wa ashita
Nihon ni kimasu (kuru) kara apāto o sōji shitai desu

MD 1 X **2** O **3** O **4** X **5** X **6** Rie-san to resutoran de
tabete, eiga o miru tsumori desu **7** Supōtsu o miru koto ga suki
da kara desu **8** Iie, dekimasen **9** Bejitarian da kara desu
10 Sushiya-san de taberu tsumori desu **11** Because she can't play
sports very well **12** She suggests watching baseball because she
likes watching sports **13** Eating shabu-shabu **14** Various restaurants 15 a She likes watching sport b He is a vegetarian

A10.1 Rainen Nihon ni ikitai no de ima Nihongo o naratteimasu.
Nihongo o hanasu koto ga mada amari jōzu ja arimasen ga Nihon
no koto ni kyōmi ga arimasu. Soshite Nihon no ryōri mo totemo suki
desu ga tsukuru koto wa dekimasen. Ashita machi de tomodachi to
atte, yūmeina resutoran de Nihon no ryōri o taberu tsumori desu

A10.2 A Miki's version 5 9 = 5 → 2 → 3 → 6 B Roger's version
5 8 → 5 → 1 → 4 → 7

A10.3 1 oyogu koto ga dekimasu **2** miru koto ga suki
desu **3** tsukuru tsumori desu **4** taberu koto ga suki
desu **5** suru koto ga jōzu desu **6** hataraku koto ga dekimasen

A10.4 **1** Byōki da kara (na no de) shigoto o yasundeimasu
2 Katie-san wa suki da kara (na no de) indo ryōri o tsukuru
tsumori desu **3** Roger-san wa mainichi renshū o suru no de (kara)
tenisu o suru koto ga jōzu desu **4** Nihongo o benkyō shitai
(naraitai) no de (kara) Nihon ni kimashita **5** Miki-san wa atama
ga itai kara (no de) ima kōhī o nondeimasu

SR Story 1 = 3; Story 2 = 4; Story 3 = 1; Story 4 = 2; Story 5 = 5

RA10.1 **1** person **2** cow **3** shellish **4** mouth **5** heart
6 water **7** fire **8** sun **9** going person **10** moon/flesh

RA10.2 **1** eat **2** drink **3** write **4** exit **5** enter **6** say/words
7 speak, talk **8** sell **9** read **10** see **11** buy **12** understand/
divide/minute **13** listen **14** go **15** rest, holiday

RA10.3 **1** c **2** d **3** f **4** g **5** h **6** a **7** i **8** j **9** e **10** b

RA10.4 **1** I eat breakfast **2** Sometimes I read the newspaper **3** Every day I listen to the news **4** I watch TV with my
father **5** Tomorrow I will go to Japan **6** I spoke Japanese
7 I bought an interesting book **8** I do the shopping on Saturdays
9 On Sunday I sold a car **10** Every day I try to write kanji

EUC **1** tsutaemasu **2** iremasu **3** dashimasu **4** okuremasu
5 gambarimasu **6** hashirimasu **7** arukimasu **8** tsukaimasu
9 okimasu **10** araimasu **11** karimasu

Unit 11

OA **1** mita, looked **2** okita, woke up **3** neta, slept/went to bed
4 kaita, wrote **5** kiita, listened to **6** nonda, drank **7** yonda,
read **8** hanashita, talked **9** ryōri shita, cooked **10** kaetta,
returned

BA **1** senshū eiga o mita **2** kesa shichiji ni okita **3** yūbe jū
niji goro neta **4** tomodachi ni tegami o kaita **5** tomodachi to
ongaku o kiita **6** yūbe bīru o ippai nonda **7** Nihongo no manga
o yonda **8** atarashii sensei ni hanashita **9** heya de indo ryōri o
tsukutta **10** kinō ryōshin wa Igirisu ni kaetta

E11.1 **1** nondeiru, nondeita **2** kaiteiru, kaiteita **3** sundeiru,
sundeita **4** itteiru, itteita **5** shiteiru, shiteita

E11.2 **1** Sashimi o tabeta koto ga arimasu **2** Fujisan o mita koto
ga arimasen **3** Nihongo de (or no) tegami o kaita koto ga arimasu

4 Nihongo no shinbun o yonda koto ga arimasen **5** Minami Amerika ni itta koto ga arimasen

E11.3 **1** bīru o nonda ato de sugu nemashita **2** shukudai o shita ato de pātī ni ikimashita **3** uchi ni kaetta ato de tomodachi ni denwa shimashita **4** konsāto no ato de bā ni ikimashita

E11.4 **1** yasai o tabeta hō ga ii desu yo **2** neta hō ga ii desu yo **3** mizu o nonda hō ga ii desu yo **4** uchi ni kaetta hō ga ii desu yo **5** e-mēru o dashita (kaita) hō ga ii desu yo; Friendlier: all the same as previous except replace desu yo with deshō

E11.5 **1** Nichiyōbi ni gorogoro shitari, shinbun o yondari, e-mēru o dashitari shimasu **2** kurisumasu ni ippai tabetari, terebi o mitari, tomodachi to (ni) attari shimasu **3** senshū Nihongo o benkyō shitari, kaimono o shitari, ōsaka ni ittari shimashita **4** asagohan ni kōhī o nondari, kōcha o nondari shimasu

E11.6 **1** Miki san no hō ga Roger-san yori majime desu **2** Roger-san no hō ga Miki-san yori supōtsu ga jōzu desu **3** Yuki-san no hō ga Eri-chan yori se ga takai desu 4 and 5 are author's personal opinion **4** supōtsu o suru hō ga supōtsu o miru yori tanoshii to omoimasu **5** bīru o nomu hō ga mizu o nomu yori ii to omoimasu

E11.8 **1** shukudai o wasurete shimatta **2** kamera o otoshite shimatta **3** bīru o nonde shimatta **4** sono hon o yonde shimatta **5** tsukarete shimatta

E11.9 **1** Nihongo no shinbun o daibu yomimashita **2** E-mēru o ippai (takusan) dashimashita **3** Ōsaka ni yoku ikimasu **4** Gohan o zembu tabete shimatta **5** Yakyū o sukoshi mimashita

MD **1** X **2** O **3** X **4** X **5** X **6** Pātī de aimashita 7 Rabu Rabu Boizu desu **8** Nihongo o oshietari, ryokō shitari shimashita 9 Kyonen no natsu shimashita **10** Ii jazu kurabu ga aru kara desu **11** 3 years ago **12** Last summer when she was living in Chicago; she thought they were really brilliant **13** A rock and jazz mix **14** Jazz **15** After they've drunk up their wine

A11.1

Script **1** Man Dōshita n desu ka. Woman Nodo ga itai n desu. Man Jā, kono kusuri o nonda hō ga ii desu yo. **2** Woman Dōshita n desu ka. Man Nodo ga kawaitta n desu. Woman Jā, mizu o nonda hō ga ii deshō. **3** Man Dō shita n desu ka. Woman Kibun ga warui n desu. Man Neta hō ga ii desu yo. **4** Woman Dōshita n desu ka.

Man kamera o otoshite shimatta n desu. Woman Atarashii kamera o katta hō ga ii deshō.   **5** Man Shōrai daigaku ni ikitai desu. Woman Jā, isshōkenmei benkyō shita hō ga ii desu yo.   **6** Woman Rainen Igirisu ni ikitai desu. Man Jā, korekara Eigo o naratta hō ga ii desu ne.   a 5   b 2   c 4   d 1   e 6   f 3

A11.2   Sequence b e h d g f c a. Missing words: **1** ippai   **2** takusan   **3** daibu   **4** sukoshi   **5** zenzen   6 amari   **7** zembu   **8** takusan/ippai

A11.3   kakimashita, tabemashita, yomimashita, ikimashita (or: iimashita), tsukimashita, kaimashita, oyogimashita

SR   Story 1 = 5 Story 2 = 3 Story 3 = 1 Story 4 = 2 Story 5 = 4

RA11.1   **1** d   **2** e   **3** f   **4** h   **5** b   **6** l   **7** i   **8** c   **9** g   **10** j   **11** k   **12** a

RA11.2   **1** father   **2** mother   **3** younger sister   **4** younger brother   **5** older sister   **6** older brother

RA11.3   **1** younger brother   **2** younger sister   **3** rain   **4** snow   **5** fine   **6** spring   **7** autumn, fall   **8** mother   **9** father   **10** heaven, sky, weather . . .   **11** summer   **12** winter   **13** older brother   **14** older sister   **15** country

EUC   **1** Minami Amerika ni itta koto ga arimasu   **2** Rabu rabu bōizu no ongaku o kiita koto ga arimasen   **3** Rokku no hō ga jazu yori suki desu   **4** Gakusei no toki konsāto ni takusan ikimashita   **5** Ōsutoraria ni sundeita toki Eigo o yoku hanashimashita (ga yoku dekimashita)   **6** Yūbe osoku neta kara (no de) tsukarete shimatta   **7** Ryōri o zembu shite shimatta   **8** Kono kamera no hō ga sono kamera yori ii to omoimasu   **9** Takeshi-san to hanashita ato de Miki-san wa Roger-san ni denwa shimashita   **10** Shūmatsu ni kaimono o shitari, eiga o mitari shimasu

Unit 12

OA   **1** miyō   **2** kikō   **3** kakō   **4** aō   **5** ikō   **6** yasumō   **7** hanasō   **8** oyogō   **9** miseyō   **10** matō

BA   **1** nyūsu o kikō ka   **2** e-mēru o kakō ka   **3** eigakan no mae de aō ka   4 ima pātī ni ikō ka   **5** yasumō ka   **6** Nihongo de hanasō ka   **7** umi de oyogō ka   8 sensei ni miseyō ka   **9** Miki-san o matō ka

E12.2 **1** Rainen Nihon ni ikō to omou (omoimasu) **2** Haha wa rainen Yūroppa ni ikō to omotteiru **3** Atarashii kuruma o kaō to omou **4** Sono e-meru o dasō to omou **5** Takeshi-san wa Miki-san ni mata aō to omotteiru

E12.3 **1** Piano o naraō to shiteiru (shiteimasu) **2** Sono repōto o kakō to shita (shimashita) **3** Chichi wa atarashii jaketto o kaō to shita **4** Kyonen Nihon ni ikō to shita

E12.4 **1** b **2** d **3** a **4** d **5** c

E12.5 **1** sushi ni shimasu **2** Jūji ni uchi ni kaeru koto ni shimashita **3** bīru o yameru koto ni shimashita **4** Kyōto ni shinkansen de iku koto ni shimashō **5** Mainichi mizu o takusan nomu koto ni shiteimasu

MD **1** X **2** X **3** O **4** X **5** O **6** Hachigatsu ni iku tsumori desu **7** Tenkin suru koto ni natta kara desu **8** Zannen desu ga ii chansu desu (or similar answer) **9** Kekkon suru koto ni shimashita **10** Pātī o suru tsumori desu **11** He tried to find another job in Tokyo **12** She thinks it's a shame, she wants to carry on working in Japan but she thinks she will go to China **13** Possibly next month but they don't know definitely yet **14** In Japan, before a transfer you're supposed to hold a farewell party **15** She's pleased and says it can be a farewell and wedding party

A12.1 **1** shinkansen (bullet train) 5 hours **2** train, 6 hours **3** on foot, 3 months **4** by plane, 1 hour **5** by car, 1 day

A12.2 Sumimasen ga konshū Nihongo wa amari benkyō shimasen deshita. Benkyō o shiyō to shiteimashita ga totemo isogashikatta desu. Getsuyōbi ni eigyō butchō to shokuji o suru koto ni narimashita. Soshite kayōbi mo suiyōbi mo osoku made kaisha de hatarakimashita. Mokuyōbi ni totsuzen watashi wa Nagoya ni shutchō suru koto ni narimashita. Raishū wa isshūkan kitto hima da to omoimasu. Dakara mainichi ni jikan gurai wa benkyō o shiyō to omoimasu

A12.3 **1** koto ni natteimasu **2** koto ni shimashita **3** koto ni narimashita **4** ni shimasu **5** koto ni natte imasu **6** koto ni shiteimasu

RA12.1 **1** j **2** b **3** g **4** c **5** e **6** d **7** a **8** h **9** i **10** f

RA12.2 **1** l **2** a **3** o **4** b **5** g **6** p **7** j **8** k **9** n **10** d **11** c **12** i **13** f **14** m **15** h **16** e

RA12.3 **1** p **2** o **3** b **4** i **5** c **6** f **7** j **8** h **9** l **10** n
11 d **12** g **13** e **14** m **15** a **16** k

RC **1** b **2** c **3** a **4** d **5** g **6** e **7** f **8** j **9** i **10** h
11 l **12** k **13** m **14** p **15** o **16** n **17** t **18** s
19 r **20** q

EUC **1** kaitai to omoimasu **2** ikō to omoimasu **3** au tsumori
desu **4** aō to shimashita **5** narau koto ni shimasu **6** kaeru
ka mo shiremasen **7** mi ni iku deshō **8** koyō to omoimasu
9 nomu koto ni shiteimasu **10** yasumu tsumori dewa (ja)
arimasen (you can also say yasumanai tsumori desu)

Unit 13

OA **1** hanasanai **2** yomanai **3** kikanai **4** tsukuranai
5 tsukawanai **6** asobanai **7** hairanai **8** oyoganai **9** minai
10 misenai

BA All answers same as OA answers with de kudasai at the end

E13.1 **1** hanasanai, hanasanakatta **2** minai, minakatta
3 yomanai, yomanakatta **4** awanai, awanakatta **5** narawanai,
narawanakatta **6** tatanai, tatanakatta **7** nenai, nenakatta
8 ikanai, ikanakatta **9** benkyō shinai, benkyō shinakatta
10 konai, konakatta

E13.2 **1** shinbun desu **2** kamera deshita **3** keitai dewa
(ja) arimasen **4** kamera dewa nai desu **5** shinbun ja nakatta
desu **6** keitai ja nai desu **7** keitai ja nai **8** kamera ja nakatta

E13.3 **1** bīru o nomanai de uchi ni kaerimashita **2** Miki-san ni
denwa shinai de resutoran ni ikimashita **3** hirugohan o tabenai de
yakyū o shimashita **4** renshū o shinai de piano o hikimashita

E13.4 **1** tabako o suwanai de hoshii desu **2** ima piano o hikanai
de hoshii desu **3** kaigishitsu ni hairanai de hoshii desu
4 Takeshi-san to asobanai de hoshii desu **5** bīru o zembu nonde
shimawanai de hoshii desu

E13.5 **1** You/I must study **2** You/I must go to work **3** You/I
must drink (take) the medicine **4** You/I must give up smoking
5 You/I must write the report

E13.6 **1–4** begin with 'it's alright if you don't/you don't have
to – 1 study Japanese this week **2** write that report **3** speak

Japanese **4** buy that expensive camera **5** I don't feel well so is it alright if I don't go to work?

E13.7 All end in hō ga ii desu – **1** Konban Roger-san ni awanai **2** Kyō kaisha (shigoto) o yasumanai **3** Shachō ni e-mēru o dasanai **4** Hondō-san ni osoku denwa shinai **5** Furui sushi o tabenai

E13.10 **1** Nihon ni ittara Fujisan o mitai desu **2** Sensei no setsumei o kiitara hayaku wakarimashita **3** Ian-san wa Chū goku ni ittara Shanghai de hatarakimasu **4** Yoku benkyō shitara Nihongo o hanasu koto ga dekimasu **5** Kirei ja nakattara dēto o shitakunai desu **6** Tabenakattara yokunai desu **7** Sumō ga suki dattara konban no shiai o mite kudasai **8** Sono eiga wa omoshi-rokattara zembu mimashita

MD **1** O **2** X **3** X **4** X **5** O **6** Chūgoku ni ikitai kara **7** Chūgoku ni iku mae ni **8** Kyū ni kekkon shitara **9** Sannin de eiga o mitari, ii resutoran de tabetari, iroirona bā de nondari shimashita **10** Miki-san wa futari no hito to dēto shimashita kara (other answers possible) **11** He tells her she shouldn't say that sort of thing **12** Before it gets hot/while it's not hot **13** She tells him not to make excuses **14** She must tell Roger about Takeshi **15** No, she thinks they are both nice people

EUC Make changes to these parts, all the rest remains the same: Kyō wa watashi no tame ni konna ni seidai na sōbetsukai (or pātī) o hiraite kudasatte arigatō gozaimasu. . . . . Raigetsu own country e kaeru koto ni narimashita ga. . . . Moshi own country ni kuru chansu ga attara, zehi renraku shite kudasai.

Japanese–English vocabulary

ā, sō desu ka	*oh, really?*
aida (ni)	*while, during*
akarui	*bright, cheerful*
aki	*fall/autumn*
amari (+ negative)	*not very, hardly*
ame	*rain*
Amerika	*America*
Amerikajin	*American* (person)
anata no koto	*you* (lit. *your things*)
anata	*you*
anatatachi	*you* (plural)
ane	*older sister*
ani	*older brother*
aneki	*older sister* (boys use)
aniki	*older brother* (boys use)
ano (ne)	*hey, erm* (friendly)
ano, are	*that, that one* (over there)
aoi	*blue*
apāto	*apartment*
are	*that (one) over there*
are	*hey!, what!*
arigatō gozaimasu	*thank you*
arimasu (1)	*have, possess*
arimasu (2)	*there is, there are* (non-living things, inanimate)
aruite	*on foot*
Aruzenchin	*Argentina*
asa	*morning*
asagohan	*breakfast*
ashita	*tomorrow*
asoko	*over there*
atama	*head*
atarashii	*new*
atatakai	*warm*
ato de	*after*
atsui	*hot*
badominton	*badminton*
bai bai	*bye bye*
banana	*banana*

bando	*band*
bangohan	*evening meal*
basu-tei	*bus stop*
Beikoku	*America*
bejitarian	*vegetarian*
bengoshi	*lawyer*
benkyō	*studying*
betsubetsu	*separately*
bijutsu	*art*
bijutsukan	*art gallery*
bīru	*beer*
boku	*I* (male)
bōringu	*bowling* (ten-pin)
bōringu jō	*bowling alley*
budō	*martial arts*
Burajiru	*Brazil*
chadō	*tea ceremony*
chairo	*brown*
chansu	*chance*
chichi	*my dad*
chiisai	*small*
chikaku	*near to*
Chūgoku	*China*
da	*is* (informal of desu)
dai	*large machinery*
daibu(n)	*greatly, quite a lot*
daigaku	*university*
daigakusei	*university student*
daijōbu	*fine*
dame	*no good, don't!*
dandan	*gradually*
dansei	*men, male*
dare	*who*
dare ka	*someone*
dare mo	*no one* (+ negative)
darō (plain of deshō)	*will probably*
de	*at/in* (after place)
de gozaimasu	= desu (humble polite form)
dejikame	*digital camera*
demo	*but*
demo	*something like or something*
denchi	*batteries*
denki	*lights, electricity*
densha	*train*

depāto	*department store*
deshō	*will probably*
desu	*am, is, are*
dēto	*date*
dewa arimasen	*is not, am not, are not*
dō	*how, what way*
dō desu ka	*how about … ?*
doa	*door*
Doitsu	*Germany*
doko	*where*
doko made	*where to*
dono, dore	*which, which one*
dōro	*street, road*
dōshite	*why*
doyōbi	*Saturday*
dōzo yorosh(i)ku	*pleased to meet you*
e = ni	*to* (a place)
ē to	*er, erm*
eiga	*movie, film*
eiga sutā	*filmstar*
eigakan	*cinema*
Eigo	*English*
eigyō buchō	*Sales manager*
Eikoku	*England*
e-mēru	*email*
en	*yen* (Japanese currency)
Fujisan	*Mount Fuji*
Furansu	*France*
Furansu no	*French* (items)
furui	*old* (things)
futari	*two* (people)
futatsu	*two items*
futatsu me	*second*
futsū	*average*
fuyu	*winter*
fuyukai (na)	*unpleasant, disagreeable*
ga	*but*
gaikoku	*abroad, foreign country*
gakkō	*school*
gekijō	*theatre*
getsu	*month*
getsuyōbi	*Monday*
ginkō	*bank*
ginkō-in	*bank worker*

gitā	*guitar*
go	*five*
gogo	*afternoon, pm*
gohan	*rice*
go-kazoku	*family* (others)
go-kyōdai	*siblings* (others)
goro	*about* (used with times)
gorufu	*golf*
go-ryōshin	*parents (others)*
go-shujin	*husband (others)*
gozen	*am, morning*
gozonji desu ka	*do you know?* (respect)
gurai	*about*
hagaki	*postcard*
haha	*mum* (own)
hai	*yes*
haiyū	*actor*
hajimemashite	*how do you do?*
hakkiri	*clearly*
hakubutsukan	*museum*
hana	*nose*
hare	*fine, sunny*
haru	*spring*
hashi	*bridge*
hashi	*chopsticks*
hayai	*quick, early*
hayaku	*early, quickly*
hazukashigari (na)	*shy, seems shy*
hazukashii	*embarrassed*
heiki	*it's cool, ok*
heta	*no good at*
heya	*room, bedroom*
hidari (gawa)	*left* (side)
hiki (piki, biki)	*small animals*
hikui	*low/small*
hima (na)	*free*
hiroi	*spacious, big* (places)
hirugohan	*lunch*
hiruma	*daytime, during the day*
hitotsu	*one item*
hitotsu me	*first*
hodōkyō	*footbridge*
hoka no	*other*
hon (pon, bon)	*long* (cylindrical items)
hontō	*real*

hontō ni	*really*
hoshii	*want*
hoteru	*hotel*
hyaku	*hundred*
ichi jikan	*one hour*
ichiban	*most, -est, number one*
ichinichi	*a (typical) day*
ichinichi	*all day*
Igirisu	*England*
ii (yoi)	*good, nice*
iie	*no*
iiwake	*excuse*
ikebana	*flower arranging*
ikura	*how much?*
imasu	*there is, there are* (animals and people)
imōto	*younger sister* (own)
imōtosan	*younger sister* (others)
Ingurando	*England*
inu	*dog*
ippai	*loads, full amount*
irasshaimase	*welcome, may i help you?*
iroiro (na)	*various*
isha	*doctor*
issho ni	*together*
isshūkan	*one week, per week*
itai	*hurts*
Itaria	*Italy*
itsu	*when*
itsuka	*sometime, one day*
itsumo	*always*
itsutsu	*ive items*
iya (na)	*awful*
ja mata ne	*see you!*
jā	*ok, right, in that case*
jānarisuto	*journalist*
jazu	*jazz*
ji	*o'clock*
jibun (no)	*oneself* (one's own)
jimusho	*office*
jin	*person* (nationality)
jitsu wa	*in fact*
josei	*women, female*
jōzu (na)	*good at, skilful*
juku	*cram school*

ka	*? (spoken question mark)*
kaban	*bag*
kado	*corner*
kai	*floors*
kai	*number of times*
kaigi	*meeting*
kaigishitsu	*meeting room*
kaimono	*shopping*
kaisha	*company*
kaisha no eigyō buchō	*company sales manager*
kaisha-in	*company employee*
kamera	*camera*
kameraman	*photographer*
kami	*hair*
kami	*paper*
kaminari	*thunder*
kamo shiremasen	*might*
kanai/tsuma	*wife* (own)
kangoshi	*nurse, medical carer*
Kankoku	*Korea*
kanojo	*she*
kao	*face*
kara	*from*
kara	*therefore, so*
kare	*he*
karera	*they*
kashu	*singer*
kayōbi	*Tuesday*
kaze	*wind*
kazoku	*family* (own)
keisatsukan	*policeman*
keitai (denwa)	*mobile (phone)*
kēki	*cake*
kekkon	*marriage*
kesa	*this morning*
ki	*tree*
kinjo no hito	*neighbour*
kinō	*yesterday*
kinpatsu	*blonde*
kinyōbi	*Friday*
kippu	*ticket*
kirai (na)	*hate*
kirei (na)	*beautiful; clean*
kiri	*fog*
kiro	*kilo*

kissaten	*coffee shop*
kitte	*stamps*
ko	*round objects*
kōcha	*black tea*
kochira	*this* (person)
kodomo no koro	*childhood*
kōhī	*coffee*
koko; soko; asoko	*here; there; over there*
kokonotsu	*9th* (date)
kompyūtā	*computer*
konban	*tonight*
konbanwa	*good evening*
kongetsu	*this month*
konkai	*this floor*
konna ni	*such*
konnichiwa	*hello*
kono, kore	*this, this one*
konsāto	*concert*
konshū	*this week*
koreji	*college*
kōsaten	*crossroads*
koto	*Japanese harp*
kudasai	*may I have . . . ?*
kumori	*cloudy*
kurabu	*club*
kurasu	*class*
kurisumasu	*Christmas*
kuroi	*black*
kuruma	*car*
kusuri	*medicine*
kutsu	*shoes*
kyō	*today*
kyōdai	*siblings* (own)
kyōmi ga aru	*have an interest*
kyonen	*last year*
kyū ni	*suddenly*
machi	*town*
mada	*not yet, still*
mado	*window*
mae (ni)	*before*
mae	*in front of*
magaru	*turn*
mai	*square-ish, flat-ish*
maiasa	*every morning*

mainichi	*every day*
maishū	*every week*
maitsuki	*every month*
majime (na)	*serious, conscientious* (person)
marui	*round*
massugu	*straight ahead*
mata	*again*
me	*eyes*
meishi	*business card*
Mekishiko	*Mexico*
michi	*road, way*
migi (gawa)	*right* (side)
mijikai	*short*
mikkusu	*mix*
minami	*south*
minasan	*everyone*
mittsu	*three items*
mizu	*water*
mo	*also*
mo . . . mo	*both . . . and*
mō	*already (no longer)*
mō sugu	*soon*
mokuyōbi	*Thursday*
mondai	*problem*
moshi	*if*
mukae	*to meet, collect (someone)*
mukaigawa	*opposite*
musuko	*son* (own)
musukosan	*son* (other)
musume	*daughter* (own)
musumesan	*daughter* (others)
muttsu	*six items*
n desu	*you see*
n ja nai deshō ka	*probably* (polite)
nagai	*long*
nagara	*while*
naka	*inside, in*
namae	*name*
nan/nani	*what*
nanatsu	*seven items*
nani ka	*something*
nani mo +	*negative nothing*
natsu	*summer*
naze	*why*

ne	*isn't it, right?*
nē	*look* (letting s/one know s/thing)
nerujikan	*sleep time*
ni	*at/for/on/in*
ni tsuite	*about*
nichi	*day*
nichiyōbi	*Sunday*
nigate	*poor at*
nigiyaka (na)	*lively, bustling*
Nihon	*Japan*
Nihongo	*Japanese*
ni-kai	*second floor*
niku	*meat*
nin	*people* (counter)
ninen kan	*2-year period*
ningyō	*doll*
niwa shigoto	*gardening*
no	*'s* (possessive)
no de	*therefore, so*
nō gekai	*brain surgeon*
nochi	*later*
Nyū Jīrando	*New Zealand*
nyūsu	*news*
obāchan	*gran*
obāsan	*grandmother*
ōdan hodō	*pedestrian crossing*
ofuro	*bath*
o-hashi	*chopsticks*
ohayō gozaimasu	*good morning*
ojīchan	*grandad*
ojīsan	*grandfather*
okagesama de	*I'm fine, thank you*
okāchan	*mum*
okāsan	*mother* (others)
ōkii	*big* (objects)
okusan	*wife* (others)
omedetō gozaimasu	*congratulations*
omoshiroi	*interesting, funny, fun*
omoshirosō	*looks interesting*
onēchan	*older sister* (informal)
onēsan	*older sister* (others)
onīchan	*older brother* (informal)
onīsan	*older brother* (others)
origami	*paper folding*

o-sake	*rice wine*
osaki ni	*before you*
osewa	*help, care for*
osoi	*late, slow*
osoku	*late*
osoku made	*until late*
Ōsutoraria	*Australia*
otonashii	*quiet* (person)
otōchan	*dad*
otōsan	*father* (others)
otōto	*younger brother* (own)
otōtosan	*younger brother* (others)
oyasumi nasai	*good night*
pātī	*party*
poppusu	*pop music*
Porutogaru	*Portugal*
pūru	*swimming pool*
rabu rabu bōizu	*Love Love Boys* (band name)
raigetsu	*next month*
rainen	*next year*
raishū	*next week*
repōto	*report*
resutoran	*restaurant*
ringo	*apple*
roketto kagakusha	*rocket scientist*
rokku tsuā	*rock tour*
roku	*six*
Roppongi	*trendy area of Tokyo*
rūru	*rules*
ryokō	*travel, trip*
ryōri	*cooking, cuisine*
ryōshin	*parents* (own)
sai	*years old*
sakana	*fish*
sake	*rice wine*
sakkā	*soccer, football*
sakka	*writer*
samui	*cold*
sannen	*3 years*
sashimi	*raw fish slices*
satsu	*book* (counter)
sayōnara	*goodbye*
se	*height/back*

se ga takai	*tall*
seidai na	*splendid*
seikatsu	*lifestyle*
sen	*thousand*
sengetsu	*last month*
senshū	*last week*
sensu	*folding fan*
setsumei	*explanation*
shabu-shabu	*table-top dish of thinly sliced beef*
shachō	*company director, president*
shiai	*tournament, contest*
shikakui	*square*
shikata	*how to do/play*
shikata ga arimasen	*it can't be helped*
shimatta (shimau)	*gone and . . . , completely*
shinbun	*newspaper*
shingō	*traffic lights*
shinjirarenai!	*I can't believe it!*
shinkansen	*bullet train*
shinsetsu (na)	*kind*
shita	*below, under*
shitsurei shimasu	*excuse me for interrupting*
shitteimasu	*I know*
shōbōshi	*firefighter*
shodō	*calligraphy*
shokuji	*meal*
shokudō	*dining room, canteen*
shōrai (ni)	*in the future*
shū	*week*
shufu	*housewife*
shujin	*husband* (own)
shukudai	*homework*
shūmatsu	*weekend*
shumi	*hobby*
shusseki suru	*attend*
soba	*alongside, by*
sōbetsukai	*farewell party*
sobo	*grandmother* (own)
sofu	*grandfather* (own)
sōji	*cleaning*
soko	*there*
soku	*pairs* (footwear)
sonna ni	*(not) especially* (+ negative)
sono, sore	*that, that one*
sorekara	*and then*

sorosoro	*shortly, soon*
soshite	*and/also*
subarashii	*wonderful, great*
sūgaku	*maths*
sugu	*straightaway*
suiyōbi	*Wednesday*
suki	*like*
sukoshi	*a little*
sumimasen	*excuse me, sorry*
sūpā	*supermarket*
Supein	*Spain*
supōtsu	*sports*
sushiya-san	*sushi bar*
suzushii	*cool/fresh*
tabitabi	*many times*
tachi	*makes certain words plural*
taitei	*generally, usually*
takai	*expensive*
takai	*high/tall*
takusan	*a lot*
tama ni	*occasionally*
tamago	*egg*
tame ni	*for*
tanoshii	*enjoyable, pleasant*
tegami	*letter*
teishoku	*set meal*
tenki	*weather*
terebi	*television*
to	*and*
to	*with*
tō	*10 items*
tō	*large animals* (counter)
toire	*toilet*
tokei	*watch* (clock)
toki	*when*
tokidoki	*sometimes*
tokoro	*place*
tokui	*good at*
tomodachi	*friend*
tonari	*next to, next door*
tōsuto	*toast*
totemo	*very*
totsuzen	*unexpectedly*
tsugi	*next*

tsuki	*month*
tsuma	*wife* (own)
tsumaranai	*boring*
tsumori	*intend to do*
uchi	*home*
uchi (ni)	*while*
uchūhikōshi	*astronaut*
ue	*above, on top*
ushiro	*behind*
utsukushii	*beautiful*
washoku	*Japanese food*
watashi	*I*
watashi no	*my*
watashitachi	*we*
ya	*and(when giving examples)*
yakyū	*baseball*
yakyūjō	*baseball stadium*
yasai	*vegetables*
yasashii	*kind, gentle*
yattsu	*eight items*
yo	*you know, I tell you*
yoko	*beside, side*
yohō	*forecast*
yōkoso	*welcome*
yoku	*often, well*
Yōroppa	*Europe*
yoru	*evening*
yottsu	*four items*
yoyaku	*reservation, booking*
yūbe	*last night*
yūbinkyoku	*post office*
yukata	*cotton kimono*
yuki	*snow*
-yuki	*bound for*
yūmei (na)	*famous*
yūsuhosuteru	*youth hostel*
zannen	*shame, pity*
zasshi	*magazine*
zehi	*be sure to*
zembu	*all*
zembu de	*altogether, in total*
zenyasai	*pre-event party*
zenzen	*not at all* (+ negative)

English–Japanese vocabulary

9th (date)	kokonoka
9 items	kokonotsu
10 items	tō
2-year period	ninen kan
a (*typical*) *day*	ichinichi
a little	sukoshi
a lot	takusan
about (used with times)	goro
about, concerning	ni tsuite
about, roughly	gurai
above, on top	ue
abroad, foreign country	gaikoku
actor	haiyū
after	ato de
afternoon, pm	gogo
again	mata
all	zembu
all day	ichinichi
alongside, by	soba
already (*no longer*)	mō
also	mo
altogether, in total	zembu de
always	itsumo
am, is, are	desu
am, morning	gozen
America	Amerika, Beikoku
American (person)	Amerikajin
and	to
and (examples)	ya
and/also	soshite
and then	sorekara
apartment	apāto
apple	ringo
Argentina	Aruzenchin
art	bijutsu
art gallery	bijutsukan
astronaut	uchūhikōshi
at/for/on/in	ni
at/in (after place)	de
attend	shusseki suru
Australia	Ōsutoraria

autumn	aki
average	futsū
awful	iya (na)
bad at	heta (na), nigate
badminton	badominton
bag	kaban
banana	banana
band	bando
bank	ginkō
bank worker	ginkō-in
baseball	yakyū
baseball stadium	yakyūjō
bath	ofuro
batteries	denchi
be sure to	zehi
beautiful	utsukushii
beautiful; clean	kirei (na)
beer	bīru
before	mae (ni)
before you	osaki ni
behind	ushiro
below	shita
beside	yoko
big (objects)	ōkii
big (places)	hiroi
black	kuroi
black tea	kōcha
blonde	kinpatsu
blue	aoi
book (counter)	satsu
boring	tsumaranai
both . . . and	mo . . . mo
bound for	-yuki
bowling (ten-pin)	bōringu
bowling alley	bōringu jō
brain surgeon	nō gekai
Brazil	Burajiru
breakfast	asagohan
bridge	hashi
bright, cheerful	akarui
brown	chairo
bullet train	shinkansen
bus stop	basu-tei
business card	meishi

bustling, lively	nigiyaka (na)
but	demo
but	ga
bye bye	bai bai
cake	kēki
calligraphy	shodō
camera	kamera
car	kuruma
chance	chansu
cheerful	akarui
childhood	kodomo no koro
China	Chūgoku
chopsticks	o-hashi, hashi
Christmas	Kurisumasu
cinema	eigakan
class	kurasu
cleaning	sōji
clearly	hakkiri
cloudy	kumori
club	kurabu
coffee	kōhī
coffee shop	kissaten
cold	samui
collect (s/one)	mukae
college	koreji
company	kaisha
company director	shachō
company employee	kaisha-in
company sales manager	kaisha no eigyō buchō
computer	kompyūtā
concert	konsāto
congratulations	omedetō gozaimasu
conscientious (person)	majime (na)
contest	shiai
cooking, cuisine	ryōri
cool/fresh	suzushii
cool, ok	heiki
corner	kado
cotton kimono	yukata
cram school	juku
crossroads	kōsaten
dad	otōchan
date	dēto
daughter (others)	musumesan

daughter (own)	musume
day	nichi
daytime, during the day	hiruma
department store	depāto
digital camera	dejikame
dining room, canteen	shokudō
do you know? (polite)	gozonji desu ka
doctor	isha
dog	inu
doll	ningyō
door	doa
disagreeable	fuyukai (na)
during	aida
early	hayaku, hayai
egg	tamago
eight items	yattsu
electricity	denki
email	e-mēru
embarrassed	hazukashii
England	Eikoku, Igirisu, Ingurando
English (language)	Eigo
enjoyable, pleasant	tanoshii
er, erm	ē to
Europe	Yōrōppa
evening	yoru
evening meal	bangohan
every day	mainichi
every month	maitsuki
every morning	maiasa
every week	maishū
everyone	minasan
excuse	iiwake
excuse me for interrupting	shitsurei shimasu
excuse me, sorry	sumimasen
expensive	takai
explanation	setsumei
eyes	me
face	kao
fall/autumn	aki
family (others)	go-kazoku
family (own)	kazoku
famous	yūmei (na)
fan (*folding*)	sensu
farewell party	sōbetsukai
father (others)	otōsan

father (own)	chichi
film, movie	eiga
filmstar	eiga sutā
fine	daijōbu
fine, sunny	hare
firefighter	shōbōshi
first	hitotsu me
fish	sakana
five	go
five items	itsutsu
floors	kai
flower arranging	ikebana
fog	kiri
football (*soccer*)	sakkā
footbridge	hodōkyō
for	tame ni
forecast	yohō
four items	yottsu
France	Furansu
free	hima (na)
French (items)	Furansu no
Friday	kinyōbi
friend	tomodachi
from	kara
front of	mae
future (*in the*)	shōrai (ni)
gardening	niwa shigoto
generally, usually	taitei
Germany	Doitsu
golf	gorufu
gone and . . .	shimatta (shimau)
good at	tokui
good at, skilful	jōzu (na)
good evening	konbanwa
good morning	ohayō gozaimasu
good night	oyasumi nasai
good, nice	ii (yoi)
goodbye	sayōnara
gradually	dandan
gran	obāchan
grandad	ojīchan
grandfather	ojīsan
grandfather (own)	sofu
grandmother	obāsan
grandmother (own)	sobo

great	subarashii
greatly, quite a lot	daibu
guitar	gitā
hair	kami
hate	kirai (na)
have an interest	kyōmi ga aru
have, possess	arimasu (1)
he	kare
head	atama
height/back	se
hello	konnichiwa
help, care for	osewa
here	koko
hey!, what!	are
hey, erm (friendly)	ano (ne)
high/tall	takai
hobby	shumi
home	uchi
homework	shukudai
hot	atsui
hotel	hoteru
hour	jikan
housewife	shufu
how about . . . ?	dō desu ka
how do you do?	hajimemashite
how much?	ikura
how to do/play	shikata
how, what way	dō
hundred	hyaku
hurts	itai
husband (others)	go-shujin
husband (own)	shujin
I	watashi
I (male)	boku
I can't believe it!	shinjirarenai!
I'm fine, thank you	okagesama de
if	moshi
in fact	jitsu wa
inside, in	naka
intend to do	tsumori
interest (*have an*)	kyōmi (ga aru)
interesting, funny, fun	omoshiroi
is	desu, da

isn't it, right?	ne
it can't be helped	shikata ga arimasen
Italy	Itaria
Japan	Nihon
Japanese	Nihongo
Japanese food	washoku
Japanese harp	koto
jazz	jazu
journalist	jānarisuto
kilo	kiro
kind	shinsetsu (na)
kind, gentle	yasashii
Korea	Kankoku
large animals (counter)	tō
large machinery	dai
last month	sengetsu
last night	yūbe
last week	senshū
last year	kyonen
late	osoku
late, slow	osoi
later	nochi
lawyer	bengoshi
left (side)	hidari (gawa)
letter	tegami
lifestyle	seikatsu
lights, electricity	denki
like	suki
lively, bustling	nigiyaka (na)
loads, full amount	ippai
long	nagai
long (cylindrical items)	hon (pon, bon)
looks interesting	omoshirosō
low/small	hikui
lunch	hirugohan
magazine	zasshi
many times	tabitabi
marriage	kekkon
martial arts	budō
maths	sūgaku
may I have . . . ?	kudasai
meal	shokuji
meat	niku

medicine	kusuri
meet, collect (s/one)	mukae
meeting	kaigi
meeting room	kaigishitsu
men, male	dansei
Mexico	Mekishiko
might	kamo shiremasen
mix	mikkusu
mobile (*phone*)	keitai (denwa)
Monday	getsuyōbi
month	getsu, tsuki
morning	asa
most, -est, number one	ichiban
mother (others)	okāsan
mother (own)	haha
Mount Fuji	Fujisan
movie, film	eiga
mum	okāchan
museum	hakubutsukan
my	watashi no
name	namae
near to	chikaku
neighbour	kinjo no hito
new	atarashii
New Zealand	Nyū Jīrando
news	nyūsu
newspaper	shinbun
next	tsugi
next month	raigetsu
next to, next door	tonari
next week	raishū
next year	rainen
no	iie
no good at	heta
no good, don't!	dame
no one	dare mo (+ negative)
nose	hana
not (*isn't . . .*)	dewa/ja arimasen
not at all	zenzen (+ negative)
not especially	sonna ni (+ negative)
not very, hardly	amari (+ negative)
not yet, still	mada
nothing	nani mo + negative
number of times	kai
nurse, medical carer	kangoshi

o'clock	ji
occasionally	tama ni
office	jimusho
often, well	yoku
oh really?	ā, sō desu ka
ok, right, in that case	jā
old (things)	furui
older brother (own)	ani, aniki
older brother (informal)	onīchan
older brother (others)	onīsan
older sister (own)	ane, aneki
older sister (informal)	onēchan
older sister (others)	onēsan
on foot	aruite
one hour	ichi jikan
one item	hitotsu
one week, per week	isshūkan
oneself (one's own)	jibun (no)
opposite	mukaigawa
other	hoka no
over there	asoko
pairs (footwear)	soku
paper	kami
paper folding	origami
parents (others)	go-ryōshin
parents (own)	ryōshin
party	pātī
pedestrian crossing	ōdan hodō
people (counter)	nin
per week	isshūkan
person (nationality)	jin
photographer	kameraman
place	tokoro
pleased to meet you	dōzo yorosh(i)ku
policeman	keisatsukan
poor at	nigate
pop music	poppusu
Portugal	Porutogaru
post office	yūbinkyoku
postcard	hagaki
president (company)	shachō
probably	deshō, darō (plain)
probably (polite)	n ja nai deshō ka
problem	mondai

question mark	ka
quick	hayai
quickly	hayaku
quiet (person)	otonashii
rain	ame
raw fish slices	sashimi
real	hontō
really	hontō ni
report	repōto
reservation, booking	yoyaku
restaurant	resutoran
rice	gohan
rice wine	o-sake, sake
right (side)	migi (gawa)
road, way	michi
rock tour	rokku tsuā
rocket scientist	roketto kagakusha
room, bedroom	heya
round	marui
round objects	ko
rules	rūru
's (possessive)	no
Saturday	doyōbi
school	gakkō
second	futatsu me
second floor	ni-kai
see you!	ja mata ne
separately	betsubetsu
serious (person)	majime (na)
set meal	teishoku
seven items	nanatsu
shame, pity	zannen
she	kanojo
shoes	kutsu
shopping	kaimono
short	mijikai
shortly, soon	sorosoro
shy, seems shy	hazukashigari (na)
siblings (others)	go-kyōdai
siblings (own)	kyōdai
side	yoko
singer	kashu
six	roku
six items	muttsu

sleep time	nerujikan
slow	osoi
small	chiisai
small animals	hiki (piki, biki)
snow	yuki
soccer (football)	sakkā
someone	dare ka
something	nani ka
something like	~demo
sometime, one day	itsuka
sometimes	tokidoki
son (other)	musukosan
son (own)	musuko
soon	mō sugu
sorry	sumimasen
south	minami
spacious, big (places)	hiroi
Spain	Supein
splendid	seidai na
sports	supōtsu
spring	haru
square	shikakui
square-ish, flat-ish	mai
stamps	kitte
straight ahead	massugu
straightaway	sugu
street, road	dōro
studying	benkyō
such	konna ni
suddenly	kyū ni
summer	natsu
Sunday	nichiyōbi
supermarket	sūpā
sushi bar	sushiya-san
swimming pool	pūru
tall	takai, se ga takai
tea ceremony	chadō
television	terebi
thank you	arigatō gozaimasu
that (one) over there	ano, are
that, that one	sono, sore
theatre	gekijō
there	soko
there is, there are	arimasu (non-living things, inanimate)

there is, there are	imasu (animals and people)
therefore, so	kara, no de
they	karera
this (person)	kochira
this; this one	kono; kore
this floor	konkai
this month	kongetsu
this morning	kesa
this week	konshū
thousand	sen
three items	mittsu
three years	sannen
thunder	kaminari
Thursday	mokuyōbi
ticket	kippu
to (a place)	e, ni
toast	tōsuto
today	kyō
together	issho ni
toilet	toire
tomorrow	ashita
tonight	konban
tournament, contest	shiai
town	machi
traffic lights	shingō
train	densha
travel, trip	ryokō
tree	ki
Tuesday	kayōbi
turn	magaru
two (people)	futari
two items	futatsu
under	shita
unexpectedly	totsuzen
university	daigaku
university student	daigakusei
unpleasant, disagreeable	fuyukai (na)
usually	taitei
until late	osoku made
various	iroiro (na)
vegetables	yasai
vegetarian	bejitarian
very	totemo

want	hoshii
warm	atatakai
watch (*clock*)	tokei
water	mizu
we	watashitachi
weather	tenki
Wednesday	suiyōbi
week	shū
weekend	shūmatsu
welcome	yōkoso
welcome, may I help you?	irasshaimase
well	yoku
what	nan/nani
when	itsu (question word)
when	toki
when I was a child	kodomo no koro
where	doko
where to	doko made
which, which one	dono, dore
while	nagara, uchi (ni), aida (ni)
who	dare
why	dōshite, naze
wife (others)	okusan
wife (own)	kanai/tsuma
will probably	deshō, darō (plain)
wind	kaze
window	mado
winter	fuyu
with	to
women, female	josei
wonderful, great	subarashii
writer	sakka
years old	sai
yen (currency)	en
yes	hai
yesterday	kinō
you	anata, anata no koto
you (plural)	anatatachi
you know, I tell you	yo
you see	n desu
younger brother (others)	otōtosan
younger brother (own)	otōto
younger sister (others)	imōtosan
younger sister (own)	imōto
youth hostel	yūsuhosuteru

Verb table

Here is a list of all the main verbs that have been included in this course. They are not included in the vocabulary lists so use this appendix when you need to find a verb in English or Japanese. They are organized first by group (group 1, group 2, **shimasu** verbs, irregular) then alphabetically within group. Group 2 verbs are listed in **masu** and dictionary form, the rest in **masu** form only – to change to dictionary form look back to Explanation 11.1; to change into other forms refer to the Index of grammar and structures.

Group 1

aimasu (au)	*meet*
araimasu (arau)	*wash*
asobimasu (asobu)	*play*
dashimasu (dasu)	*send, take out, submit*
erabimasu (erabu)	*choose*
(ame ga) furimasu (furu)	*rain falls*
hairimasu (hairu)	*enter*
(kutsu o) hakimasu (haku)	*wear (shoes)*
hanashimasu (hanasu)	*talk, speak*
hatarakimasu (hataraku)	*work*
hikimasu (hiku)	*pull, play*
hirakimasu (hiraku)	*organize, hold*
kaimasu (kau)	*buy*
kakimasu (kaku)	*write, draw*
keshimasu (kesu)	*switch off, erase*
kikimasu (kiku)	*listen*
kowashimasu (kowasu)	*break*
machimasu (matsu)	*wait*
mochimasu (motsu)	*hold*
naraimasu (narau)	*learn*
narimasu (naru)	*become, get, will be*
nomimasu (nomu)	*drink*
nugimasu (nugu)	*take off*

okonaimasu (okonau)	*hold (an event)*
okurimasu (okuru)	*send, post, mail*
omoimasu (onou)	*I think*
otoshimasu (otosu)	*lose, drop*
oyogimasu (oyogu)	*swim*
sagashimasu (sagasu)	*look for*
shinimasu (shinu)	*die*
shiru (shirimasu/shitteimasu)	*know*
sugoshimasu (sugosu)	*spend time*
tabako o suimasu (suu)	*smoke cigarettes*
tsukimasu (tsuku)	*arrive*
tsukurimasu (tsukuru)	*make, build*
utaimasu (utau)	*sing*
wakarimasu (wakaru)	*understand*
yasumimasu (yasumu)	*rest, take holiday*
yomimasu (yomu)	*read*

Group 2

(shawā o) abimasu	*take a shower*
aiteimasu	*is open*
dekakemasu	*go out, set off*
dekimasu	*can do*
demasu	*leave, exit, go out*
kaerimasu	*return*
kimemasu	*decide*
mimasu	*watch, see, look*
misemasu	*show*
mitsukemasu	*find*
mukaemasu	*meet, receive, collect (s/one)*
nemasu	*go to bed*
okimasu	*get up*
oshiemasu	*teach*
shitteimasu	*know*
sundeimasu	*live*
tabemasu	*eat*
tsukaremasu	*tired*
tsukemasu	*switch on*
wasuremasu	*forget*
yameru	*give up*

Shimasu (suru) verbs

aiteimasu	*is open*
benkyō shimasu	*study*
denwa shimasu	*make a phone call*
doraibu shimasu	*drive (go for a drive)*
ensō shimasu	*perform*
gorogoro shimasu	*chill out, laze around*
gorufu o shimasu	*play golf*
kaimono shimasu	*do shopping*
kansha shimasu	*appreciate*
kekkon shimasu	*get married*
renraku shimasu	*make contact*
renshū shimasu	*practice, practise*
ryokō shimasu	*travel, take a trip*
sakkā shimasu	*play football*
sampo shimasu	*go for a walk*
sanka shimasu	*take part in*
setsumei shimasu	*explain*
shigoto shimasu	*work (do a job)*
shinpai shimasu	*worry*
shokuji shimasu	*have a meal*
shukudai shimasu	*do homework*
shusseki shimasu	*attend*
shutchō shimasu	*take a business trip*
sōji shimasu	*do the cleaning*
sotsugyō shimasu	*graduate*
tenkin suru	*transfer*
yoyaku shimasu	*make a reservation*

Irregular verbs

asobi ni ikimasu (iku)	*go and visit*
asobi ni kimasu (kuru)	*come and visit*
ikimasu (iku)	*go*
kimasu (kuru)	*come*
shimasu (suru)	*do, make, play*

Index of grammar and structures